To Neil

To B. A.

C

J Corey.

To Neil
Good Luck
William Russell

Neil
Love
Michael Cozy

For Neil
Gerald Armtard

To Neil
Love
Wendy Padbury
x

Neil
love
Yvonne Wills

Tors Mores

FROM A TO Z

GARY GILLATT

BBC

Guide to full-page illustrations:

A William Hartnell as the Doctor
B Ian (William Russell) and Susan (Carole Ann Ford) with a Dalek in *The Daleks*
C The Doctor (William Hartnell) trades with Ben Daheer (Reg Pritchard) *The Crusade*
D Dodo (Jackie Lane) in trouble in *The Gunfighters*
E Carmen Munroe as Fariah in *The Enemy of the World*
F Patrick Troughton as the Doctor
G A Silurian in *Doctor Who and the Silurians*
H Jon Pertwee and Katy Manning in a publicity still from *The Dæmons*
I Jon Pertwee's Doctor in drag in *The Green Death*
J Jo (Katy Manning) and her fiancé, Cliff (Stuart Bevan)
K Sarah (Elisabeth Sladen) and the Doctor (Jon Pertwee) disguised as monks in *The Time Warrior*
L Tom Baker as the Doctor
M Paul Crompton's front cover art for the 1977 *Dr Who Annual*
N Peter Pratt as the decaying Master in *The Deadly Assassin*
O Tom Baker and Lalla Ward in Paris for *City of Death*
P Lalla Ward dresses as the Doctor
Q Adrian Gibbs as the Watcher in *Logopolis*
R Tom Baker on Brighton beach
S Peter Davison as the Doctor
T Peter Davison as the Doctor
U A Cyberman perishes in *The Five Doctors*
V Oscar (James Saxon) is mourned by Peri (Nicola Bryant), Jamie (Frazer Hines) and Anita
(Carmen Gomez) in *The Two Doctors*
W The Doctor (Colin Baker) with Mr Popplewick (Geoffrey Hughes) in *The Trial of a Time Lord*
X Sylvester McCoy as the Doctor
Y Gian Sammarco as Whizzkid in *The Greatest Show in the Galaxy*
Z Paul McGann as the Doctor

Published by BBC Worldwide Ltd
Woodlands, 80 Wood Lane, London W12 0TT
First published 1998
Text © Gary Gillatt 1998. The moral right of the author has been asserted

Original series broadcast on the BBC
Format © BBC 1963
Terry Nation is the creator of the Daleks
Doctor Who, TARDIS and the Daleks are trademarks of the BBC

ISBN 0 563 40589 9

Imaging and design by *eyetoeye* Design Consultants © copyright BBC 1998
Edited by Stephen Cole

Colour originations by Radstock Reproductions Limited, Midsomer Norton
Printed by Cambus Litho, East Kilbride
Bound by Hunter & Foulis Limited, Edinburgh
Jacket printed by Lawrence Allen Limited, Weston-super-Mare

For my mother and father, the wisest, kindest
and most generous of parents

And for Andrew Pixley – a scholar, a gentleman,
and a friend – for his unparalleled research
and unwavering support

AUTHOR'S NOTE

In the thirty-five years since *Doctor Who*'s distinctive theme music first curled and hissed from the tinny speakers of the TV sets of Britain in 1963, a host of serious tomes have painstakingly catalogued almost every detail of the series' production for the programme's many loyal fans.

Doctor Who: From A to Z is not one of them.

Each chapter of this book tells a story. Together, and read in order, they tell an even bigger story – a tale of *Doctor Who*'s rise and fall and rise and fall in popularity, of its effect on the lives of its followers, of what it can tell us about the broader cultural backdrop to its three decades on television. It may be offered as a 'celebration' of *Doctor Who*, but it does not shirk from drawing your attention to the weaknesses and crudities of the series any more than it stints on the praise for its subtleties and triumphs.

Twenty-six topics have been chosen, one for each letter of the alphabet and each year the series was in continuous production at the BBC. The themes under analysis here were selected at an early stage and then assigned to a letter and a year when a significant event in the show's history occurred in relation to that aspect of the programme. Some, such as the discussion of ethnicity in *Doctor Who* in Chapter E, consider their subject matter in relation to the entire history of the series. Others, such as the look at the background to *Doctor Who*'s temporary suspension of production in 1985 in Chapter W, may focus on a single moment, but it will be one that had long-term consequences for the series as a whole. Some chapters will dwell on a single month, a single episode or single individual for 1,000 words, then skip over twenty years, fifty serials or a host of other production personnel in just a few lines; that's because this book is telling a story.

The most appropriate examples and facts are selected throughout to illustrate arguments. This is not a completist, 'tick off the names' work. I have felt under no obligation to quote all relevant information relating to a subject in any given chapter. In the discussion of romance in Chapter J, for example, Leela's hasty marriage to Andred in the 1978 serial *The Invasion of Time* is mentioned only in passing, as any points that it may raise can be considered in a more interesting way by studying the behaviour of Susan in *The Dalek Invasion of Earth* (1964) or Jo Grant in *The Green Death* (1973).

This work is more discursive than most on the subject, and, as a result, more opinionated. I have tried throughout to cite appropriate evidence before any conclusions. You may disagree with some of those conclusions, and the reasoning that takes me to them. That's good – if this book provokes a response, be it nodding agreement or head-shaking anger, then I have done my job.

Finally, although most of the readers of this work are likely to be very familiar with the details of the subject matter, I have tried not to assume that knowledge is possessed at any stage in order to keep the 'story' as accessible as possible. To this end I have avoided 'jargon' – stories are identified by their year of broadcast or the identity of their lead actor, rather than blithely referring to 'the Season Six serial *The Dominators*' – an identifier that would place the story within the series' history perfectly well for a dedicated fan, but would be meaningless for someone whose interest in the production of *Doctor Who* is more casual. For the Hartnell stories that lack overall titles on-screen, I have used those adopted by *Doctor Who Magazine* and by BBC Books' *Doctor Who – The Televison Companion*, aside from opting for *The Daleks*, rather than *The Mutants*, as a title for the monsters' first serial, to avoid confusion. If this hair-splitting seems incomprehensible to any of you, that's fine – it's much better not to worry about it.

As a side effect of this 'easy access' approach, you may encounter some minimal repetition of information. The chapters of this book are best read sequentially, but each has been written to stand alone, so companion Barbara Wright may be referred to as a 'schoolteacher' on several occasions, as I can't guarantee that a reader will retain that information from its first statement. On the plus side, you may derive some vicarious pleasure from the obvious fun I have had in finding different explanatory adjectives for the vicious Voord, for example (there's another one).

Some parts of this dramatised history may be familiar, some of the facts may be as well known to you as your telephone number. I hope, however, that there is also much that is new. And certainly, I hope you find that I have brought a fresh point of view to the material and that, by the end of my *Doctor Who* alphabet, you find yourself viewing much of the series in a different light.

It's a big, bold, sad, mad, funny and fascinating story. Enjoy the ride.

Gary Gillatt
July 1998

ACKNOWLEDGEMENTS

There are a number of individuals without whose help this book would have been 160 blank pages.

Steve Cole, my editor at BBC Books, who has put up with the most ridiculously flaunted deadlines in the history of *Doctor Who* publishing, a stream of feeble excuses and endless transparent attempts to change the topic of conversation, without allowing any of it to get in the way of a great friendship. His faith, his comments on the manuscript and his editing of my windy prose – along with the wise additions and subtractions made by his genius assistant Lesley Levene – have made an immeasurable contribution to the finished product.

For useful conversations regarding subject matter, I'd like to thank: Alan Barnes, who for some months had to stand as *de facto* editor of Marvel's *Doctor Who Magazine* while I frittered away my time – his lunchtime insights have never been less than inspirational; Scott Gray and Jason Quinn, fellow Marvel-ites, who each helped with parts of the first draft; Gary Russell, for unceasing support, a computer, annuals, comics, videos, audios and lots of 'do you really think so?'s which helped to marshal my arguments; Rupert Laight, whose earlier, first-class work made Chapter I possible; Edward Salt, for being such a great mate, for endless arguments on and around these twenty-six topics, and for getting me out of Brixton Hell.

For moral support during tense moments: Gary Burd, Grayson Fuller, Peri Godbold and all at Marvel, Mike Tucker, Robert Dick, David Darlington, Robin Pembrooke, John Ainsworth, Jim Sangster, David Bailey, John Binns, Simon Moore, Michael Bryan-Brown, Neil Corry, Robert Franks, Michaels Cregan and Park, Clayton Hickman and He Who Cannot Be Named.

Various *Doctor Who* factual books by others have been unashamedly plundered for useful data, and I can wholeheartedly recommend them all to interested readers: the *Doctor Who Production Guide* by Andrew Pixley, David Brunt and Keith Armstrong (published by DWAS), *Doctor Who – The Sixties*, *The Seventies* and *The Eighties* by David J. Howe, Mark Stammers and Stephen James Walker (Virgin) and the *Doctor Who Handbook* series from the same authors (Virgin). Thanks to all those trail-blazing authors.

Other factual contributions and insights came from David Brunt, Jan Vincent-Rudzki and Martin Wiggins.

Recognition is also due to dozens of *Doctor Who Magazine* writers down the years, but particularly to Marcus Hearn and Philip MacDonald, whose erudition exceeds mine and lit the way. Thanks also to Peter Griffiths, the magazine's most talented interviewer, for always having asked just the right questions.

Thanks to the staff of the BFI Library and Bobbie Mitchell and the team at the BBC Photo Library.

No thanks at all to: Sony Playstation, Jack Daniels, *This Morning with Richard and Judy* and *EastEnders*.

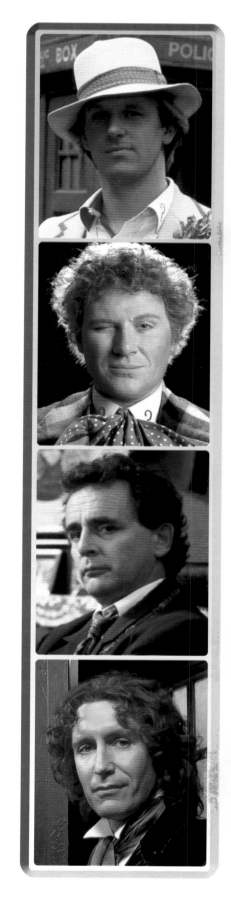

FROM A TO Z

CONTENTS

It was all made official on the night of Sunday 3 November 1996.

Exactly sixty years earlier, soprano Adele Dixon had belted out 'A mighty maze of mystic magic rays is all about us in the blue' from Alexandra Palace and so launched BBC Television: the world's first regular high-definition television service. At that time many had felt that television didn't have a future and would prove to be a here-today, gone-tomorrow medium; a busy, migraine-inducing blur of too-bright images that could never truly supplant the wireless in the nation's affections. Even John Reith, bullish, obsessive first Director-General of the BBC, seems not to have been very inspired by the thought of television: his diary entry for 2 November 1936 reads simply, 'To Alexandra Palace for the television opening. I declined to be televised or take part.'

Of course, everyone was very, very wrong, and after sixty years as the world's favourite broadcaster, Auntie Beeb thought it was time to show off a bit, to hitch up her skirts and dance. The on-air celebrations were to be led by a special series of programmes, broadcast under the banner title *TV60*.

At the core of this – among the more heavyweight documentaries and social histories – was the affectionate and nostalgic *Auntie's TV Favourites*, a weekly compilation of clips from the best of the Corporation's drama, comedy and light entertainment. After each programme, viewers were offered the chance to make a telephone vote for their favourite series, actor or presenter in each category, choosing from a short-list compiled by television writers and senior industry figures. Winners would receive a special award, an 'Auntie', at what BBC publicity suggested would be a 'glittering televised gala, staged before a celebrity audience in early November'.

The 11 October edition of *TV Favourites* offered a review of the BBC's finest drama series and serials. Vying for supremacy as favourite drama serial were heavyweight, critically applauded offerings such as *I, Claudius* and *The Boys from the Blackstuff*. A second category, favourite popular drama, brought together programmes from the Beeb's more bread-and-butter populist output, the ten nominations including such classics as *Bergerac*, *Colditz*, *The Onedin Line*, *When the Boat Comes In* and *Z Cars*, and the then-current hit *Ballykissangel*. The tipped favourites, however, were the mild, green vet series *All Creatures Great and Small*, the often controversial but always phenomenally successful soap *EastEnders*, and the blood-splattered and ratings-grabbing medical drama *Casualty*. The tenth nomination, and a surprise to everyone, including the programme's most loyal fans, was the fantasy adventure series *Doctor Who*, which, bar a one-off TV movie earlier that year, had ceased regular production in 1989. Surely *Doctor Who* was just silly sci-fi stuff? Shouldn't it be in some kids' TV category?

That 'glittering gala' was recorded at BBC Television Centre on the evening of 27 October and broadcast exactly one week later in a prime Sunday evening slot. Shoulder to shoulder in the front rows of the audience were dozens of familiar BBC faces – that family of presenters and performers who, no matter how many times they appear on other channels, no matter where their television career began, will always be 'BBC people'. Many, such as Ronnie Barker, Noel Edmonds, Terry Wogan,

Above: A Dalek, perhaps the most potent symbol of *Doctor Who*, out and about in London's Shepherd's Bush during an early photocall

Far right: Doctors Sylvester McCoy (right) and Peter Davison with their 'Auntie' award

Harry Enfield and Victoria Wood, were nominated for an award or two; others were there to watch colleagues' faces as they won or lost; and perhaps some just came along for a free dinner in the BBC canteen and a chance to flirt with the producer of the network's next big costume drama.

Noel Edmonds took the stage to reveal which programme the nation had chosen as their favourite popular drama to be produced by the Beeb in its sixty years as the rarely surpassed master of the art. In the audience, actress Wendy Richard – who as bitter mother-of-three Pauline Fowler had been the locus around which all of *EastEnders* had revolved since its launch in 1987 – put a hand up to check her hair. Co-star Barbara Windsor leaned forward in her seat, ready to stand. Noel fumbled with the envelope, slid out the card bearing the winning name... and a look of utter astonishment flicked across his face. One beat later, and with a tremor of quizzical doubt in his voice, he softly announced, 'It's *Doctor Who.*'

EastEnders star Brian Croucher threw back his head and laughed. His fellow cast members, along with those from *Casualty* and the rest, smiled thin smiles as former *Doctor Who* leads Peter Davison and Sylvester McCoy stepped down to the stage to receive their 'Auntie'. The applause was generous but hardly deafening, and the audience seemed a little partisan – even Peter Davison looked somewhat sheepish, as if he'd voted for *All Creatures Great and Small* himself – but the result was clear: *Doctor Who* was officially the most popular drama series to be produced by the BBC. Ever.

But why?

It's likely that more has been written about and around *Doctor Who* than any other television programme. Even ignoring the mass of novelisations of television episodes and the something like 13 million words of professionally published original fiction that have followed on from the series' de-commissioning in 1989, the scale of non-fiction study of the series is astonishing. Marvel Comics in the UK has offered a monthly magazine on the subject for just short of twenty years, and dedicated fans have filled the pages of around 2,500 amateur fanzines, ranging in tone from the sombre to the psychedelic. The books looking at the production minutiae of the series could probably stack up to the height of a man, each in turn logging the who, when and how of *Doctor Who*'s scripting and recording. The clever researcher can pick almost any date between 1963 and 1989 and discover exactly which scenes were being shot that day, who was appearing in them, on what date an actor's contract was signed, who made their costume, what they made it from and from which shop they bought the fabric; interviews might reveal every detail of the performer's preceding and proceeding career and even, perhaps, where their favourite place to have a picnic is.

But in these pages we're going push the 'who's, 'when's and 'how's into the background, and concentrate on the 'why's. Why did *Doctor Who* prove so popular and so enduring? Why, in its heyday, did over 13 million people in the UK alone choose to tune in to the antics of the Doctor and his menagerie of monsters, villains and companions? Why, in its last years, did the audience dwindle to less than a quarter of that figure? And even then, why was it that, seven years later, the audience was still loyal enough to allow Peter Davison and Sylvester McCoy to collect that 'Auntie'?

We'll have to take a look at *Doctor Who* from a wide variety of perspectives. We'll consider the best, the worst, the most mundane, the most strange of its episodes. We'll meet some of the people who brought them to life and consider their contribution to the whole, for better or for worse. We'll look at its ever-changing popularity with the public and the press. We'll leaf through the comic strips, novels and annuals, and play with some of the toys. We'll pretend to be Daleks in the school playground.

Then, perhaps, we'll be able to answer some of these questions, and discover the true position *Doctor Who* holds in the hearts and minds of a generation. ◖

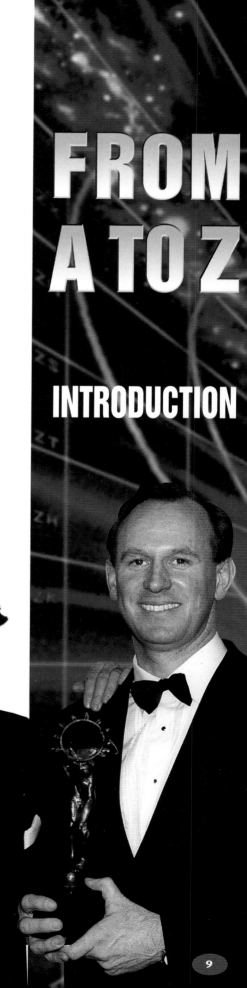

INTRODUCTION

Well before the first episode of *Doctor Who* had reached the TV screens of Britain, much of its core philosophy had been sketched out by just one man – a writer forever uncredited...

ADVENTURES IN SPACE AND TIME

Coronation Street was created by Tony Warren. *Star Trek* was created by Gene Roddenbery. *Dad's Army* was created by Jimmy Perry and David Croft. The provenance of each of these three television series – in their own way, among the most popular ever to reach the screen – is certain and unchallenged, the names of their prime movers plainly and proudly stated in their on-screen credits.

Throughout its history, *Doctor Who* bore no such credit. Always seen as the brainchild of an ever-changing committee of early 1960s BBC staff members and freelances, it has seemed impossible to lay the honour, or indeed the blame, for the creation of this slice of hectic nonsense at the door of any single individual.

But then, perhaps it's just that no one has really searched in the right place. If you look past the devisers of the trimmings and the gimmicks, the TARDIS and the title, it becomes clear that *Doctor Who* does have an unsung creator, and it is well past time he received the recognition he deserves.

Doctor Who's very first episode, *An Unearthly Child*, opens with a caption slide declaring it to be 'written by Anthony Coburn'. So would it be reasonable to assume that Coburn, who presented us with many of the characters and motifs which appear to define the series – the mysterious Doctor, his confused companions, the time-travelling phone box – also stands to receive the kudos for their creation? Well, no. Back in 1963, Coburn was just a jobbing writer recruited from the then-recently reorganised BBC script department. Originally intended to feature later in *Doctor Who*'s initial batch of stories, Coburn's script was pulled forward by Head of Serials Donald Wilson to stand as the series' opening adventure. He was therefore called upon to introduce *Doctor Who*'s central characters and format – elements which had already been defined at an earlier stage in production.

But by whom? The BBC's internal 'Production as Broadcast' notes for *An Unearthly Child* – a standard document drawn up by the Corporation listing salient details of any production – assign copyright for that first episode to both Coburn and one C. E. Webber.

Another member of the Script Department, TV and radio writer Cecil Edwin Webber was charged by Wilson to formulate *Doctor Who*'s central characters and framework and to write what was intended to stand as the programme's pilot serial; this was later abandoned for practical reasons and merged with Coburn's serial. Late in April 1963, he was responsible for the first draft of a document entitled 'General Notes on Background and Approach', which stands as a clear manifesto of both the format and many of the trappings of the series. Describing the central character of 'Dr Who', Webber writes: 'A frail old man lost in time and space. They give him this name because they don't know who he is. He seems not to remember where he has come from; he is suspicious and capable of sudden malignancy... he has a machine which enables them to travel together through time, through space, and through matter... He remains a mystery. From time to time the other three discover things about him, which turn out to be false or inconclusive... They think he may be a criminal fleeing from his own time.' Although very basic, surely this still stands as a fair description of the Doctor as he reached the screen.

On the subject of this enigmatic stranger's 'machine', Webber adds, 'When we consider what this looks like, we are in danger of science-fiction or fairytale labelling… If we scotch this by positing something humdrum, say, passing through some common object in the street such as a night-watchman's shelter to arrive inside a marvellous contrivance of quivering electronics, then we… have a version of the dear old Magic Door.' Although the name 'TARDIS' and its disguise as a police box would be the inspiration of Coburn, Webber's suggestion of a 'common object' full of 'quivering electronics' must surely allow him to claim credit for the central conceit of *Doctor Who*'s distinctive, attention-grabbing time machine.

Webber also describes the series' associate regular characters. There is a fifteen-year-old girl, Bridget or 'Biddy', who is 'with it… eager for life, lower than middle class' and has a 'neutral accent laced with the latest teenage slang'. This description is gradually amended by the production team, the girl's name is later set as Susan, and she becomes the Doctor's other-worldly granddaughter; a young woman of curious manner and prodigious scientific knowledge. But, ironically enough, here we see that Webber was a man ahead of his time. His own simpler outline for the 'young girl companion' stands more or less as the model used by many a future *Doctor Who* production team. Indeed, it can be read equally well as a description of Ace, the Doctor's last regular BBC-created companion in the 1980s, even down to the informal nickname. Webber's other creations, the teachers Miss Lola McGovern and Cliff, are also sketched using language that will define the series central character interactions for the next thirty years. Lola is 'twenty-four, timid, but capable of sudden rabbit courage... Modest with plenty of normal desires. Although she tends to be the one to get into trouble, she is not to be guyed; she is also a loyalty character.' Miss Lola may become history teacher Barbara Wright before *An Unearthly Child* airs, but she will in later years be seen again as Polly, Jo Grant, Sarah Jane Smith, Mel and Peri, among others. Cliff is 'twenty-seven or twenty-eight... physically perfect, strong and courageous, a gorgeous dish. Oddly, when brains are required, he can even be brainy, in a diffident sort of way.' Although *Doctor Who* has used relatively few regular male supporting characters in its long run, and given that the description 'a gorgeous dish' comes down to a matter of individual taste, the character of Cliff stands equally well for the courageous and diffidently clever Ian Chesterton, Steven Taylor, Ben Jackson, Brigadier Lethbridge-Stewart and Harry Sullivan. Indeed, aside from the high-concept companions from alien worlds or Earth's own past who would find favour at various points in the *Doctor Who* saga, Lola, Cliff and Biddy stand as the archetypes for almost every fellow traveller to join the Doctor in his TARDIS.

As if this isn't enough, Webber further outlines the 'Quality of Story' for this developing series. 'We are not writing science fiction,' he tellingly asserts. 'We shall provide scientific explanations too, sometimes, but we shall not bend over backwards to do so, if we decide to achieve credibility by other means. Neither are we writing fantasy: the events have got to be credible to our three ordinary people who are our main characters... I think the writer's safeguard here will be if he remembers that he is writing for an audience aged fourteen... the most difficult, critical, even sophisticated, audience there is for TV. In brief, avoid the limitations of any label and use the best in any style or category as it suits us, so long as it works in our medium.'

And there, in that very last sentence, we have the key. Webber had, probably quite unwittingly, outlined the criteria that did then and certainly will always uniquely define *Doctor Who*.

This outline document was subsequently amended by Donald Wilson and Head of Drama Sydney Newman. Although names of characters change and many of Webber's other more bizarre flights of fancy regarding 'Dr Who's secrets' were swiftly abandoned, its core principles and values remained.

This is not to downplay the significant contributions made by both Newman and Wilson. It was Newman who first suggested that a half-hour science fiction serial for a family audience would enhance the Saturday night line-up on BBC Television. It was Wilson who charged Webber with the task of developing a suitable outline for such a serial. Both Newman and Wilson worked hard on shaping Webber's embryonic ideas and curbing some of his more whimsical excesses. It appears that the name of the series sprang fully formed from the brain of Newman (in much the same way as the title for *The Avengers*, one of his earlier commercial television successes, had done), and it was Newman who first ruled that a time machine should form the central gimmick of this new venture, and that it should be piloted by a difficult old man.

Far left: Ian (William Russell), Barbara (Jacqueline Hill), Susan (Carole Ann Ford) and the Doctor (William Hartnell) meet Arbitan (George Coulouris), the Keeper of the Conscience machine of Marinus in 1964's *The Keys of Marinus*

Main: Vicki in the grip of her bizarre guardian Koquillion (Ray Barrett) during a photocall for her debut story, 1965's *The Rescue*

But these were just trappings. Was it really important that the series was shown on Saturdays, with episodes twenty-five minutes long, featured a time machine and a pensionable alien, or even happened to be called *Doctor Who*? All these elements, along with the intelligent casting, the spooky theme music and the imaginative set design perhaps helped the series to become a hit, but they made no real philosophical or spiritual contribution to what the series actually *is*. No, such elements are to be found in the musings of Cecil Webber and, for the thirty-five years that have followed, it is almost certainly his name that should have been scrolling past on the end credits of hundreds of episodes, or noted in the fine print on the opening pages of countless novels. Sadly, the words 'created by C. E. Webber' were never to been seen on a single episode of *Doctor Who*; not even the very first instalment that so casually and confidently employs almost all his core ideas.

In retrospect, it is interesting that Webber took time to state plainly in his outline that 'we are not writing science fiction' – especially when Newman had expressly commissioned just such a series. What was this science fiction that wasn't really science fiction that Webber had in mind? And what, for that matter, can possibly be more 'science fiction' than an alien time traveller?

Certainly, from a current-day perspective, *Doctor Who* is most commonly described as a science fiction series, bracketed by the press and the public alongside such space-going fare as *Star Trek*, *Star Wars* and *Blake's 7*. But this is a lazy categorisation coloured by perceptions of what *Doctor Who* became later in its life. Initially, there was a conscious attempt to avoid the trappings and clichés of science fiction – at the time a genre most closely associated with the three hugely popular *Quatermass* serials produced by the BBC between 1953 and 1959, which told the story of the driven rocket scientist Professor Bernard Quatermass and his battles with malign or simply amoral forces from outer space. Monsters and evil aliens were, at first, far from the thoughts of *Doctor Who*'s initial alchemists, and although, in an attempt to find that 'addictive' quality, the series took its basic format from the hectic pace and unlikely cliffhanger endings of the 'tuppenny rush' Saturday morning film serials of the 1930s (which made heroes of Flash Gordon, Buck Rogers, Zorro and the Rocket Man for a generation of pre-teen, scuffed-kneed cinemagoers), it was hoped that *Doctor Who* would offer something more sophisticated. Only one in three of the Doctor's adventures was designed to even take him into space; the rest would guide him on enlightening safaris to key points on the modern secondary-school history syllabus – to the Third Crusade, to the French Revolution or even, as Webber suggested, to Bethlehem – or on trippy-sounding journeys into strange dimensions offering consciousness-enlarging, almost Orwellian commentaries on the human condition.

It was the tastes of the viewing public which drew *Doctor Who* towards the motifs of science fiction – huge spacecraft gliding overhead, marauding aliens shooting lasers – but even then this was to be largely just a superficial dressing. In truth, *Doctor Who*'s mood, manner and moral attitude are all drawn from a different genre of fiction: the children's fantasy novel.

It is from works such as *Alice's Adventures in Wonderland*, *The Hobbit* and, perhaps most significantly, C. S. Lewis's Narnia books that *Doctor Who* takes much of its central ethos; stories of ordinary children and adults catapulted from comfortable lives into a crazy, mixed-up world where everyday objects and people become strange and alien, where turtles can stand on their hind legs and offer you a drink. We, as viewers, are happy to follow our unlikely heroes on their surreal quests, and we can dream of stepping out of our own mundane lives by stumbling through a magical portal and into a world of adventure.

Here we come back to Webber's suggestion that a 'good old Magic Door' could stand as the Doctor's

means of travel rather than a glittering spaceship or flying saucer. In 1950, C. S. Lewis's *The Lion, the Witch and the Wardrobe* took two boys and two girls through the doors of a seemingly ordinary wardrobe into a series of strange lands, where they, at least on one level, fought an arch-villain who was bad just for the sake of it. Lewis, of course, famously used his innocent adventure as a means of conveying a range of moral and spiritual issues to young readers. This appears to be very similar to the style that Webber envisaged for *Doctor Who*. The series would purloin some of the trappings of science fiction and fantasy – much as Lewis's work disguised itself in the unassuming clothing of children's fairytales – but would, in reality, busy itself with higher concerns. Science fiction that wasn't really science fiction.

C. S. Lewis died on 23 November 1963, the same day that the uncredited work of C. E. Webber first reached British TV screens. In this opening half-hour, the Doctor, his granddaughter, Susan, and her teachers, Ian and Barbara, step through the doors of an everyday police box on the first stage of a voyage through bizarre and surprising worlds. At first they just want to get back home, but soon, overtaken by the thrill of it all, they set about fighting injustice and righting wrongs. Lewis himself would probably have been a fan…

The new series received only moderate pre-launch publicity, and just a small feature in the *Radio Times* for the week. On its listings page for that Saturday night, no synopsis was offered for the first episode, just the detail '*Doctor Who* – An Adventure in Space and Time'. The simplicity of that description left the series free to paint its picture on the broadest canvas possible; to 'avoid the limitations of any label and use the best in any style or category…'

Doctor Who had all of space and time to play in, and, over the next thirty-five years, it was certainly going to make the most of it.

CINDERELLA, CHRIST AND JACOB MARLEY

Although C. E. Webber was undoubtedly the father-creator of *Doctor Who*, he was prone to making some hair-raising flights of fancy. Here are some of his other early thoughts on the series, almost all politely declined by Sydney Newman and Donald Wilson.

○ 'In his own day, somewhere in our future [Doctor Who] decided to search for a time or for a society or for a physical condition which is ideal, and, having found it, to stay there. He is thus an extension of the scientist who has opted out, but he has opted out farther than ours do. And having opted out, he is disintegrating.'

○ '[He has a] hatred of scientists, inventors, improvers. He can get into a rare paddy when faced with a caveman trying to invent a wheel. He malignantly tries to stop progress (the future) wherever he finds it, while searching for his ideal (the past).'

○ 'Think about Christmas: what seasonable setting shall we take our characters into? Bethlehem? Was it by means of Doctor Who's machine that Aladdin's palace sailed through the air? Was Merlin Doctor Who? Was Cinderella's Godmother Doctor Who's wife chasing him through time? Jacob Marley was Doctor Who slightly tipsy, but what other tricks did he get up to that Yuletide?'

Main: The travellers flee to their ship at the conclusion of their first adventure

Inset: A year on, the regular cast celebrate the sale of *Doctor Who*'s initial fifty-two episodes to Canada, Australia and New Zealand, the future of the series secure

Far left: Barbara meets a Menoptra, a denizen of *The Web Planet* (1965)

Put on your Dalek playsuit and load up your Anti-Dalek Fluid Neutraliser from the kitchen tap: it's 1964, and the Dalek Invasion of England is about to begin. Their weapons? Marketing, clever PR and money-spinning licensing agreements...

The date: Friday 20 November 1964. The place: any British primary school playground.

The fragmented white lines of the concrete tennis court mark out the boundaries of the petrified forest. Outside of these, Billy isn't supposed to be able to see Geoff and Lee – his Rangerscopes can't reach that far – so his friends are giggling by the baseline, daring only to stick one foot at a time into the edge of his magnificent city. Geoff, owing to his rough mop of blond hair, is stuck with playing 'Thal' again. Lee, who is always in charge of the games, is Ian Chesterton. Billy, chiefly because he isn't the highest-scoring letter in the Scrabble bag, is very happy with his role as ten different Daleks – after all, he gets to do the funny voices.

Less than five minutes later, after much frantic scuffling, the entire Dalek force on the planet Skaro is being held down by a non-specific Thal and a bullying pre-pubescent version of a science teacher, having dirt rubbed into his face.

Game over. Thirty–nil to the anti-Dalek taskforce. Normally they would now go and play something else – perhaps *Dr Kildare* if Geoff's little sister will agree – but not this time; nothing but 'Daleks' is being played this lunch hour. After all, everyone knows they are back on TV tomorrow.

The Daleks changed everything for *Doctor Who*. From their first full appearance in the fledgling series' sixth episode, *The Survivors*, the monsters became synonymous with the programme. Although they received little pre-publicity in themselves, the Daleks instantly gained popular currency in both schoolyard and office. Their sinister and ruthless ways (the inspiration of scriptwriter Terry Nation), their striking design (all kudos to Raymond Cusick) and their easy-to-mimic squawking voices (stand up, Peter Hawkins and David Graham) all contributed to the appeal.

Positive word of mouth spread and brought millions of new viewers to the series. The recorded rating for the final episode of the first Dalek-free adventure was 6.4 million homes, but by the time the monsters had done their work, *Doctor Who* was being watched in 10.4 million homes, and the majority of these stayed with the programme even after the time travellers had left Skaro with the Daleks vanquished.

The *Daily Mail* took a particular shine to the Daleks and in the first months of 1964 barely a week passed without some kind of Dalek-related story in its pages. If it wasn't a tale of how some eager enthusiast had assembled his own robot out of Austin Traveller hubcaps, it was a celebration of the donation by the BBC of two of the original props to a Dr Barnardo's children's home in Essex.

The BBC's own press information, sent out to prospective overseas purchasers of the show in the mid-1960s, captured some of the cheery madness of those days. 'Eighty-five per cent of letters to the BBC's popular *Points of View* TV programme concerned the Daleks,' it gleefully noted. 'In Scotland, one viewer proposed forming a society for the Prevention of Cruelty to Daleks. In Birmingham, a little girl constructed a model Dalek out of egg boxes and silver paper. A bevy of Dalek-deprived damsels appealed to the BBC to let them adopt one of the models, to make their lives complete, although two teenagers from Wiltshire added, "We don't want to buy a Dalek, but we wouldn't mind a couple of handsome Thals."'

BOYS AND GIRLS COME OUT TO PLAY

Apparently with little sympathy for the emotional well-being of those lonely 'damsels', the BBC was to slow capitalise on the Daleks' overnight stardom. When entrepreneur and commercial exploitation expert Walter Tuckwell contacted the BBC after the broadcast of *The Survivors*, offering to help make both the Corporation and himself a fortune through the sale of licences to produce Dalek merchandise, he was curtly told, 'Forget it, Doctor Who is going to finish them off after six episodes and then he is off to China with Marco Polo.'

A few weeks later, however, the BBC had a better measure of the Daleks' success. A memo from the Head of Business for Television Enterprises to the drama department dated 20 February 1964 inquired politely but pointedly if there were any plans for a rematch between the 'phenomenally popular' creatures and the Doctor. Head of Serials Donald Wilson replied four days later, 'We have in mind, of course, to try and resurrect the Daleks, but... it is hardly likely to happen until well on in the summer. I am asking [producer] Verity Lambert to keep you informed of any possible exploitation ideas.' In fact, publishers Frederick Muller Ltd had already asked the production office if the rights to produce novelisations of some early episodes were available. Walter Tuckwell had his call returned.

Less than a month later, on 17 March, Terry Nation was commissioned to write a new set of scripts which evolved under the title *Return of the Daleks*. The ever-eager *Daily Mail* must have been well connected, however, as they had confirmed the Daleks' comeback four days earlier!

Throughout the summer of 1964, levels of interest in Nation's 'children' remained high. Even before this second Dalek serial went into production, the BBC took time to trundle its plywood stars around Madame Tussaud's and the London Planetarium for the benefit of Her Majesty's press in a sensible drive for early publicity. Further hype came on 12 November, when magazine *Kinematograph Weekly* announced the impending production of a Dalek movie. In principle, *Dr. Who and the Daleks* would star Peter Cushing and Roy Castle, although they would be little more than warm props beside the chief robotic attraction. Production of what co-producer Milton Subotsky said would be 'a science-fiction comedy' began almost immediately.

Saturday 21 November saw the return of the Daleks to TV in *World's End*, the first episode of the retitled *The Dalek Invasion of Earth*. The creatures blazed across the cover of *Radio Times* and most of the daily newspapers ran associated stories. Some 11.4 million homes tuned in – *Doctor Who*'s highest figure so far – rising to 12.4 milion for the second episode. This pushed the series into the

Top 10 programmes of the week for the first time – quite a feat, considering that the programme's debut episode didn't even make the Top 100.

The Daleks had obviously been talked up enough to make the independent television channel feel somewhat threatened. As is still the case today, ITV was divided into separate regional stations, each of which could broadcast their own choice of competition to *Doctor Who*. In 1964 this would often take the form of *Thank Your Lucky Stars,* a pop music magazine show that had been successful enough to be awarded the title of 'Best TV Pop Show' by *Melody Maker* magazine in 1962.

The edition of *Thank Your Lucky Stars* broadcast opposite the Daleks' return would be special in two ways. First, it would be shown simultaneously across the whole ITV network. Second, it would feature the Beatles. The pop sensations were at the height of their popularity and in the middle of their still-unbeaten run of eleven consecutive No. 1 singles. It was one of those hits, 'I Feel Fine', that formed the centrepiece of their pre-recorded set for *Thank Your Lucky Stars*, although the song would not actually be released until 3 December. But even against this stiff competition, the Daleks won the battle of the 1960s icons, actually stealing 2 million viewers from the music show's regular audience.

In the following weeks Daleks popped up in all kinds of places, but their most remarkable and era-defining moment must have been an appearance on the *The Black and White Minstrel Show*. One of the most popular television series of the 1960s, the *Minstrel Show*'s crowd-pleasing mix of song-and-dance and variety had won the first Golden Rose of Montreux television award for the BBC in 1961. It was in the midst of a typical selection of light-hearted mayhem that the Daleks made their second appearance of the evening of 12 December, the fourth episode of *The Dalek Invasion of Earth* having been shown just a few hours before. Thus the fearsome pepper pots, who earlier in the evening had been busy mining out our planet's magnetic core, took time off to join in the Minstrels 'first space shot'. The Daleks tap-danced with Benny Garcia and had 'This Can't Be Love' sung to them by Tony Mercer, before finally carrying Margaret Savage off set as she belted out 'Whatever Lola Wants'!

Christmas arrived, but unfortunately would-be Dalek merchandisers had not been quite quick enough off the mark – perhaps due in part to that early inertia of the BBC's – which meant that few Dalek goodies were on the shelves in time for the big day. What was available sold quickly: two Dalek badges, available exclusively from Woolworths stores, reportedly sold over a million units; Frederick Muller's hardback novelisation of their first TV adventure, penned by series' story editor David Whitaker, went to a swift reprint; parents clamoured for a PVC Dalek dressing-up costume (on sale for the king's ransom of £8 15s 6d), but supply was cut off abruptly when the manufacturing plant reportedly burnt to the ground shortly before Christmas.

The hype continued through 1965, although *Doctor Who*'s production team attempted to distance the series somewhat from the phenomenal popularity of the Daleks, thus making it less reliant on their regular appearance. Interviewing producer Verity Lambert for the *Daily Mail* during the broadcast of *The Dalek Invasion of Earth*, writer John Sandilands reported that she became 'positively forbidding' and 'chilly' when he suggested that the Daleks might take over *Doctor Who*. Lambert added, 'I feel in no way obligated to bring them back for a third time even if this present story is a tremendous success.'

'STRANGE... BUT TRUE'

Some bizarre 'facts' from mid-1960s Dalek books:

○ Entertainment on Skaro consists of mock battles, displays of new weapons and television programmes that show the glorious history of the Daleks.

○ Daleks cannot die from 'natural causes' as long as their tissue is exposed to neutron radiation. It is not unusual to find Daleks over a million years old.

○ The colour red is unknown on Skaro, so during a Dalek attack it is advisable to wear bright red clothes.

○ On a flat surface, a Dalek can move at over 2,000 miles per hour, so it could travel between London and Birmingham on the M1 in under two minutes.

○ The Abominable Snowmen in the Himalayas are actually crashed Daleks which have crawled out of their casings and now live in the mountains.

○ Because of the lightness of its metal, a Dalek weighs only two and a half Earth pounds.

○ Using their Rad-etheric Magniscope, the Daleks could read the text on this page from over a million miles away.

○ The Loch Ness Monster is just the top of a periscope of a giant Dalek submarine.

Far left main: The Daleks are shunted around Shepherd's Bush market on their first official photocall
Far left inset: The following summer, a waxen Queen Victoria and friends remain unamused by a press and Dalek jaunt to Madame Tussaud's

Top: Nearly thirty-five years before the Spice Girls pull the same stunt, some listless Daleks stroll through Cannes to publicise their upcoming first feature
Middle: A scene from the full-colour, full-on *Dr. Who and the Daleks* film
Bottom: The movie Daleks' chief co-star, Peter Cushing

As the Daleks demonstrated their own independence by taking a trip to the Cannes Film Festival in May, *Doctor Who*'s television scriptwriters struggled to broaden the series' appeal by creating new monsters that would similarly capture viewer and press attention. They had tried and failed with the alarmingly fetishistic rubber-clad Voord from 1964's *The Keys of Marinus*, and would fail again in early 1965 with the giant, ant-like Zarbi from *The Web Planet*. A third attempt would come with the chunky robotic Mechanoids, also created by Terry Nation and pitted against the Daleks themselves in his third Dalek serial, *The Chase*, that June. Unwieldy in the studio and unconvincing on screen, the Mechanoids would be soon forgotten after the serial's undisputed stars polished them off in a kamikaze away win on the planet Mechanus.

The day before this fiery small-screen battle, the Daleks also blasted their way to big-screen success as the *Dr. Who and the Daleks* film received its London première. Even if reviews were mixed – 'Dr Who and his enemies seem a good deal sillier than they did on television,' said the *Financial Times*; 'Peter Cushing's Doctor is a pale shadow of the TV grouch,' agreed the *Sunday Telegraph* – box-office takings were high. As the film reached the regions in early August, its distributors launched a carefully plotted publicity campaign, offering tie-in features to local newspaper editors and taking both specially made Daleks and replicas of the film's sets on a promotional tour around John Lewis department stores across the country. Major branches of Woolworths also joined in the lucrative fun, ensuring that there was barely a high street in Britain that didn't have windows full of Dalek toys, books and games.

And that was how, in the summer and autumn of 1965 – through separate but mutually sustaining hype from the TV series, a film and dozens of merchandisers – the Daleks conquered the United Kingdom. By the following Christmas, nearly ninety different Dalek products had been licensed by the BBC, with the Corporation more than happy with its 5 per cent of the wholesale price of each item. Due to a canny joint copyright agreement, Terry Nation received a similar amount, allowing him to move from a small London flat to an Elizabethan mansion in Kent. In September, *The Times* revealed that a stage play called *The Curse of the Daleks* would run in London over Christmas. In December, Aaru Films announced the imminent production of a second Dalek movie. The press would casually present the Daleks alongside the Beatles and James Bond as defining popular icons of the decade.

But having been inflated by such unceasing hype and marketing hot air, the bubble could only burst.

The backlash began slowly, with the *Sunday Telegraph* one of the first off the blocks. In June 1965, critic Philip Purser said of *The Chase*, 'The Daleks, recalled with increasing frequency and increasing desperation, are fast losing their ancient menace; one of them has acquired a south London accent and another is undoubtedly queer.' What could he have meant? The following August, even in the teeth of 'Dalekmania', the *Daily Mail* suggested that the Daleks were soon to be supplanted in children's affections by none other than Winnie the Pooh, noting that the bear was receiving the Walt Disney treatment ready for the summer 1966 UK release of the animated film *Winnie the Pooh and the Honey Tree*. Other sources touted Batman, now in his camp Adam West TV incarnation, as the next big thing.

Christmas 1965 was straddled by the twelve-episode *The Daleks' Master Plan*, a sprawling tale of a Dalek scheme to conquer the entire galaxy. It also witnessed the symbolic handover to the true successor to *Doctor Who* and the Daleks in the affections of British children: a new American TV adventure series that was, in many ways, to be more popular than Terry Nation's monsters had ever been.

Paying a visit to the *Doctor Who* set during the recording of the ninth episode of *The Daleks' Master Plan* on 17 December was Sam Rolfe, creator/producer of *The Man from U.N.C.L.E.* This one-hour film series, recounting the tongue-in-cheek adventures of spies Napoleon Solo and Ilya Kuryakin of the United Network Command for Law Enforcement, debuted in the US in 1964 and came to BBC1 in June 1965. Outstripping *Doctor Who*'s viewing figures by a healthy margin, the series spent twelve weeks in the list of Top 20 programmes in 1965 while the home-grown serial managed just two. *U.N.C.L.E.* stayed in the chart for a further twenty-three weeks the following year.

While *Doctor Who* saw only three novelisations of episodes published before the end of 1966, *The Man from U.N.C.L.E.* had nine all-new novels, each often seeing up to three reprint runs in a month, some even published with the smug note 'reprinted before publication'. An offer of an U.N.C.L.E. membership card on the last pages of the books elicited a phenomenal response and extra

Top: *The Man from U.N.C.L.E.* producer Sam Rolfe gloats on the set of *The Daleks' Master Plan*
Bottom: Robert Vaughan, David McCallum and the flirtatious forces of T.H.R.U.S.H. from the chart-topping spy saga

Main picture: The TARDIS crew and some amphibian allies fall foul of a diffident Dalek in 1965's *The Chase*

secretaries were drafted in by the handling company to cope after requests topped 200,000. A series of theatrically released 'double episode' films helped to maintain the momentum.

So at the same time as Sam Rolfe was seen posing with Daleks in photographs featured in a February 1966 edition of *Radio Time*s – publicity for *The Man from U.N.C.L.E.* that was presumably trying to say 'anyone who likes the Daleks must know a good thing when he sees it, so watch his show' – he was also officially receiving the 'fantasy favourite' baton on behalf of his series from the now-flagging monsters, confirming a shift in juvenile loyalties that had actually begun a few months before.

As if in confirmation, the film *Daleks – Invasion Earth 2150 AD* opened the following summer to significantly smaller audiences – and an even more nonplussed reaction from the critics – than its predecessor. The day of the Daleks was over.

And so, as the Daleks are back at the local cinema, mining the core of the Earth again, only this time in colour, we can go back to the school playground.

Lee is in full strut as Napoleon Solo, and Geoff, owing to his rough mop of blond hair, is Ilya. As they shout into their felt-tip-pen communicators and wield invisible guns, Billy hops around his outline secret base, ready for their inevitable attack. No one suggests playing Daleks.

But that was, of course, by no means the end of the line. *Doctor Who* would see great success and popularity again – without the help of the Daleks – and would still be on television when Geoff, Lee and Billy reached their mid-thirties. And perhaps when the Daleks appeared for the final time in the 1988 Sylvester McCoy serial *Remembrance of the Daleks*, it was Billy's own son or daughter racing around that same schoolyard with both arms held out stiffly in front, shouting 'Exterminate!'

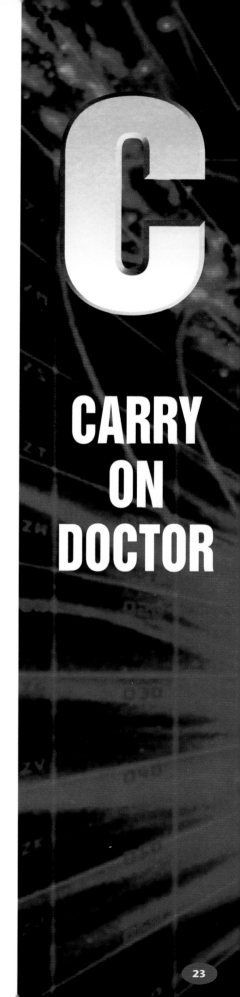

CARRY ON DOCTOR

Humour – both broad and sly – made an important contribution to the long-term popularity and success of *Doctor Who*. The funny thing is, it was added during the series' second year almost as an afterthought...

Under the suffocatingly hot lights, a bead of sweat tickles at the edge of the young comedian's eye, causing him to blink, fidget and mistime his punchline.

He prays for laughter, but there is none. Instead, a babble of distracted conversation rises across the tables of the club, joining with the sound of rummaging fingers wrestling with chicken-in-a-basket. The comedian has ten minutes' more material planned, but quickly decides to flee before the crowd's apathy shifts up to outright hostility. He mumbles his name, a thank-you and goodnight, and passes the microphone to the startled manager.

Off stage, he pulls together his things, pats his jacket pocket in search of car keys and heads for the back door, quietly pleased to be out of the spotlight and heading home to Tottenham.

'I was watching your act,' says a voice from behind. 'You were terrible.'

Open-mouthed, the comedian turns to see a small, unassuming man smiling at him. 'I'm sorry,' says the man, still grinning, 'but you were. The name's Harry by the way. You're Dennis, aren't you?'

Dennis knows that Harry was a hit tonight, so rather than attempting a stinging reply, he just lets his shoulders slump in admission of the truth of the more successful comic's criticism.

'The delivery was shocking but the material was great,' continues Harry. 'Who writes your jokes?'

'They're all my own.'

'Great. I've got a radio show coming up, which can be a bit difficult for a ventriloquist. Do you feel like putting together a sketch for me?'

This chance meeting with Harry Illingworth at a club in Stanmore, Middlesex, in 1954 was to change the life of twenty-two-year-old would-be comedian Dennis Spooner. Having recently completed his National Service, Spooner had returned to England from a troubled posting near Suez without a trade, qualifications or prospects – his education, along with his childhood, interrupted by the Second World War. Having written humorous sketches since his time in the Boy Scouts – even appearing on stage at the London Palladium in a Gang Show – and having continued to perform his own material on Forces radio, Spooner tried his hand at stand-up comedy. Touring working men's clubs across London, Spooner met with little success and was on the verge of giving up when Illingworth made him that offer he couldn't refuse.

A comedy ventriloquist, Illingworth's star was rising rapidly. Soon to shorten his name to Harry Worth, he was to become one of the most popular TV and radio comics of the 1960s. Spooner would rise part of the way with him as a gag writer before his career took a different course. Working with Worth on the Sunday evening light entertainment series *Val Parnell's Star Time* brought Spooner into contact with fellow sketch writer Terry Nation. The pair became friends, writing material for such forgotten comedy series as *Tell it to the Marines* for the princely sum of £200 an episode each. The launch of commercial television in 1955 had created a huge increase in openings for TV writers, and would offer Spooner a raft of opportunities to work on straight drama. Scripts for the popular police series *No Hiding Place* led in turn to work on some of the more restrained early series of *The Avengers*.

By autumn 1963, Terry Nation had begun work on the first of his scripts for the embryonic *Doctor Who*. His creation of the Daleks, which catapulted the series to near the top of the ratings charts within its first six weeks, effectively guaranteed him a place on the regular writing team for as long as he wanted it. Nation was already overstretched by other commitments, however, and suggested to story editor David Whitaker that his friend Spooner would be a valuable asset to *Doctor Who*. Still a gag man at heart, Spooner brought a fresh breath of comedy to the series, a move that would come to redefine the boundaries of *Doctor Who*'s style of storytelling for the rest of the series' broadcast life.

It began quietly. Spooner's first script of the series was 1964's *The Reign of Terror*, ostensibly a bleak tale of the events surrounding this particularly grisly period of post-revolutionary French history. Following much the same path as the earlier and almost entirely chuckle-free *The Aztecs*, the Doctor and his friends find themselves cut off from the TARDIS and fighting to save their own lives, powerless to intervene in history or prevent the seemingly senseless carnage taking place around them. Spooner added a distinctive new spin, however – something that was to become a trademark *Doctor Who* motif – by introducing the series' first consciously comedic character.

Imprisoned in the Conciergerie prison in Paris, Barbara and Ian meet their jailer – an unhygienic and unsavoury little man with ideas above his station. While an earlier *Doctor Who* story would perhaps have made this character as sadistic and inhuman as possible, Spooner instead opted to draw upon the inherent comedy in his tactless, vainglorious behaviour, lingering on his mugging double-takes as he is outwitted first by his prisoners, and later by a swaggering, confident Doctor.

As *Doctor Who* has always studiously avoided answering the question of why all its characters seem to speak English (be they from far-off planets or France), it is interesting to note that this drunken, ludicrous Parisian jailer was played by actor Jack Cunningham with a Yorkshire accent, while all the other French characters offer classic 1960s BBC received pronunciation – a broad Northern twang being, of course, a familiar if somewhat offensive TV shorthand for 'comedy working class'. This small touch, not specified by Spooner in his script but instead indicative of a production team happily rising to his bait, was also a first for *Doctor Who*, and the jailer was to be one of dozens of clumsy, amusing, regional characters to follow over the next two decades.

The Reign of Terror also saw a significant shift in the series' treatment of the Doctor. For the first time in nearly forty episodes, the Doctor was shown to be having a great deal of fun on his adventures – dressing up, pitching in and extracting a gleeful delight from his outwitting of bumbling human beings.

Finding himself caught up in a roadside labour gang, he challenges the authority of the bullying foreman, who replies with, 'I suppose you think you're clever?' The Doctor's answer – 'Well, without any undue modesty, yes!' – is, although not exactly side-splittingly funny, far lighter in tone than the more antagonistic responses he would have offered in any previous story. Later dismissing the foreman as 'a common fellow', the Doctor uses the man's clearly signposted greed to distract him – pretending to find coins buried in the road – before laying him out cold with a whack over the head from a spade. This is both the Doctor's and *Doctor Who*'s first use of seemingly pain-free cartoon violence, and another tweak of the series' template by Spooner. In the years to come, many a threat would be dispatched with a wine bottle over the head or a swift side-step that would allow an attacker to cannon into a wall, often followed by a self-satisfied quip from a Doctor obviously having a whale of a time.

Setting out his scripting philosophies in a 1981 interview, Spooner said, 'I tried to do it fairly light. *The Reign of Terror* was three hours long, six half-hour episodes, and you know that there are places in episode two where you don't want to get any further into the story because you don't want certain things to happen until episode four. So if you can introduce a character or an element of humour, then it can become a marvellous way of padding the show without boring the audience or breaking up the plot. If I'd had a straight jailer and had to do three minutes on him it would have turned out terrible. The audience will always watch "a funny bit" and quite like it.'

Spooner was obviously in tune with the thoughts of the production team, as he was swiftly appointed David Whitaker's successor as *Doctor Who*'s overall story editor just as *The Reign of Terror* concluded production in August 1964. Swiftly commissioning himself for a second script exploring a bloody time in European history, Spooner was encouraged by producer Verity Lambert to play the comedy element to the hilt: a brave shift in format for a series not yet a year old.

1965's *The Romans* brings the TARDIS troupe of the Doctor, Ian, Barbara and Vicki to the Rome of Emperor Nero in AD 64 and, as usual, quickly separates them from the ship and each other. The tone of the serial seems markedly different from the outset, as we watch the lazy travellers relaxing and joking in a purloined villa. Vicki even bemoans the lack of excitement – a far cry from the regular characters' usual desire to avoid danger and run away home. When Barbara replies, 'The adventures come without us looking for them,' it seems odd to hear her often terrifying, always-near-death exploits described by such a light and juvenile term as 'adventures' – the line sounding like it has escaped from the opening chapter of an Enid Blyton *Famous Five* romp.

Far left: The regular cast joking on set for the sombre 1964 historical serial *Marco Polo*...

Left: ...but by the end of the year, humour became a staple ingredient of the final product. Here, the Doctor (William Hartnell) tries to outwit the slovenly jailer (Jack Cunningham) in *The Reign of Terror*

What follows was intended by Spooner and colleagues as a spoof of the 1951 MGM Roman movie epic *Quo Vadis*, but a more appropriate cinema comparison becomes quickly apparent.

Living near Spooner at the time he was working on the scripts of *The Romans* was actor Jim Dale, already established as one of the leading men of the popular British *Carry On* movie comedies, of which Dale was busy working on the tenth, *Carry On Cleo*. A typical *Carry On* tale of confusion and single entendre – in this case set in Rome and the palace of Queen Cleopatra – the film would be best remembered for Amanda Barrie's wide-eyed and sexy Cleo and Kenneth Williams's definitive nostril-flaring performance as a flouncing Julius Caesar. Replete with trademark punning – 'Infamy, infamy… they've all got it in for me!' – and 'safe' sexual innuendo, it has much in common with Spooner's Roman *Doctor Who* runaround. Indeed, while writing his script, Spooner not only visited the set of *Cleo* at Dale's invitation, he also employed the services of the movie's historical researcher.

The Romans was *Doctor Who*'s first serial to offer a consciously joke-led script, and one that builds towards ever more absurd and comedic moments. The story proper begins when the Doctor and Vicki find the body of an itinerant lyre player, Maximus Pettulian. Picking up the musician's discarded instrument, the Doctor is mistaken for Pettulian by a Roman centurion – a confusion the time traveller is happy not to correct as it offers him a chance to visit Nero's court. Maintaining the deceit, the Doctor introduces Vicki to the soldier with a knowing wink and the line, 'The girl, she travels with me. She looks after all the lyres' – *Doctor Who*'s first genuinely appalling pun.

The Doctor and Vicki reach Rome, as do, separately, Ian and Barbara. On the way, each party becomes involved in a full-on slapstick fight, with amphoras smashed on heads and a would-be assassin accidentally falling out of a window. In Nero's palace, the Doctor and Vicki remain unaware of Barbara's presence – and she of theirs – as she disappears around the next corner pursued by a lustful, flabby Nero every time her friends step into a corridor; theatrical farce in its purest form.

William Hartnell's performance as the Doctor is irreversibly changed by the actor's obvious enjoyment of the comedy of *The Romans*. The actor fluffs almost every line when called upon to deliver traditional plot details, but never misses a beat on the

delivery of punchlines or skipping through some amusing physical 'business'. Through Spooner's work, the moody and quietly dangerous Doctor of the first year is banished for ever, to be replaced by a more likeable, childish but clever adventurer whose worst character trait is a tendency towards vanity and petulance. This ingenious, pompous Doctor was the one viewers would come to love through the 150-plus serials that were to follow – whatever his face looked like – and again it was Spooner who made the change.

Viewers at the time responded rather negatively to *The Romans*; some were even quoted in an internal BBC Audience Research report as saying the serial was 'so ridiculous, it's a bore!' and 'only suitable for morons'. Years later, even Verity Lambert herself described it as a failure, saying, '*The Romans* worked for me but not for the audience... At the time, *Doctor Who* was serious. It wasn't considered a humorous programme. For us to introduce comedy in a farcical four-parter as opposed to the odd laugh in an episode was something that people weren't really ready for.'

However, although a small lesson about restraint was learned – leaving *The Romans* as *Doctor Who*'s sole excursion into the realm of out-and-out farce – the production team were confident enough of the wisdom of maintaining a thread of humour not to pull away from the idea completely. It crept from its testing ground in the historical stories into the science-fiction episodes. Spooner's *The Time Meddler* later that year offered a time-travelling foe disguised as a monk whose interference in history included such trivial antics as banking £200 in 1968 London and collecting 'a fortune in compound interest' 200 years later. Terry Nation's third Dalek serial, *The Chase*, even undercut the series most menacing foe by presenting one of their number as a stuttering stooge whose response to a difficult question begins, 'Um... err...'!

Spooner's legacy lived on most clearly in Donald Cotton's two late William Hartnell serials *The Myth Makers* and *The Gunfighters*. The former was a more moderate version of *The Romans*, this time set during the Trojan War, and sticking to a similar *Carry On* template by offering characters from history with suspiciously modern senses of humour, sarcasm and irony – a rich vein tapped by many a TV comedy, most notably *Up Pompeii* and the *Blackadder* series. *The Myth Makers* even had an excruciating pun of an episode title – *Small Prophet, Quick Return* – which is so contrived and self-conscious, one might almost suspect the episode was plotted around it.

Guest stars better known for their comedy work were a regular feature of 1980s *Doctor Who*...
Top: Hale and Pace with Sylvester McCoy in *Survival* (1989)
Above: Elisabeth Spriggs and Richard Briers in *Paradise Towers* (1987)

The Gunfighters, meanwhile, although labelled by *Doctor Who* fans as another full-strength comedy, is really quite a different kettle of fish from its two rib-tickling period predecessors. All but one of the supporting characters in this Wild West story are cold-blooded killers on one side of the law or the other, and they don't stop to make droll observations. Strangely, it is only the regulars who play the serial as a comedy – larking around with guns, silly pseudonyms and double-taking at everything in sight – only calming down in later episodes as the body count increases. By the time of the final gunfight at the OK Corral, no one is laughing. *The Gunfighters* offers at one extreme a wittily framed shot of the Doctor standing in front of a saloon sign with only the letters 'LOON' visible over his head, and at the other both a ranting lynch mob and the sudden and shocking murder of a likeable babbling bartender.

Through the rest of the 1960s, 1970s and 1980s, *Doctor Who* would continue to serve up the majority of its episodes with a liberal sprinkling of gags, puns and witticisms. Later writers, particularly the skilful Robert Holmes, would recognise the same need for amusing characters and light by-play that Dennis Spooner identified back in 1964. In Holmes's 1977 serial, *The Talons of Weng-Chiang*, every other line is a joke of some form, although the story remains tense and involving. That said, only *Hitch-Hiker's Guide to the Galaxy* creator Douglas Adams, writing and script-editing episodes for Tom Baker at the end of the 1970s, would come close to focusing on comedy to quite the same degree as Spooner – particularly in his own *The Pirate Planet* and the co-written *City of Death*.

Spooner's influence on *Doctor Who* was far-reaching and vitally important to the programme's long-term success. It was also no accident: 'After the first year we realised that the show was destined to run a long time. And in a TV show you have to learn very quickly what you are going to get away with, because once it becomes at all established then you cannot change it... With that second year of *Doctor Who* we knew that whatever we could establish would set the boundaries for a long time to come.'

It is to Spooner's credit that those boundaries were set so wide, and it was to *Doctor Who*'s lasting benefit that comedy was the element he pushed for the hardest, the series' resultant longevity standing as testament to the talent of this 'terrible' comedian. ◖

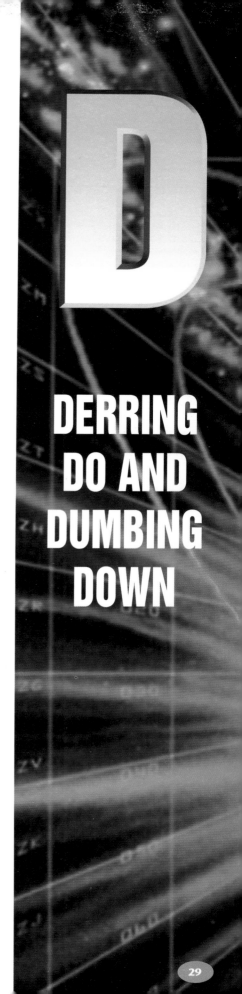

D

DERRING DO AND DUMBING DOWN

In its fourth year, the format of *Doctor Who* was streamlined and simplified to offer viewers a little more of what they wanted. The first casualty of this gentle repositioning was to be the monster-free adventures set in Earth's history...

It has often been said that *Doctor Who* was principally designed to be an educational programme for young people carefully disguised as an action adventure series; and that the TARDIS was created as a device to either take its occupants on trips into Earth's history – allowing them to explore its key battles and tragedies – or slip them into the future, there exploring issues of science and technology equally pertinent to a different section of the secondary-school curriculum. It is also said that the phenomenal success of the Daleks irretrievably changed the expectations of viewers, making them hungry for monsters and fantastical alien planets, and pushed the series away from this laudable crusade to educate and towards the more whimsical gimmicks of pulp science fiction.

This is only partly true. Certainly, the appeal of the Daleks was so great that they eclipsed the popularity of the series as a whole in the mid-1960s, but it would be wrong to say that they unilaterally changed the direction of *Doctor Who*. Looking through production-office paperwork from before the series' launch, there is little evidence that *Doctor Who* was ever intended to be coldly educational. It was dressed as a high-energy adventure series not to sugar a tutorial pill for youngsters but simply because it *was* a high-energy adventure series. The Doctor's journeys into Earth history were not designed to form some kind of moving, cathode-ray textbook, but rather to allow the production team to hedge their bets. In the early 1960s, science fiction was a largely untested television genre and one in which the BBC had little faith; even *Doctor Who* represented a very cautious expansion into the field.

It has further been suggested that, perhaps for added security, *Doctor Who*'s historical adventures were modelled on such successful filmed independent television action series as *The Adventures of Robin Hood*, *The Adventures of Sir Lancelot* and their ilk, which had dominated the television ratings charts in the years immediately following ITV's launch in 1955. But this is also unlikely for two reasons. By the time *Doctor Who* arrived in 1963, it must have been clear within the BBC that the popularity of these undemanding period swashbucklers was in steep decline – most, in fact, had long since been cancelled. Audiences were craving slightly more sophisticated fare, and had perhaps realised that the likes of *Robin Hood* – with its minimal number of sets, repetitive storylines, extended hokey fight sequences and familiar extras cropping up in multiple roles even within the same episode – were little more than cheap production-line schedule fillers. Moreover, *Doctor Who*'s forays into the past actually did very little to ape the exploits of Sir Lancelot or Robin Hood. The early TARDIS travellers were never seen swinging into the great hall of a castle on a velvet curtain, never leapt into the air to grab a spinning sword hurled by a comrade, and never clinked together flagons of foaming ale to toast the defeat of an evil sheriff. Well, not for a few years at least...

And so, neither drily educational nor thigh-slappingly frivolous, the historical *Doctor Who* story was a curious creature and one that, for as long as it was employed, would change its form several times as successive production teams struggled to find an angle – a level – for the action. The principles of story editor David Whitaker – overseeing the series' first year – set the initial tone. In Whitaker's view, interference in what was judged to be established history was strictly forbidden, *impossible* even. This meant that whatever events were documented in the textbooks and learned works consulted by the series writers – and by implication the Doctor himself – were, unquestionably, what happened. Why exactly history was judged by the Doctor – or Whitaker – to have 'finished' in 1963 remains a moot point, and even the normally questioning and querulous Barbara didn't stop to ask her temporal pilot why, if she was unable to civilise the Aztecs and prevent their massacre at the hands of the Conquistadors in the sixteenth century, it was still perfectly fine for the Doctor to prevent the Dalek invasion of Earth in 2167.

In a number of serials, the Doctor has referred in passing to many other historical events at which he has been present, and a whole host of famous figures he has claimed to have met...

◯ The Doctor has... met Theseus at the time of his battle with the Minotaur; marched with Alexander the Great; caught fish on the River Fleet with the Venerable Bede; heard Genghis Khan speak; been present at the battle of Agincourt; been imprisoned in the Tower of London after throwing a parson's nose at Henry VIII, from where he was rescued by Susan; attended the coronations of Queen Elizabeth I and Queen Victoria; met Sir Francis Drake just before the arrival of the Spanish Armada; encouraged Shakespeare to take up writing; shared a cell with Sir Walter Raleigh; fished with Izaak Walton; stood as a founder member of the Royal Geographical Society; climbed a tree and dropped apples on Isaac Newton's head before explaining gravity to him over dinner; borrowed a lockpick from Marie Antoinette; told Napoleon that 'an army marches on its stomach'; witnessed the charge of the Light Brigade; taken a coat from Gilbert and Sullivan; seen the eruption of Krakatoa in 1883; studied medicine under Lister in Glasgow; sparred with John P. Sullivan; attended the relief of Mafeking and the Battle of Gallipoli; watched Capablanca play chess in 1927; learned magic from Mescalin; and joined Mao Tse-Tung on the Long March.

◯ In addition, the Doctor claims to have met Pyrrho, Archimedes, Hannibal, Cleopatra, Dante, William Tell, Christopher Columbus, Mr and Mrs Pepys (she makes a great cup of coffee), the Duke of Marlborough, Lord Nelson, Beau Brummell, Isambard Kingdom Brunel, Thomas Huxley, Alexander Graham Bell, Puccini, Harry Houdini, Marie Curie, Albert Einstein, Donald Bradman, Dame Nellie Melba and Edward VII.

As this approach could serve to stifle a story's dramatic potential – since all must be left 'as it was' by the time the travellers depart from any given time period – *Doctor Who*'s opening forays into the past kept to the byways and B-roads of history. *100,000BC* saw a visit to a Palaeolithic tribe facing the onset of the Ice Age. *Marco Polo* followed the eponymous traveller on a journey to Cathay in 1289. *The Aztecs*, as mentioned, explored the culture of a group of fictional – but no less well drawn – warriors and priests.

Each of these early outings sees our painfully unlucky travellers cut off from their ship, fighting to escape bondage and get all four of their number back to the TARDIS at the same time – a task that for many months would generally prove a good deal more difficult than you might expect. In this time, they would each be unavoidably caught up – to a greater or lesser degree – in the politics of their captors. At the end of the day (or the end of the 120th day in the case of the lengthy, continent-crossing tale of *Marco Polo*), the historical status quo would remain and the game group would escape being written into the history books.

Although these tales were not designed to be principally educational, both *The Aztecs* and *Marco Polo* are still highly erudite and carefully realised pieces of work. Both were written by John Lucarotti and both are meticulously researched.

Marco Polo is a good candidate for closer study. Here, Lucarotti was writing about a subject close to his heart, and one that he had already explored in great detail in a fifteen-part 1956 Canadian radio series. The seven-episode script is crammed with period detail, all of it referenced, some quoted almost verbatim, from Polo's own memoir, *The Description of the World* (well, almost his own – he dictated it to a cellmate while imprisoned in Genoa in 1295).

The journey depicted in the *Doctor Who* serial closely follows that of Polo's first expedition from Venice to Cathay, which he began in 1271. The Doctor, Ian, Barbara and Susan join his caravan on the plain of Pamir and follow the Silk Road to Lop before crossing the Gobi Desert and eventually reaching Kublai Khan's 'stately pleasure dome' at Shang-Tu. Throughout the journey they are threatened by the machinations of Mongol warlord Tegana (a name lifted from the real memoirs) and learn a great deal of local history from Ping-Cho, a sixteen-year-old girl travelling to Cathay to wed a seventy-five-year-old man – a subplot based on a similar episode detailed in Polo's writing. From *Marco Polo* the interested viewer can also learn about the terrible cold of the Pamir mountains, Khan's love of stallions and hunting, the strange illusions to be seen and heard in the desert of Lop and, in a lengthy look-and-learn interlude in the third episode, the entire history of Ala-eddin and his Hashshashin assassins.

This is all edifying stuff, but at least Lucarotti doesn't always feel the need to let facts get in the way of his story. Polo made no such journey in 1289 – the year in which the serial claims to be set

– and probably wasn't nearly so significant a figure at the court of Kublai Khan. These are churlish observations, however, and such dramatic necessities do nothing to distract from the laudable splendour and intelligence of the serial.

The next few years, however, were to see a steady slide in the standard of research and a shift in priorities on the part of a changing production team. As it became clear that the futuristic and monster-driven stories were more popular with the viewing public, the historical adventures became a testing ground for new experiments with the series' style and content. Writer Dennis Spooner's work on *The Reign of Terror* and *The Romans* not only brought comedy to the fore – as discussed earlier (see Chapter C) – but also saw the main characters caught up in far more specific historical events: the imprisonment of Robespierre and the rise of Napoleon in the former, and Nero's purported burning of Rome in the latter. This incident was also to mark a further watershed for the series when we see the Doctor accidentally – or, just possibly, deliberately – inspiring the Emperor to destroy the city when he sets fire to Nero's plans for his new capital, Neropolis. When his companion, Vicki, chides the Doctor about his influence on history, inadvertent or otherwise, the Doctor chuckles to himself, amused by the idea – a long way from his hectoring of Barbara in *The Aztecs* over the impossibility of such action. In the years to follow, the Doctor would accidentally affect a wide range of human events, from the writing of *Hamlet* to the extinction of the dinosaurs, with such meddling by others becoming a key element in dozens of plots.

Following the Roman shenanigans, *Doctor Who*'s second and third years saw the historical interludes move further away from straight drama as the series embraced pastiche. There were two important exceptions, however, in the form of 1965's *The Crusade* and the following year's *The Massacre of St Bartholomew's Eve*, both in their own way stylistic hangovers from the series' previous administration. David Whitaker's *The Crusade* saw the time travellers once again taking the role of beleaguered bystanders caught up in an intrigue over which they ultimately have no influence and will be lucky to escape with their lives. There is still a notable shift in tone from those icier early stories like *The Aztecs* in that the level of action is upped somewhat and, as such, the story comes close to the territory of those aforementioned ITV filmed series as we see Ian battling Saracen warriors and murderous bandits (hurrah!) in his quest to save his damsel-in-distress from the wicked El Akir (boo!).

The Doctor's adventures in history...
Above: With Kublai Khan and Marco Polo

Far left: At the preparations for an Aztec blood sacrifice

Below: With Vicki (left) and Princess Joanna at the court of Richard I during the Third Crusade

The Doctor's adventures in 'bad' history...
Above: Polly cradles Ben in a seventeenth century Cornish inn, a favourite haunt of smugglers, pirates and thieves.
Below: The Clanton brothers, ready to face their destiny at the OK Corral.

The Massacre of St Bartholomew's Eve is *Doctor Who* history at its most bleak and traumatic. The serial depicts the events leading up to the slaughter of around 3,000 Protestant Huguenots in Paris during the Feast of St Bartholomew on 24 August 1572, a massacre ordered by the Catholic King Charles IX under the influence of his forceful and manipulative mother, Catherine de Medici. Written by John Lucarotti, it was more than merely a throwback to his serials from the show's first year in that the events depicted were far more shocking, due to their depiction of real characters and events and the TARDIS crew's complete lack of influence over the unfolding tragedy. The Doctor is absent for the bulk of the story, and his coincidental likeness to the Abbot of Amboise – a fictional Catholic involved in the otherwise accurately depicted plot – is used only as a device to move his confused companion Steven from event to event, allowing him, and hence the viewer, to stand mute witness to all aspects of the developing conspiracy.

The Massacre of St Bartholomew's Eve was to be not only *Doctor Who*'s last straight historical serial but also its most extreme and uncompromising. It was unpopular with viewers and saw the series almost touching the bottom of the week's Top 100 programme's for the first time ever. This type of story was to make way for two new genres of *Doctor Who* serial. The period pastiche, as given a dry run in *The Romans*, was tried again in gentler form in *The Myth Makers*, *The Gunfighters*, *The Smugglers* and *The Highlanders*. The new idea that human history was flexible and not an absolute – also mooted in *The Romans* – led the series to derive great mileage from placing assorted incongruous aliens into historical settings. It had begun with the Daleks clearing the decks of the *Marie Céleste* in one instalment of 1965's *The Chase* and seen fruition in *The Time Meddler*, where one of the Doctor's as yet unnamed own race generously attempts to help King Harold win the Battle of Hastings with atomic bazookas, believing this will speed the development of human civilisation.

Although often listed as 'historicals' alongside the likes of *Marco Polo* and *The Crusade*, the pastiche serials *The Myth Makers* (1965), *The Gunfighters*, *The Smugglers* and *The Highlanders* (all 1966) are very different beasts and – with the exception of the first – pretty much represent a more simplistic, less meticulously researched, 'dumbed-down' version of the genre. The 1966 serials take their origins from literature and film rather than accurate historical records. *The Gunfighters* takes much of its structure and content from the 1957 movie *über*-Western *Gunfight at the OK Corral*, even to the point of recording its own musical narration, 'The Ballad of the Last Chance Saloon', featuring the uncertain vocal talents of actress Lynda Baron – to replace a similar offering from Frankie Laine in the film. *The Smugglers* – all 'A-haa, me hearties' pirates, lost treasure and seventeenth-century Cornish smuggling – takes its inspiration from the work of Daphne du Maurier and

Robert Louis Stevenson, the latter author's *Kidnapped* also forming the basis for *The Highlanders*, with its tale of young Jacobites sold into Caribbean slavery.

The Myth Makers is slightly different in that it doesn't go for the crude gung-ho adventure of its successors, but is instead just as learned as *The Massacre* or *The Aztecs* in a less obvious way. It takes the stories of Homer and populates them with a series of flawed, vain or silly versions of his great heroes, offering a series of in-jokes for those familiar with the original text. Alas, however wittily intelligent the story was, by this stage in *Doctor Who*'s development, viewers seemed to know what they wanted from the programme and that was the Daleks, or, as second choice, whatever other marauding monster the production team could spoon-feed to them. Moreover, dwindling ratings suggested that even these elements were declining in potency. As *Doctor Who* attempted to reposition and re-energise itself in its fourth year, even the days of the historical pastiche were numbered, and nothing as intelligent and honest as *The Massacre* would come close to being contemplated again.

From that point on, endless alien invasions would be the order of the day, with period settings being used only as so much set-dressing or as a chance to use cheap costumes from BBC stock. The TARDIS would still take the Doctor and friends on many a jaunt into English history, but on arrival they wouldn't be forced to wrestle with the complex moral issues attendant to human sacrifice or to take sides in a religious war. Instead, there'd just be a shape-changing android to nobble or a vengeful time traveller to unmask. Little pain and little gain.

Looking back, it's a shame that the palette of possible *Doctor Who* stories was so drastically narrowed so early in the series' long run. But the public must get what the public wants, and if in order to survive that fourth year the show had to sacrifice some of its brain and part of its heart, at least it kept enough of both to ensure that even the simpler of the stories it went on to tell would be, in their own way, worthwhile.

Tales of time meddlers...
Top: A crafty fag during rehearsals for Kevin Lindsay as Linx, *The Time Warrior* (1973)
Middle: The Doctor in fifteenth century Italy. *The Masque of Mandragora* (1976)
Bottom: The Rani, gloating over the Doctor as her genetic experiments trigger a Luddite uprising. *The Mark of the Rani* (1985)

Left: Hector and Achilles do battle on the plains of Troy. *The Myth Makers* (1965)

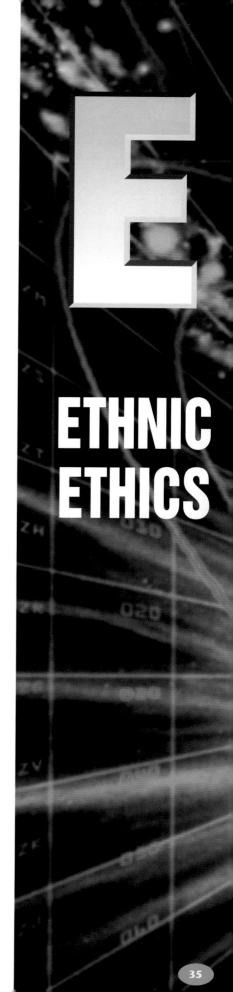

The Doctor explores the entire universe and all kinds of futures, meeting countless go-getting scientists and fearless leaders. But why do these brave new worlds consistently contain a predominance of white faces?

ETHNIC ETHICS

'Sometimes I felt that I was being used. I thought they were using me because they needed a scene to look dressed up – the "we're going to have a black person, and it's going to be really wonderful" sort of attitude. I had to become the person that the director really wanted.

'But I also understood what the overall situation was. Not to understand that would have caused me a great deal of pain… Those were struggling days, the days when you felt that you had to make a difference with whatever you did.'

This is how Guyanan actress Carmen Munroe described her feelings towards her appearances on British television during the mid-1960s for the book *Black and White in Colour* – a collection of interviews with black and Asian actors compiled by the British Film Institute. It is relevant here because in 1967 Munroe appeared as bodyguard Fariah in the Patrick Troughton *Doctor Who* story *The Enemy of the World*.

The serial follows the rise and downfall of the amoral dictator Salamander in the early twenty-first century. Fariah is his servant and food-taster, and nurses a secret loathing for her 'employer' – the inverted commas required as Fariah is effectively Salamander's slave, held in thrall by some unknown blackmail. Fundamentally, *The Enemy of the World* is *Doctor Who*'s attempt to 'do' James Bond, with a story of plot and counterplot, helicopter and hovercraft chases, and a Blofeld-type villain engineering volcanoes as part of a scheme for world-domination. Extending the James Bond comparison further, Fariah clearly takes the role of 'second girl' – the agent of the enemy who changes allegiance, delivers vital information to the hero and then tragically dies. So Carmen Munroe's suggestion that, as a black African, she was often used in the 1960s purely as 'dressing' may well be true of her *Doctor Who* role, with her colour being employed merely to convey more of the globe-trotting, exotic feel of the Bond films. *The Enemy of the World*'s guest female lead, Astrid Ferrier, is more 'safely' blonde and fair-skinned – her primary status confirmed by the fact that she is honoured with a surname when introduced. (David Whitaker's script does give Fariah a surname – lazily spelt variously as Neguib or Neguid, which indicates that the decision to make the character African, or Afro-Caribbean, in origin was his – but it is not used on screen.) Misgivings about the possible token nature of Munroe's casting aside, the actress can at least claim to be the first black actress to play a strong, key character in a *Doctor Who* serial. In her own words, 'Small it might have been, but you were there, you felt that what you were doing was going to make a difference.'

Overall, *Doctor Who* has a shockingly bad record on the use of black or Asian characters, and the employment of appropriate actors to play them. Even on the few occasions when they do appear, it is rarely in a role that does anything other than present them as a common racial stereotype – the slave, the native or the entertainer – or make their colour a token plot point in itself.

Ethnic stereotyping is a thorny and emotive issue. While we can gain through *Doctor Who* an interesting, if depressing, insight into three decades of slowly shifting attitudes and priorities in both British television and the nation at large, it is important to consider the series within the ever-changing broader social and media context of its time.

Black entertainers and actors had been appearing on BBC Television regularly since the service's inception in 1936 (the American song and dance team Buck and Bubbles formed part of the very first broadcast from Alexandra Palace). In the years following the Second World War, a number of television plays – chiefly adaptations of the works of Nobel Prize-winning American writer Eugene O'Neill – managed to offer good roles for the relatively few black actors working in Britain at the time.

The 1950s saw the ethnic mix of Britain transform dramatically. The mass migrations of Asian, African and Caribbean citizens from former colonies helped to rebuild the UK's war-torn national infrastructure and economy. But although British citizens now came from a swiftly broadening variety of ethnic backgrounds, little of this shift was reflected in the images of British life presented by the BBC. Although the television magazine programme *Tonight* managed to give Britain its first *bona fide* black 'star' in the form of Cy Grant, who sang the news in calypso every night, the image that most TV viewers had of any form of 'black' culture came from the phenomenally popular sing-along variety series *The Black and White Minstrel Show*, which didn't employ any black performers at all, but instead used 'blacked-up' white artistes in the American South musical tradition. The *Minstrel Show* came to TV in 1958 – developing from twenty-five years of successful BBC Radio forebears, including one whose theme signature actually invited listeners to 'come on and listen to the gay white coons' – and was a huge hit. It would run for twenty years before the appropriateness of its content and presentation in a multiracial culture were finally called into question.

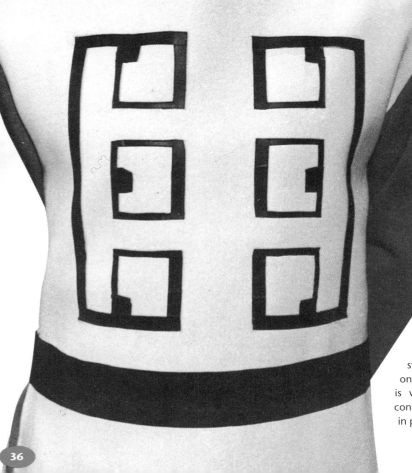

'Blacking up' white performers was not confined to light entertainment. *Doctor Who*, in its third serial, *Marco Polo*, used several Caucasian actors made up to appear Chinese, most notably Martin Miller as Kublai Khan and Claire Davenport as his empress. Actors of genuine East Asian extraction were allowed to take roles as extras and non-speaking walk-ons, although the lead female role of courtesan Ping-Cho was at least given to young actress Zienia Merton, whose mother was Burmese.

Several other 1960s *Doctor Who* serials – most notably *The Aztecs* and *The Crusade* – also gave the key roles to white actors in heavy make-up, while allowing black or Asian actors to fill background parts. *The Daleks' Master Plan* (1965) was casually offensive on two levels. Not only did the script describe one of its central characters – *Doctor Who*'s first 'super-villain', Mavic Chen – as being 'clearly part oriental', lazily using a Fu-Manchu 'yellow peril' shorthand for 'evil', but the production team went on to cast a white actor, Kevin Stoney, to play him.

These observations are not intended to imply any conscious racism on the part of the *Doctor Who* team of those days; their thoughtlessness was just a measure of the times. In the book mentioned earlier, *Black and White in Colour*, Pakistani-born actor Zia Mohyeddin comments on the approach of BBC directors in the 1960s, 'It was somehow assumed that black and Asian actors weren't good enough, I heard this again and again: "Oh well, you're all right, but you know that blacks can't act – their style isn't right. So it's much better to have Joe Bloggs putting on reams of greasepaint and trying to pretend he's Asian." This is why some people who were not even remotely Asian constantly played Asian parts. And because they had specialised in playing these parts, the directors felt more comfortable using

them. I don't know whether that was because they knew these people, or because they couldn't cope with the real thing.'

So accepted was this technique that Patrick Troughton was even said to have considered playing the role of the Doctor 'blacked up' and wearing a turban. As this form of make-up – and its consequent denial of roles to genuine black actors – has rightly come to be seen as morally unjustifiable, we should be thankful that Troughton settled on a different 'look', thereby saving *Doctor Who* from the same shameful fate as *The Black and White Minstrels*.

By the mid-1960s, there were signs that television was becoming both braver in its depiction of racial issues and happier to offer more imaginative roles to black performers in drama. John Hopkins's controversial 1965 play *Fable* explored inter-racial relations in the context of a Britain viewed as an imaginary apartheid state, but with black and white roles reversed. Transmission was briefly delayed by a jittery BBC after questions were asked in the House of Commons concerning the 'appropriateness' of the play's content – the planned broadcast date coincided with a by-election in the East London constituency of Leyton, and Conservative campaigning was focusing on the image of Harold Wilson's new Labour government as being 'soft on immigration'.

However, little of this new bravery seemed to filter down to light entertainment and more trivial drama – particularly not to *Doctor Who*. *The Savages* (1966) tells the story of a dictatorial élite ('the Elders') on an unnamed alien planet who employ machinery to tap off the fundamental 'life force' of an enslaved lower class ('the Savages'). The serial was developed under the working title *The White Savages* – suggesting, perhaps, that savages must otherwise be black by definition. It would be nice to believe that the serial was *Doctor Who*'s attempt to produce a racial role-reversal drama after the manner of *Fable*, but that is probably too generous. Beyond a simple 'message' in the serial about the barbarity of slavery, there are few clues to suggest anything more subtle is going on. Even though Jano, the leader of the Elders, is dark-skinned, as the part is played by another 'blacked-up' white actor, it would be difficult to ascribe a higher agenda to the production team.

Left: The 'clearly part oriental' Mavic Chen, Guardian of the Solar System, from 1965's *The Daleks' Master Plan*, played by Kevin Stoney in heavy eye make-up

Below: The Doctor (William Hartnell) with the dark-skinned Jano (Frederick Jaegar) in 1966's *The Savages*

Doctor Who's fourth year made more use of black and Asian actors than ever before, some in highly stereotyped roles, others in a more laudable attempt to portray a better, less prejudiced future. In the first category, there is the babbling, eye-rolling pirate 'Jamaica' in 1966's *The Smugglers* (he gets to deliver such empowering dialogue as 'The old man, cap'n. He put a spell on me. It was the black arts, cap'n. Spare me!') and the servant Toberman in the following year's *The Tomb of the Cybermen*. Toberman represents a string of clichés – the slave, the silent strong man, the noble savage who gives up his life to save his white masters – and even the Doctor talks to him as if he's a child.

Top: Terry (Callen Angelo) and Williams (Earl Cameron) fight for control of their Zeus V rocket in *The Tenth Planet* (1966)

Above: Ralph (Mark Heath) is attacked by a Cyberman in *The Moonbase* (1967)

Main: A scene from *The Mutants* (1972), featuring Rick James as Cotton

On the other side of the scale, both 1966's *The Tenth Planet* and its 1967 near re-run *The Moonbase* feature futuristic scientific outposts staffed by skilled personnel from around the globe. In the former, director Derek Martinus cast Bermudan actor Earl Cameron as astronaut Glyn Williams. The script specified the character was Welsh, and it's nice to note that Martinus didn't change the name, recognising that it is possible to be both black and Welsh. Five years later, a similar piece of casting in the Jon Pertwee serial *The Mutants* saw black actor Rick James cast as a cockney guard on an Earth Empire space station. This time perhaps a name-change would have been appropriate. Choosing an Afro-Caribbean actor to play a character called 'Cotton' is, at best, somewhat tasteless.

The late 1960s and early 1970s saw racial issues kept high on the political agenda. Wilson's Labour government had been elected with a majority of just four, and faced a rough ride until it fell to the Edward Heath-led Conservatives in 1970. During this time, one of Labour's staunchest critics had been Tory MP Enoch Powell, most notably in his 1968 speech on immigration policy which famously employed the words of Virgil to predict nothing less than a race war in Britain: 'As I look ahead, I am filled with foreboding. I seem to see the river... foaming with much blood.'

'Powellism' offered a formal political voice for all manner of deep-seated prejudice, feeding a growing sense of national anxiety. In the television industry, programmers backtracked and headed for safer ground. This confrontational tone hardly fostered creative expression and most of the black or Asian faces to be seen on TV at this time were in a host of dull documentary programmes attempting to 'justify' aspects of immigrant life in Britain to what was perceived as a fundamentally xenophobic audience.

Against this general background, it is hardly surprising that there was no broadening of *Doctor Who*'s casting policy. Even as late as 1977's *The Talons of Weng-Chiang*, a white actor was employed to play a Chinese villain under heavy eye make-up. Strangely, many fans of this popular serial are still surprised that it hasn't had a recent terrestrial repeat.

By the 1980s, the barriers were beginning to fall again. Many of the major soap operas began regularly to feature sympathetic black characters – a confidence perhaps drawn from the limited but significant success at the close of the 1970s of the drama *Empire Road*, the UK's first television series to be written by a black writer for a black cast.

As an ever-more enlightened decade progressed, one might have expected *Doctor Who*'s attitude to providing creative and interesting roles for non-Caucasian actors to improve. Given that much of the series' key audience was made up of young children or adolescents, it could also be argued that the programme had a duty to show

characters from a broader ethnic background – even *Doctor Who*'s BBC fantasy stablemate, *Blake's 7*, added a self-possessed black character, Dayna Mellanby, to its regular line-up in its 1980 run. But *Doctor Who* was lagging far behind.

The programme's final decade saw a scattering of black and Asian characters, but somehow the production team still managed to frequently fumble the ball. *Resurrection of the Daleks* (1984) employed a large number of actors from different ethnic backgrounds as the crew of a space station, but cast white actress Rula Lenska as their glamorous chief scientist. *Remembrance of the Daleks* (1988) used 1960s racism as a major plot theme – offering parallels with the Daleks' own desire to exterminate in an attempt to package racial themes for a family audience. Nevertheless, the serial's only black character is given just one scene in a café and dialogue that is purely of and about his ethnic background ('My father, he was a cane-cutter!').

The series refused to go all the way and cast a non-Caucasian companion. The spin-off comic strip in Marvel's *Doctor Who Weekly* had casually and confidently used such a character in the form of Sharon – a black working-class schoolgirl – in 1980 and, even better, felt no need to make any reference to her background. What very small leap of faith and insight would it have taken to cast a black actress as the very similar TV character of Ace in 1987? Or as Mel, Peri, Tegan or Nyssa for that matter?

As each *Doctor Who* serial offers around five major guest roles, making roughly 800 significant supporting characters, it's embarrassing to note that only around two per cent of these parts were taken by non-white performers; and among those, not a single black or Asian companion (until the 1996 stand-alone TV movie), lead Time Lord (although one does appear fleetingly in a crowd scene in 1976's *The Deadly Assassin*), chief scientist or guest villain.

Above: Ling Tai and Angela Bruce, with Sylvester McCoy in *Battlefield* (1989)

Left: John Bennett as Li H'sen Chang in *The Talons of Weng-Chiang* (1977)

But at least *Doctor Who* had a remarkable final, redeeming year. In the 1989 run of episodes, *Battlefield* offers two good supporting roles – most notably for Angela Bruce as Brigadier Bambera of UNIT, but also Ling Tai as the feisty Shou Yuing. The show's final regular serial, *Survival*, gave us Ace's Asian friend Shreela, played by Sakuntala Ramenee. The backgrounds of Bambera and Shreela were not remarked upon or made an issue of, and both actresses were allowed to play forthright, aspirational characters.

It had taken *Doctor Who* a long time to get this far. Who knows, if it had had a few more years, it might have finally offered us that black companion or even, perhaps, a black Doctor. ◖

Many *Doctor Who* stories offer convoluted and complex plots. Some require the viewer to do most of the work in unravelling the meaning of the things they've seen or heard. A few others, however, are just downright weird...

A cloud of poisonous mercury fumes is rising from the TARDIS console, choking the Doctor, Jamie and Zoe. Outside, a tide of lava is about to engulf the vessel. If they are to survive, the Doctor knows his only option may be to operate the TARDIS's hitherto untested Emergency Unit – but he can only guess at the dangers of lifting his ship from the time-space dimension altogether. In a panic, Jamie seizes the initiative. Placing his hands over the Doctor's, he forces the Unit into place on the console. With a painful shrieking and howling, the TARDIS dematerialises...

So, in quite traditional mode, begins the first episode of the 1968 Patrick Troughton adventure *The Mind Robber*. What follows, however, is anything but run of the mill.

Although the TARDIS seems to land, the scanner shows nothing outside the ship but a white void, and the Doctor can tell his companions only that they are 'nowhere... and it is only the unknown that worries me'. Appearing genuinely scared by his situation, the Doctor makes his friends promise not to leave the TARDIS, then sets about repairs before the time limit on the Emergency Unit runs out.

Watching the scanner, his young companions each see a view of their respective homes – a misty Scottish glen for Jamie and an ultra-modern twenty-first-century city for Zoe. The girl is unable to resist the temptation to investigate, so persuasive are the images on the screen. She runs through the main doors and vanishes into the opaque expanse of white. Despite the Doctor's protests, Jamie sprints after her.

The youngsters find each other, but have no sense of the way back to the TARDIS. Large white robots appear from nowhere to menace them, and Jamie and Zoe are shown spectral images of themselves dressed entirely in white who beckon the travellers towards them. The Doctor, meanwhile, is trying to resist a persuasive voice in the TARDIS telling him to 'follow and save them'. Eventually he gives in and leaves the ship – now also white – to find the sinister, silent robots and his companions, who have seemingly been entranced and replaced by their colourless *doppelgängers*. Slowly but surely, he manages to persuade them to go back into the TARDIS.

Seemingly safe, the Doctor sets the vessel back in flight as Jamie falls instantly asleep. The Doctor's concern about troubling readouts on the console soon become irrelevant as a steady whining vibration builds up inside the control room. Jamie wakes, babbling about a unicorn in his dream. The noise rises to a deafening scream before we see the TARDIS shatter into pieces in space. Jamie and Zoe cling to the console as it spins downward into the void. The Doctor hurtles off into the darkness as Zoe screams...

The Mind Robber was something of a break from the norm for the Patrick Troughton years. After two series of monster-driven 'invasion' stories, with a host of creatures or alien intelligences attempting to conquer the Earth or Earth-like planets – be they Daleks (twice), Cybermen (three times), giant crabs, shape-changing aliens, Yeti (twice), Ice Warriors, sentient seaweed, mad scientists or dictators – *Doctor Who* took a brief turn away from the familiar motifs of science fiction and made an attempt at producing an out-and-out fantasy.

F
FAR
OUT

The Mind Robber's remaining four episodes take our heroes on a journey through a realm that is pure Lewis Carroll territory. The Doctor is initially greeted by a succession of bizarre characters. There's a 'traveller' in a tricorn hat who replies to questions only in gibberish. 'I must retire in as private a manner as I came,' he says before vanishing into thin air (*pace* the Cheshire Cat). A group of children in Edwardian clothes challenge the Doctor with riddles including, 'Where was Moses when the lights went out?' and 'How many beans make five?' (very Mad Hatter). Later, finding a cardboard cutout of Jamie, the Doctor has to rebuild the Scots lad's face like a jigsaw – only he gets it wrong and Jamie appears with entirely different features. Zoe is discovered trapped in a jar – which is, of course, what a door is when it isn't a door.

After encountering the unicorn from Jamie's dream, followed by the similarly mythical Minotaur and Medusa, the Doctor is convinced that they are in a domain where characters from literature and folklore appear real. He deduces that the enigmatic traveller they keep bumping into is none other than Lemuel Gulliver from Jonathan Swift's 1726 satirical novel *Gulliver's Travels* – indeed, his strange speech patterns are explained by the fact that he can use only the words that Swift wrote for him in the book.

As the serial progresses, things begin to conform more and more to the *Doctor Who* formula. Once the Doctor has deduced the nature of their surroundings, the serial keeps to its own internal logic. Eventually a computer brain is discovered to be controlling the bizarre environment; it even threatens the seemingly mandatory invasion of Earth. There is still fun to be had as the Doctor fights to rewrite the computer's stories to allow him and his companions to escape, and a host of other out-of-copyright fictional characters – including musketeer D'Artagnan, Blackbeard the pirate, Sir Lancelot and Cyrano de Bergerac – are summoned up to fight for either side. However, those first two episodes, before a cogent plot is unravelled, remain especially compelling and stand as one of the few examples of *Doctor Who* steadfastly refusing to offer the viewer any hints about what is going on.

It's interesting to note that *The Mind Robber* was developed during a time of behind-the-scenes instability on *Doctor Who*. The preceding story, *The Dominators*, had been cut at the eleventh hour from six episodes to five following a dispute between the production office and writers Mervyn Haisman and Henry Lincoln over revisions. Peter Ling's *The Mind Robber* was at that point planned to run for just four instalments and would have been set entirely within the Land of Fiction proper. With a slot now spare, script editor Derrick Sherwin had little option but to write a new opening episode to Ling's story. There was no cash left in the budget and no actors available other than the regulars under contract. With only a white studio cyclorama and the TARDIS interior to use as sets, and some robot costumes left over from a 1967 episode of the BBC2 science-fiction anthology series *Out of the Unknown*, Sherwin created that baffling excursion into 'nowhere'.

Almost five years earlier, another story produced using only a limited number of cast members and sets had also compensated for a lack of visual incident with a similarly uneasy atmosphere and equivocal plot. *Doctor Who*'s third serial, the two-part *Inside the Spaceship*, came from the pen of the series' first story editor, David Whitaker. Developed, it seems, to allow the series to see more cost-effective use of the expensive TARDIS interior set, *Inside the Spaceship* was a startlingly brave experiment. With viewers having only

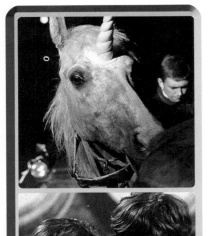

Three images from
The Mind Robber (1968)
Top: 'Goldy the Wonder Horse' is made-up as Jamie's unicorn prior to filming
Bottom: The Doctor (Patrick Troughton) and Jamie in an out-of-control TARDIS

Right: The Doctor encounters Gulliver (Bernard Horsfall) in the Land of Fiction

just begun to get to know the regular characters of the Doctor, Ian, Barbara and Susan, Whitaker's tale deliberately undercuts any such burgeoning feelings of security and familiarity...

When the TARDIS is rocked by an explosion, the four travellers are thrown off their feet and knocked unconscious. As each in turn comes round, they do not seem to be quite the same people. They apparently recognise one another, but have no memory of who they are or how they come to be there.

'You're working late tonight, Miss Wright,' says Ian calmly when he awakes, seemingly in the belief that he is still at Coal Hill School. They voice little alarm at their predicament and the most serious of questions are asked without any sense of urgency. Ian points to the still-unconscious Doctor. 'Shouldn't we help him?' he says, but no one moves. Characters stare at each other strangely, coming and going in silence. Each speaks slowly at first, enunciating their words carefully. Susan collapses, holding her head in pain. She is taken to bed, but then wakes in a hysterical state, threatening her companions with scissors before stabbing her couch in a vicious frenzy. The cloying silence of the TARDIS, coupled with talk of an unseen presence having invaded the ship, gives the opening episode the mood of a ghost story. 'I've never noticed the shadows before,' says Susan of her room. In a surreal Dali-esque moment, they find that the face of the large clock in the control room, along with those of their watches, has

Travellers in trouble *Inside the Spaceship* (1964)
Top: Susan, driven to one of *Doctor Who*'s most violent outbursts
Left: The Doctor, unwilling to trust Barbara and Ian, despite the fact they have already saved his life several times

melted. The TARDIS doors open and close by themselves; there is only a white light outside. The scanner screen shows a seemingly random collection of images.

Each of the crew members gradually returns to something like his or her former self, but the sinister, dream-like atmosphere remains. The Doctor initially accuses Ian and Barbara of sabotage and even attempts to drug them to prevent them interfering with his investigation.

The mystery is unravelled only as they begin to trust one another more, and the reason for the bizarre events is finally revealed. The TARDIS is attempting to warn them that the ship has been accidentally set on a course that will cause its destruction and is offering clues to the exact fault. The second episode ends with the travellers united by their experience, and much of the mistrust that had dogged their early adventures has eased. They have had to work together to save themselves and from now on they will be friends, with concern for each other's welfare as important as their own.

The first episode of *Inside the Spaceship* is, without doubt, the most strange and sinister ever to be broadcast in the name of *Doctor Who*, and remains startlingly effective to this day. If, in the eighties, *Twin Peaks* director David Lynch had been invited to work on the series, he would not have created anything so quietly dislocated and uncanny. Sadly, the show would never attempt quite such a brave experiment again.

The unfamiliar and the unexpected are the bread and butter of *Doctor Who* but, as discussed elsewhere in this book, most of the series' plots follow a straightforward, logical progression. What *Inside the Spaceship* and *The Mind Robber* have in common is that, at first, there appears to be absolutely no logic to the events taking place, and both stories maintain that sense for much longer than is traditional. In the end, they offer rationales of a sort for what we've seen, although in both cases some of the events still defy explanation at the close of the tale.

Another episode that may be classed as 'surreal' within this definition must be *The Feast of Steven*, an episode of the epic *The Daleks' Master Plan*, broadcast on Christmas Day 1965, which sees the TARDIS crew caught up in a series of slapstick chases around a Liverpool police station and a 1920s Hollywood film studio. However, as the episode doesn't attempt to tell a dramatic developing story and is obviously intended to be just a bit of disposable fun, it would be something of a cheat to say it was testing the boundaries of the series' format in any real way. The fact that the Doctor wishes viewers at home 'a merry Christmas' at the episode's conclusion is perhaps a clue that we're not to take it seriously!

While some serials surprise and delight by seeming to cast off logic from the beginning, a few others have taken the Doctor into environments where reasonable laws of cause and effect break down while still managing to keep one foot on the floor of reality, as it were. The best example of this is the 1976 Tom Baker serial *The Deadly Assassin*.

Attempting to track down a traitor on his home planet of Gallifrey, the Doctor links himself into the APC Net, a powerful computer that contains the thoughts and memories of all the Time Lords who have ever lived. His opponent is also connected to the system, and we watch as their battle is played out in the Doctor's dreams. Although the images we see are metaphors for their more abstract mental confrontation, they are, for the Doctor and his foe, dangerously real – if someone dies in this domain, they will die in the real world too.

Before the Doctor pulls himself together, his shadowy adversary has the upper hand, plunging him through a succession of bizarre scenarios, containing some quite disturbing images. When the Doctor brushes away sand on the ground looking for water, he finds only a polished mirror and

Top: The Doctor ponders the dangers of the Matrix mindscape...
Right: ...and suffers a surprise attack In *The Trial of a Timelord* (1986)

a clown's face cackling back at him. The sound of a war builds up around him as a soldier and horse, each wearing a gas mask, advance slowly through the mist. He finds himself on an operating table in the middle of a plain as a masked surgeon wields an enormous syringe. A biplane strafes him with bullets. His foot becomes trapped in railway points as a silent goggle-wearing driver accelerates a train towards him...

Remarkably, *The Deadly Assassin* lingers in the fantastic world of the APC Net for more than a whole episode, a brave decision by its writer and producer. But, as ever, the environment becomes gradually more logical and recognisable as time passes and the Doctor exerts his will. The surreal dream images are left behind as the Doctor and his enemy adopt the role of game hunters, attempting to track and outwit each other in a forest. It remains very effective stuff – and it's fascinating to see the Doctor forced to become a more physical hero and fighter – but it shows that the series can't avoid having to play by its own rules for long.

In 1986 the Colin Baker serial *The Trial of a Time Lord* took the Doctor back into this Gallifreyan dreamscape, also for more than a whole episode. The first scenes in this twisted world are very similar in style: the phantom voices of unseen children swirl through the air; a pair of hands emerge from a water barrel and try to drown the Doctor; dozens of arms pull him into quicksand. As before, however, the Doctor begins eventually to take control and the setting becomes less unpredictable – if still somewhat incomprehensible.

A final category of story comprises those that offer a few surreal moments in the midst of an otherwise traditional narrative. These generally occur in the form of visions or dreams experienced by the Doctor or his friends. One of the best examples of this can be found in the 1982 Peter Davison story *Kinda*.

While Nyssa is sleeping in the TARDIS, the Doctor, Tegan and Adric explore the forest world to which the ship has brought them. After they have discovered a huge crystal windchime suspended between the trees, Tegan becomes separated from her friends and finds the lulling sounds of the chime drawing her into a trance-like sleep. We enter the dream with her and find ourselves in a black void...

At first, Tegan seems to be experiencing a twisted re-creation of recent events. Just as, a few minutes before, she passed the TARDIS to find Adric and Nyssa playing a game of draughts, here she rounds a sinister-looking metal structure – its function unclear – of about the same dimensions as the TARDIS to discover a man and woman playing chess. It may seem familiar, but this dream couple are old and nightmarishly ugly, with a manner that is anything but friendly. Denying that Tegan even exists, the couple bicker and hiss through red-stained teeth before vanishing into the darkness. Then, just as the Doctor had earlier stepped from the TARDIS to join his young companions, a third figure appears on the threshold of the metal shack. He has the same stained mouth and sinister manner as the chess players, and begins to taunt and manipulate the girl...

Eventually we discover that the people in the dream are personifications of the Mara, a demonic force for evil trapped in the unconscious – 'the dark places of the inside', as it is later put – that uses the dream to take over Tegan's physical body and become a corporeal being. This, once again, is where the serial's consistent internal logic takes over and events proceed in a more predictable *Doctor Who* fashion.

Kinda is a highly rewarding story for the more mature viewer, weaving themes from Buddhism, Christianity and Carl Jung's theories of analytical psychology into a traditional *Doctor Who* setting of 'alien settlers threatened by apparently primitive but unexpectedly powerful natives'. *Kinda* still offers its younger viewers a pay-off in the form of a twelve-foot-long snake, but it was a measure of the series' self-confidence that it could take time to explore a setting as atmospheric and oblique as Tegan's dream.

So, while *Doctor Who* has contained any number of strange and entertaining moments that you'd never find elsewhere, and told many stories that could be classed as offbeat, 'way out' or even plain preposterous, there are few occasions on which it has completely suspended its own rules and internal logic and became plain 'weird'. When it has, however, the results have always been a delight.

'THEY USED TO HOP LIKE KANGAROOS'

Some of the Doctor's most bizarre adventures may number among those he has referred to on screen but we never actually got to see. Here are some of the odder things that the Doctor claims to have got up to, and the stories in which they were mentioned...

● He and Susan met the telepathic plants of the planet Esto (*The Sensorites*). He once trained a fighter called the Mountain Mauler of Montana (*The Romans*). He visited the planet Delphon, where the natives communicate using their eyebrows (*Spearhead from Space*). He learned never to trust a Venusian Shanghorn with a Perigosto Stick (*The Green Death*). He became a member of the Alpha Centauri Table Tennis Club (*Robot*) and President of the Intergalactic Flora Society (*The Seeds of Doom*). He gave the Droge of Gabrielides cause to offer a star system for his head (*The Sunmakers*). He learned how to walk on fire in Bali (*The Armageddon Factor*). He visited Magla, a planet-sized amoeba with a hard crust (*Destiny of the Daleks*). He helped Shakespeare with the first draft of *Hamlet*, the playwright having sprained his wrist writing sonnets (*City of Death*). He learned Vortex Swimming from an ancient mystic in the Quantocks (*Shada*). He's battled the terrible Zodin, whose servants used to hop like kangaroos (*The Five Doctors*).

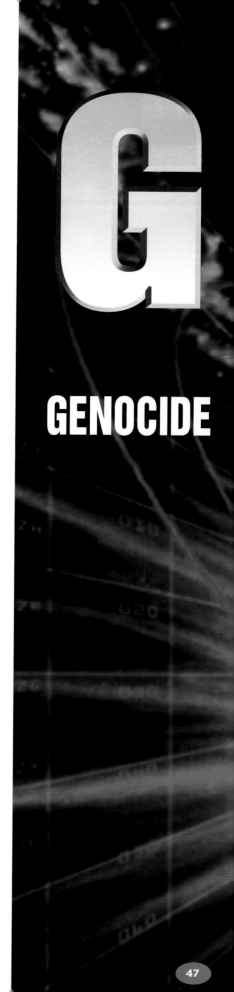

GENOCIDE

It's very rare that *Doctor Who* will call upon its lead character to justify his actions or to ponder their moral consequences. Considering some of the dubious choices he makes, perhaps that's a good thing...

It goes without saying that most *Doctor Who* stories have a happy ending. A cruel enemy is comprehensively quashed and a triumphant Doctor engages in idle banter with new friends – cracking a joke about the silliness of humans, planning a holiday or wondering what's for supper. Only a handful of stories fade out on a consciously downbeat note, and of those that do few are as thought-provoking as the 1970 Jon Pertwee serial *Doctor Who and the Silurians*.

In this tale, the Doctor and his military colleagues at UNIT are called upon to investigate unexplained power losses at an underground nuclear research centre in modern-day England. Exploring a nearby cave system, the Doctor is attacked by a tyrannosaur-like creature, discovering later that the dinosaur is no more than a guard dog for a race of intelligent, humanoid reptiles – soon to be christened 'Silurians' by the humans.

The Silurians have been in extended hibernation deep beneath the Earth for millions of years, hiding from a predicted natural disaster that never occurred. While they slept, the race of wild apes they had once treated as vermin evolved into *Homo sapiens* and developed a civilisation and technology of their own. The humans' atomic facility has accidentally revived some of the reptiles, and they are now ready to stake a claim to the planet they believe to be theirs by right.

Doctor Who and the Silurians formed part of *Doctor Who*'s seventh block of serials and fell at the end of a year that had already seen big changes for the series. In an ongoing narrative, the Doctor found himself in exile on Earth and trapped in an initially uneasy alliance with the military investigation team of UNIT, led by the sometimes open-minded, sometimes reactionary Brigadier Lethbridge-Stewart. This new, seemingly permanent setting placed additional demands on the series' writers, challenging them to keep fresh and surprising a format which had to see UNIT and their Time Lord scientific adviser confront and defeat a different threat to humanity and the Home Counties every few weeks. With no opportunity to distract viewers' attention from the unavoidable repetition inherent in this narrower format by taking a trip to a gimmicky new alien planet, a different sleight of hand was necessary to keep them engaged. With this in mind, the series began bravely to probe a variety of moral issues pertaining to the Doctor's actions – essentially, for the first time since the early William Hartnell serials.

Beyond its status as a simple parable of entrenched racism, *Doctor Who and the Silurians* shows a far more adult and anguished Doctor than ever before, tortured by his conscience as he struggles to prevent needless deaths – and, indeed, all-out war between the two races. The Time Lord – now more clearly identified as an alien than ever before – refuses to take sides, merely offering soothing words of peace to both parties. Among the humans, he has the support of his assistant Liz ('Just because they're an alien species doesn't mean we have to kill them') but comes into conflict with the less enlightened authority figures, including Lethbridge-Stewart himself. Although not directly belligerent, the Brigadier won't consider confronting the reptiles without a platoon of armed men at his side. His first question to the Doctor regarding the creatures is, 'What weapons do they have?' Adding fuel to the fire, the reactions of humans are affected by a feeling of deep-seated revulsion triggered by an ancient race-memory fear of the Silurians, and the Brigadier's ultimate 'shoot first, ask questions later' approach is crystallised by the reaction of emotional scientist Miss Dawson, whose lover has just been killed by a wounded Silurian he was holding captive: 'We must destroy them before they destroy us!' The Doctor's protestations that the creatures have so far killed only in self-defence fall on deaf ears.

Alien invasions repulsed by the Doctor, with all the would-be conquerors killed...

Top: A Krynoid, seeking to consume all animal life on Earth in 1976's *The Seeds of Doom*

Above: A Terileptil from 1982's *The Visitation*, one of four alien fugitives who plan to wipe out humanity with the Black Death

Main: The Zygons, harbingers of mass invasion in 1975's *Terror of the Zygons*

Far right: Roger Delgado as the 'evil' Master

What this serial offers – and it's rare in *Doctor Who* – is an opportunity to see representatives of an alien race as creatures wrestling with moral dilemmas of their own, rather than as just the usual militaristic clones, collectively hissing or squawking threats. The Silurian leader is willing to listen to, and eventually support, the Doctor's pleas for peace, in the process taking a more reasonable position than any of the humans; but a young pretender to his throne adopts exactly the same hawkish attitude as, and even unknowingly paraphrases, Miss Dawson and the Brigadier. The Doctor almost manages to secure his peaceful settlement before the younger Silurian kills his leader and attempts to wipe out mankind with a plague. From this point on the Time Lord is on a hiding to nothing with his preaching of pacifism and it is all he can do to prevent further bloodshed, be it the warm blood of the humans or the cold blood of the reptiles. This he does by curing the plague and forcing the Silurians temporarily back into hibernation by means of a cunning ruse.

In the closing scenes of the story, the Doctor insists that the Brigadier promises not to disturb the Silurian base while he leaves to seek help with the task of reviving the reptiles one by one, hoping for an opportunity to negotiate with them calmly and so guarantee a lasting armistice. But as the Doctor and Liz drive away, a series of explosions echoes across the countryside. The Brigadier has sealed the Silurians underground once more. The Doctor is appalled, whispering to his friend, 'That's murder. They were intelligent alien beings – a whole race of them, and he's just wiped them out.' The viewer feels something of the Doctor's shock and shame.

If this was the first time that such moral uncertainties clouded the traditionally gung-ho ending of a *Doctor Who* story, it was also one of the last. By the following year, the production team had plunged the Doctor back into more helter-skelter, undemanding adventures. Whereas *Doctor Who and the Silurians* (and the preceding few stories) attempted to find ways to disguise the fact that this new Earth-bound *Doctor Who* had only three plots at its disposal – 'alien invasion from space', 'mad scientist endangering civilisation' and 'innocent people possessed by evil force' – the rest of the Doctor's exile brought stories that wholeheartedly embraced this limitation. Moreover, with the introduction of a new regular foe for the Doctor in the form of his nemesis-by-numbers, the Master, writers happily wove those three plots together – week in, week out – in the form of 'mad scientist possesses innocent people and endangers civilisation with alien invasion from space' (*Terror of the Autons*, *The Mind of Evil*, *The Claws of Axos*... repeat to fade). There was little need to dwell on any moral shades of grey because we were regularly assured that the Master was simply 'evil' and so had to be defeated. Although now screened in colour, *Doctor Who* was as black and white as ever.

The concept of fundamental 'evil' has always been a useful moral get-out clause for *Doctor Who* writers – or writers of fantasy in general. In fact, it could be argued that the very use of the word actually defines a television programme, film or book as 'fantasy'. Consider any police or detective drama: an episode of *The Bill* or *Columbo* could be judged 'realistic' because the motives of the villains are always very human – generally greed, lust or envy. But if, when a murder has been committed, the investigators at any point suggest the culprit was merely 'evil', then you are instantly in the realm of *Twin Peaks* or *The Avengers*. No further meaningful psychological study or character insights are required, and all the heroes can pitch themselves, without hesitation, into the thrill of the chase and the inevitable execution.

A useful demonstration of this in *Doctor Who* can be found by comparing that Jon Pertwee Silurian tale with the early Tom Baker serial *Terror of the Zygons*. Both have plots that could be summarised thus: a group of aliens hidden on Earth for centuries want to claim the planet for their own, ultimately seeking to alter the environment to suit their needs, destroying mankind in the process. Even many of the incidental details are the same: the Doctor is called in by UNIT to investigate a mystery where he finds a sole surviving babbling witness to a significant earlier tragedy; both the Silurians and Zygons protect themselves using a pet dinosaur; and one of each of their number finds itself cornered by humans in a barn. However, despite these similarities, the Doctor's position and attitude in the two tales could not be more different. The Fourth Doctor says nothing about the possibility of peaceful cohabitation of the Earth by Zygons and humans, let alone

attempting to negotiate such a settlement. Instead he taunts the Zygon commander about the ludicrous scale of his designs upon the Earth ('Isn't it a bit large for just about six of you?') or his duties as a ruler ('You've got to come out on the balcony sometimes and wave a tentacle'). Furthermore, the Doctor happily accepts the Brigadier's ultimately fruitless plan to bomb the Zygon ship, before finally destroying the vessel, and all but one of its alien occupants, himself – casually killing those half-dozen Zygon 'troops' who could quite easily have been captured instead.

But the Doctor's actions in this later story appear to be justified within the narrative because the Zygons, unlike the Silurians, have already been labelled 'evil': their leader identifies himself very early on as a 'Warlord', they are presented as soldiers rather than scientists (*Doctor Who*'s general celebration of science means that its exponents are rarely 'evil', just mad or misguided) and they never show any sympathetic dissension in their ranks. Evil beings are allowed to be killed in *Doctor Who* with no questions asked and no moral justification required. There's no way that *Terror of the Zygons* – or any of the countless other *Doctor Who* stories with similar structure or character motivation – is going to end with the Doctor bemoaning the 'murder' of 'intelligent alien beings'. The Silurians were privileged indeed.

Of course, the use of the word 'evil' is not the only indication that a TV series is a fantasy. *Star Trek*, for example, hardly uses it, and always assigns its aliens more everyday motives for their murderous enterprises – generally something to do with political powerplay. In so doing, it ensures that its characters spend time discussing the moral issues contingent to their decisions and actions. Starfleet Command, the interstellar organisation that employees Captains Kirk, Picard *et al.*, even has a series of standing orders that govern and moderate the actions of its officers, central to which is the 'Prime Directive' prohibiting Starfleet personnel from interfering in the normal development of any society, and much plot mileage in the various *Star Trek* series is drawn from its characters' need to stand by this rule.

Doctor Who's own galactic authority, the Time Lords, have a similar directive – one of their 'Laws of Time' – which prevents their number from influencing the affairs of other peoples and planets. Significantly, in 1969's *The War Games* we discover that it is for the *breaking* of this very rule that the Doctor has been on the run from his own people, and his punishment for this crime is the aforementioned exile to Earth. In many ways, this demonstrates the key difference between *Star Trek* and *Doctor Who*. Whereas the American series celebrates heroes who are very much part of the establishment and abide by a clear moral code, the Doctor is presented as a loner who lives outside and in opposition to the system – a renegade, and an unpredictable and inconsistent one at that.

The motives behind the Doctor's regular interference in Earth history warrant investigation. Early in his televised travels, the Time Lord informed his companions that it was 'impossible' to alter the course of established history. As we later discover that his own people actually need to have a rule forbidding such activity, we must assume that the Doctor was either badly informed or lying. When the Doctor meets the first in a long succession of temporal manipulators – another time traveller trying to help King Harold win the Battle of Hastings in 1965's *The Time Meddler* – he goes out of his way to prevent such improper interference. However, on several occasions – his ignition of the Great Fire of London in 1982's *The Visitation* is a prime example – he creates 'established' history himself (in this case while preventing the alien Terileptils conquering the Earth in 1666). What absolute record of time does the Doctor have access to in order to be allowed to make such choices? The Terileptils hadn't travelled through time to the pervert the course of history, and they were merely trying to save themselves at the expense of mankind. Who is the Doctor to say that humanity has the right to survive this accidental early contact with aliens – to decide who lives and who dies – just because he happens to be passing?

Even in serials set in the present day, we regularly see the Doctor quickly taking sides when the moral issues are surely more complex. Invaders such as the Daleks or the Cybermen can be dismissed as 'evil' and sentenced to death by the laws of *Doctor Who* natural justice, but how can the Doctor justifiably rule that the carnivorous Krynoid plants that almost consume the Earth in 1976's *The Seeds of Doom* have no right to do so? Surely they are just doing what Krynoids do, so why should the vehicular vegetables be cut down for responding to an instinct to feed when man happens to be on the menu?

In *Genesis of the Daleks* – just three serials prior to his casual extermination of the Zygons – we get to see the Doctor agonising over his right to destroy his deadliest enemies at the moment of their creation. His dialogue – 'But if I kill... wipe out a whole intelligent life form – then I become like them. I'd be no better than the Daleks' – is consistent with his response to the Brigadier's actions in *Doctor Who and the Silurians*, but largely out of step with his own attitude on many other occasions. In 1980's *State of Decay*, he destroys the last of a species of giant vampires; in 1986's *Trial of a Time Lord*, he wipes out the only examples of the Vervoid race of intelligent plant life; in 1988's *Remembrance of the Daleks*, he manipulates events towards the destruction the Daleks' entire home planet and almost cruelly taunts what appears to be the last surviving member of the race into suicide without a second thought.

Issues of mass extinction...
Top: Aukon and Camilla, servants of the last of the Great Vampires, destroyed by the Doctor. *State of Decay* (1980)
Above: A Vervoid, a new intelligent species wiped out in an attack by the Time Lord. *Trial of a Time Lord* (1986)

Far left: The Doctor ponders his right to wipe out the Daleks in 1975's *Genesis of the Daleks*...

Left: ...before finally doing just that in 1988's *Remembrance of the Daleks*

From just these few examples, there is no doubt that the Doctor is a meddler on a breathtaking scale. In the real world, 'meddling' is not seen as a likeable personality trait. Those who snoop, intrude upon or interfere with our business are not generally welcome, and uninvited advice or intervention is rarely tolerated. It's interesting that *Doctor Who* can make a hero out of such a character. The fight against unquestionable 'evil' allows him a certain amount of latitude, but even then, as we've seen, many of his actions remain a bit ethically dubious. So what sleight of hand does the series' production team use to keep us on the Doctor's side?

In truth, this unpredictable and contradictory behaviour ultimately serves to make the Doctor even more mysterious and captivating. Because we feel we can never truly understand his alien and universe-spanning moral perspective – and we so desperately want him to have a consistent perspective – he is allowed to make these grand choices between right and wrong on our behalf. In many ways, the Doctor is defined by our distance from him. Unlike the leads in *Star Trek* and its ilk, we are rarely given access to his thought-processes or motivations, which in turn only adds to the character's enigmatic appeal.

So, in many ways, *Doctor Who* has benefited from not lingering on the moral high ground of *Doctor Who and the Silurians* for too long. In a series with a primary goal to entertain through a steady stream of showdowns between the Doctor and multifarious monsters, it would never have paid to dwell on the Doctor's doubts and insecurities for too long. That would force both the Doctor and his audience to grow up and face the fact that it's a messy and often unjust world. By staying, for the most part, in the clear-cut, black-and-white realm of fundamental 'good' and 'evil', the Doctor is liberated from such dreary and mundane concerns as duty or conscience. And so, during those more innocent half-hours, are we.

Doctor Who **was created as entertainment for the whole family. The kids were easy to snare with monsters and action, while the adults could be caught up in the often sophisticated plots and knowing humour. But the teenagers were harder to please, and when the series tried to talk their language it had an alarming tendency to say exactly the wrong thing.**

'But, Doctor, it really *is* the dawning of the Age of Aquarius!'

On one level, companion Jo Grant's opening words to the Doctor in 1971's *The Dæmons* serve purely as an opportunity to introduce the basic dilemma of the plot. An ancient burial mound near the village of Devil's End is about to be opened and the media are playing up prophecies of diabolic consequences. The Doctor, meanwhile, stands up for science and reason, casually dismissing superstition, black magic and the occult before finally exposing alien interference and another megalomaniacal plot by the Master.

Sadly, however, Jo's line also stands as a classic example of *Doctor Who's* sometimes crude and often inadvertently hilarious attempts to employ the interests and language of its teenage and young adult audience in an attempt to appear 'with it'.

Here, 'This is the dawning of the Age of Aquarius' is recognisable as the chief refrain of the most memorable song from *Hair*. First staged in New York in October 1967, *Hair* was a virtually plotless, anti-establishment 'love-rock' musical which followed the drug-fuelled antics of a group of hippies and flower children celebrating the new Age of Aquarius – a time when peace and free love would reign. The show gained notoriety in the UK for its on-stage nudity and a failed attempt by the Lord Chamberlain to ban its performance in London, where it eventually opened in the summer of 1968. It's pretty typical of *Doctor Who* that, in an attempt to give a serial a contemporary edge, the writer plumps for a reference which is already at least three years out of date. But then, the series always was a bit hit and miss in that department...

The earliest attempt to capture the mood of the moment came in that very first episode, *An Unearthly Child*, shown in November 1963. We see a corridor in Coal Hill Secondary School. The contemporary checkpoints are offered straight away: two fashionably dressed schoolgirls – almost early-teen versions of Profumo girls Christine Keeler and Mandy Rice-Davies – are chatting as they walk. One shows the other a photograph, perhaps a fashion page from a magazine, and we can just hear their exchange: 'Oh, no, that's horrible!' 'No, it's not, it's fabulous.' After a sarcastic remark from a boy, they roll their eyes, Christine whispers something caustic to Mandy, and they sweep off, plastic handbags swinging.

H

HIP AND GROOVY, BABY...

Of course, this grounding of the story in the here and now was very important. After all, the two schoolteachers we are about to meet, Ian and Barbara, are intended to be the eyes and ears of the viewer, so we must be sure we can relate to their everyday world and Everyman experiences. This set-up is quick and neatly done, and is free from the self-consciousness that would dog similar scenes later in the series' life.

Through Ian and Barbara we come to meet their troubling pupil Susan Foreman. Unaware that her teachers are nearby, Susan is alone in a classroom, dancing – well, waving her hand – to some twanging guitar music on her transistor radio. Her gestures are so mannered and ill-suited to the track she's listening to, they can be taken only as a deliberate attempt to convey her soon-to-be revealed status as the extraterrestrial junior of the episode's title. The music isn't alien, however: 'It's John Smith and the Common Men,' she tells Barbara when the teacher interrupts. 'Aren't they fabulous?' (Note that the word 'fabulous' has already been used twice in the series' opening five minutes.) Sadly, *Doctor Who*'s budget for that first episode seems not to have been able to run to a rights payment for a real pop song, so something from BBC stock had to do. The track, 'Three Guitars Mood 2' by the Arthur Nelson Group, sounds like a supermarket Muzak version of The Shadows, but that kind of thing must have been popular in the reality of *Doctor Who*, as Susan tells us, 'They've gone from 19 to 2', thus proving that she's a hip chick with her finger on the pulse of popular culture. (Out of interest, the real chart No. 2 on the week of *An Unearthly Child*'s transmission was the Beatles' 'She Loves You'). Ian then shows that he takes time to read the tabloid papers in the Coal Hill staff room by informing a bemused Barbara, 'John Smith is a stage name used by the Honourable Aubrey Waites. He started his career as Chris Waites and the Carollers.'

Thankfully Ian and Susan's pop-music banter in these early scenes is quite realistically handled and entertaining. Ian's next attempt to show that he's a hip guy, however, forms part of one of the most gruesome attempts the series ever made to look up to the minute.

May 1965 saw the broadcast of *The Executioners*, the first episode of *The Chase*, in which the Doctor, Ian, Barbara and Vicki (a recent recruit after Susan's departure) are pursued across the Universe by the Daleks. Before the mayhem proper begins, the Doctor takes time to demonstrate his new Time Space Visualiser – a gift from the new curators of a 'Space Museum' the team encountered during their previous adventure. The Visualiser has the useful but rather absurd ability to 'tune in' to any event in history. Typically, Ian and Barbara plump for pure secondary school syllabus material – in line with *Doctor Who*'s half-hearted mission to educate – and ask to see Lincoln's Gettysburg Address and Shakespeare at the court of Elizabeth I. But Vicki, bless her, asks to see the Beatles, the 'classical music' of her twenty-fifth-century home. As the device serves up a performance of 'Ticket to Ride', Ian proceeds to lose all his cool and laid-back credentials by dancing like a middle-aged dad at a wedding reception.

What was so important about this scene in its original context was its incredible immediacy. *The Executioners* was broadcast on 22 May 1965 when 'Ticket to Ride' was still in the top ten, having just spent three weeks at No. 1. In fact, the Time Space Visualiser actually selected an edition of *Top of the Pops* screened just five weeks before. The brief 'turn-around' time of *Doctor Who* episodes in the 1960s – about four weeks in this case – would allow such contemporaneous material to be dropped in with ease, particularly considering that the *Top of the Pops* concerned was recorded in the London Riverside Studio Two, so the *Doctor Who* team, working in Studio One, effectively had only to tune their visualiser to the room next door. From a present-day perspective, the idea of the Beatles appearing on *Doctor Who* seems an amusing curiosity, but it remains one of the most crude crowd-pleasing stunts the series has ever pulled. It is difficult to imagine Tom Baker's Fourth Doctor agreeing to show Sarah Jane the video for Queen's 'Bohemian Rhapsody' during *The Brain of Morbius* in 1976, or the Sixth Doctor and Peri stopping to watch Band Aid perform 'Do They Know It's Christmas?' before the main action of *Attack of the Cybermen* in early 1985!

The 1960s swung on. By 1966 London was the most 'happening' city in the world. For young women, fashion designer Mary Quant and celebrity hairdresser Vidal Sassoon had created a whole new look, while Twiggy and

Jean Shrimpton showed how to carry it off. Years of post-war austerity had given way to a new boom, and thoroughly modern Millicents revelled in their new spending power. In London, Kensington Church Street and the King's Road became their Mecca, as shops such as Biba, Granny Takes a Trip and Quant's own Bazaar offered a miniskirt and Lurex uniform for the young, and Terence Conran's new Habitat store provided the bean bags and globe chairs essential to any new pad.

When dreaming up the first of two new companions for the Doctor in early 1966, producer Innes Lloyd and story editor Gerry Davis looked to this new London for inspiration. Their creation, Polly, was to be one of the most carefully thought-out regular characters ever to feature in the series, although more effort was put into the details of her background than finally showed on screen – as can be discovered from a production office writers' guide put together around the time of her introduction.

The notes explain that Polly was to be twenty-four and the only daughter of a large middle-class family. Having secured her independence at an early age, she spent time as a travel courier and a model (which she found 'irksome') before becoming a secretary. She would have few of the then traditionally female practical skills such as cooking or sewing, and instead loved sports cars, motor racing and skiing. The writers specified that she had a flat on London's Gloucester Road, in Kensington, which put her in the heart of 'swinging London'.

With her blonde hair and big eyes, actress Anneke Wills also brought to Polly the perfect look of the time – the waifish awkwardness of model Twiggy, but with the lanky teenage androgyny replaced by a shade of the sex appeal of French actress Brigette Bardot.

Since *An Unearthly Child*, only a handful of other serials had brought various TARDIS crews back for generally brief visits to modern-day Earth. Polly's introductory serial, *The War Machines* – broadcast in England's World Cup-winning summer of 1966 – represented the first occasion that the series had really tried to go out and about in 1960s London and touch some contemporary cultural checkpoints. Aside from the novelty of seeing the Doctor riding around in a black cab and battling a deadly robot in Covent Garden fruit market (these days, the piazza), we also see him dropping in at the nearby Inferno discotheque – 'the hottest nightspot in town', according to Polly – for a drink on the house.

The Inferno is a brave try on the part of the production team. Its paint-splattered walls and sub-Dante styling are cool enough, but its bright lighting and questionable music policy leave a little to be desired. There are no Rolling Stones or the Who to be heard – not even Nancy Sinatra – just a selection of tracks from a Johnny Hawkesworth stock music album.

We meet Kitty, barmaid and seemingly sole member of staff, who is pleased to see the Doctor because 'it isn't every day we get the over-twenties in here' – a flagrant lie, as the average age of the crowd swaying randomly on the dance floor is patently around thirty-four. The dialogue in the Inferno scenes is 'safe' for a family audience. Kitty 'digs' the Doctor's 'fab gear' and thinks he 'looks like that disc jockey' (presumably Jimmy Saville). There are hints of a darker undertow, however. A rowdy 'lad' obviously keen to celebrate the new sexual liberation makes a play for Polly, shouting, 'C'mon, darling, I know your type!' But our spirited new friend proves not to be a girl of easy virtue. Later, when the Doctor's friend Dodo goes missing, the authorities aren't called in because Kitty 'don't want the police round 'ere'. What does she have to hide? Perhaps the Inferno's middle-aged, middle-of-the road front room is just a cover for more libidinous goings-on out back?

A young sailor, Ben Jackson, is sitting alone the bar at the Inferno, amusingly wearing a hat emblazoned with the words 'HMS Teazer'. Thought up by the same team that created Polly, Ben was to be the second new companion introduced in *The War Machines*. When we first meet him, he is morose about being confined to shore duties as his ship and crew sail off to exotic climes. Very much the devoted naval man, he speaks of little else, and the production team fumble a chance to throw another 1960s archetype into the mix. Michael Craze, playing Ben as a full-on cockney, gives the character the look and sound of Michael Caine in the 1965 film *Alfie*, or Ray Brooks in the same year's *The Knack* – two hit films of the time which told tragi-comic stories of wide-boy London Lotharios. However, *Doctor Who*, with its family audience, couldn't hope to present a character as frank and sexual as Alfie, so instead we get a doggedly loyal and scrupulously moral sailor. Polly and Ben would come to bridge the first recasting of *Doctor Who*'s lead character in November 1966. Sadly their 'shock of the new' quality, which successfully threw William Hartnell's Doctor into sharp relief, didn't sit as easily with Patrick Troughton's younger, more spirited version. After a few more months they slipped quietly away.

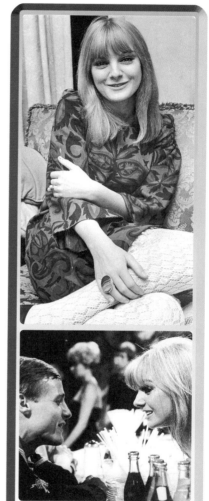

Top: Actress Anneke Wills meets the Press in 1966

Above: Polly (Wills) and Ben (Michael Craze) come together over a line of Coke in the alcohol-free Inferno nite-spot

Far left: Carole Ann Ford practises 'coquettish' during an early publicity shoot as Susan

'HERE COMES JOHNNY REGGAE...'

Top ten hits used in *Doctor Who* (cover versions by session musicians not included):

○ 'Ticket to Ride', the Beatles* reached No. 1 in May 1965 and features in *The Chase*, May 1965

○ 'Paperback Writer', the Beatles* reached No. 1 in July 1966 and features in *The Evil of the Daleks*, May 1967

○ 'Oh Well', Fleetwood Mac* reached No. 2 in November 1969 and features in *Spearhead from Space*, January 1970

○ 'Johnny Reggae', Piglets* reached No. 3 in November 1971 and features in *The Sea Devils*, March 1972

○ 'A Whiter Shade of Pale', Procul Harum reached No. 1 in June 1967 and features in *Revelation of the Daleks*, March 1985

○ 'Lollipop', the Mudlarks reached No. 2 in May 1958 and features in *Remembrance of the Daleks*, October 1988

*still in chart when *Doctor Who* episode broadcast

Main: 'It' girls Isobel (Sally Faulkner) and Zoe (Wendy Padbury) lie down on the job in a behind-the-scenes shot from *The Invasion*
Inset: Faulkner on her flirty cornfield press call

The Second Doctor was to be an irregular visitor to contemporary Earth, but few attempts were made to embrace any of the trends of the day. A brief stop-off at the pop-art Tricolour coffee shop in 1967's *The Evil of the Daleks* allowed the Doctor and Jamie to catch the Beatles' latest No. 1 and ogle some miniskirted girls shaking their thing to the Seekers, but in most other stories England was too busy being invaded to show off its latest fashions. The chief exception is 1968's *The Invasion*, in which the Doctor, Jamie and Zoe befriend young Isobel Watkins, another spirited socialite from the same mould as Polly.

Like her predecessor, Isobel was in her twenties, middle class and living in fashionable Kensington. She had also tried her hand at modelling in the past, but was determined to forge a career as a photographer. Their main difference was that while the character of Polly had been more or less on the ball in 1966, Isobel, just three years later, seemed a cliché. 1967 had brought the 'Summer of Love' to the USA: drugs guru Timothy Leary had challenged a generation to 'turn on, tune in and drop out', the Beatles had shed their 'boy next door' image and even shared the bill at the Monterey Pop Festival with Jimi Hendrix and the Grateful Dead, while all the *de rigueur* pop music was written under the influence of LSD. Isobel didn't seem up with any of this; listening to music on a retro-chic wind-up gramophone while she worked, she eschewed Pink Floyd in favour of 'The Teddy Bears' Picnic'.

Isobel was, however, given a bit more substance in that she was allowed to employ the dialogue of an ardent feminist. It was six years since psychologist Betty Friedan's *The Feminine Mystique* had been published and become an influential text of second-wave feminism, and Isobel was obviously still an ardent follower, dismissing the Brigadier on one occasion for making 'bigoted, anti-feminist, cretinous remarks'. One can imagine her keenly snapping up a copy of Germaine Greer's more confrontational and controversial *The Female Eunuch* the following year. (Then again, Isobel's staunch views are somewhat undercut by her materialism: one of her first questions to 'dolly soldier' and possible suitor Captain Turner is, 'Are you stinking rich?')

As Patrick Troughton gave way to Jon Pertwee, the Doctor found himself exiled to Earth, although the producers made surprisingly few attempts to deliberately use modish references to make *Doctor Who* seem cool. These Earth-bound stories make some play of being set either a few years into the future or on a slightly different version of Earth. References to 'BBC3' or British rocket missions to Mars do what they can to push the series into a fantasy world of its own design, even though all the fashions, settings and concerns are solidly contemporary.

After a year assisted by buttoned-down physicist Liz Shaw, the Third Doctor was soon to pick up a new helpmate in the form of bubbly Jo Grant. If the production team of the time had Twiggy in mind when 'designing' Polly, then Jo's creators were obviously thinking Goldie Hawn. The American actress had been a hit as the vivacious but vacuous blonde stooge on the energetic US TV sketch show *Rowan and Martin's Laugh-In* in the late 1960s, and seen greater fame as the seemingly dizzy waif who eventually outsmarts her 'protector' in the 1970 Peter Sellars film *There's a Girl in My Soup*. Actress Katy Manning's performance as Jo drew on many of the same qualities.

But if Jo was a girl of the 1970s, she rarely shouted about it, give or take the dated reference that opened this chapter or her misquoting of the Beatles' 'I am the Walrus' in 1973's *The Three Doctors*. Her clothes spoke louder than words, showing that in one area at least she was truly 'hip'. (But then, hot pants were even accepted in the royal enclosure at Ascot in 1971.) Finally, always cursed to be slightly behind the times simply because her life was scripted by middle-aged men, Jo eventually left the Doctor in 1973 to live with a hippie – only four years after Woodstock.

Jo was succeeded by Sarah Jane Smith, who, bar the odd nod in the direction of Womens' Lib in ways that were even less convincing than those tried with Isobel Watkins six years earlier, was given very few consciously modern tastes or concerns. With the Doctor's exile over, fewer stories returned the TARDIS to present-day Earth, a trend that continued after Tom Baker took over in 1974. Sarah Jane was followed by a long run of alien companions who felt no need to quote pop-song lyrics at the drop of a hat. In 1980 Australian air hostess Tegan Jovanka proved herself a modern girl, taking a lead from the aggressive 'stand on your own two feet' Thatcherism of the early 1980s – all shoulder pads and big hair – but her successors, Peri and Mel, again seemed to have few links with present-day ephemera.

Sadly, *Doctor Who*'s last attempt to create a modern companion with an identifiable real-life background was, seemingly as ever, to be fudged. Saddled from the outset with a name from an already out-of-date slang, Ace – who accompanied Sylvester McCoy's Doctor – employed a similarly moribund vocabulary (all 'wicked' and 'well dodgy') for her first year and a half which was already crashingly uncool. Her teenage-girl-rapper zipped-up bomber jacket and stereo helped her to look the part – suitably Salt'n'Pepa – but could never compensate for her cringeworthy dialogue.

With Ace in tow, *Doctor Who* made its last significant trip to the modern day in its final regular serial – and at fifty-nine minutes past the eleventh hour showed it really could get it right if it tried.

In 1989's *Survival*, Ace asks the Doctor to take her home to the outer London suburb of Perivale so she can catch up with old friends. The first episode brilliantly evokes the lifestyle of disaffected suburban youth. When Ace tells the Doctor that her 'crowd' used to climb a local hill just to 'light a fire, muck about – y'know', it's easy to imagine their dismal Metroland existence in run-down youth clubs and vandalised parks – with only the challenge of mastering the fruit machine in the local pub to allieviate the ennui. We meet Ace's friend Ange, a hunt saboteur with string-tied dreadlocks, who details the exploits of Ace's other mates – as a teenager in Perivale in the late 1980s, it seems, you can aspire to becoming a window-cleaner, marrying a plumber or, perhaps at best, moving to Birmingham. We even get to see the Doctor's first visit to a council tower block, and it's something of a shock to see him surrounded by the clutter of the unemployed, rather than safe in the institutional and rural milieux that had always seemed his home.

Steeped in pathos, *Survival* is perhaps *Doctor Who*'s best attempt to capture on screen the real world of its teenage viewers.

From well-spoken kids discussing 'fabulous' things in a school corridor in 1963 to a listless 'crusty' shaking a collecting tin on an empty street corner in 1989, *Doctor Who* offers a series of interesting snapshots of the lifestyles of British youth across three decades. As we've seen, the picture is often distorted and shouldn't be taken entirely at face value, but sometimes – just sometimes – contains a grain of truth. ◖

Images of 1980s modernity...
Top: In control and not-for-turning, Janet Fielding power-dressed as Tegan Jovanka
Middle: Sophie Aldred as Ace, streetwise kid with a heart of gold
Above: Ace catches up with trusty crusty pal Ange (Kate Eaton) in 1989's *Survival*

I'M FREE!

There's the bumbling Brigadier and his ineffectual troops. There's the eccentric scientific adviser. There's the pretty but dippy assistant. It could be an outline for a very silly sitcom...

'I'll nip out, find a phone and tell the authorities exactly where we are. I'm fairly sure that's Cromer...'

To some, 1972's *The Three Doctors* is an important and worthy slice of *Doctor Who* which intelligently deconstructs its hero while still offering a fast-paced adventure to appeal to the most discerning of viewers. To others, it's a gaudy send-up that's as camp as Christmas. And Christmas 1972 must have been very camp indeed.

The *Oxford English Dictionary* defines camp as 'affected, effeminate', 'homosexual' or 'done in an exaggerated way for effect'. In many ways this is a simplistic and inaccurate summary of a very subjective adjective. Camp is different things to different people. To some, it does indeed suggest the catty, effeminate comedy of Julian Clary or Kenneth Williams, with their rambling stand-up routines brimming with double entendre, or John Inman's Mr Humphries gaily calling 'I'm free!' in the sitcom *Are You being Served?*. To others, it's the exaggerated and theatrical stage performances of the likes of Shirley Bassey, Bette Midler and Diana Ross. It can invoke images as varied as Victoria Wood's *Acorn Antiques* skits, Elvis Presley in his Las Vegas years, Elsie Tanner storming out of the Rovers Return in *Coronation Street*, the architecture of Disneyland or Abba chiming 'A-ha' throughout the chorus of 'Knowing Me, Knowing You'.

Camp's lazy conflation with homosexuality further muddies the waters. Of course, many of the performers and characters quoted above are immensely popular figures within gay culture, and many of their routines have been assimilated into the collective consciousness of the many gay men who can quote whole chunks of dialogue from *Absolutely Fabulous* or *Sunset Boulevard* at the drop of a hat. But to suggest that campness is wholly derived from, or purely for the entertainment of, gay men would be wrong. There is no doubting, for example, the inherent campness of the musical *Evita* or the outrageous Dame Edna Everage, but the followings of both these phenomena include more ladies of a certain age than gay men.

The word 'camp' possibly originates from the French '*se camper*', meaning to present oneself in a flimsy manner, like a tent. 'Flimsiness' suggests overtones of vanity, theatricality, trashiness and sexual provocation, some or all of which are certainly common to the mainstream cultural references above. A further defining quality of camp must also be its presence only in the eye of the beholder: one man's 'camp' is another's 'clean-cut early evening game show'. Further, to recognise or label something camp implies that there is fun to be had from being part of the cognoscenti, a select group which is in on some subtle joke that others are missing.

How, you may ask, can any of this possibly be relevant to something as innocent and earnest as *Doctor Who*? The programme offers few effeminate characters and little in the way of conscious sexual double entendre. What can the adventures of a Time Lord possibly have in common with a Kenneth Williams monologue or an Abba single?

The answer is very little, at least on the surface, because so far we've only really looked at *deliberate* camp – sexual suggestion, cross-dressing or arm-waving theatricality employed to calculated effect. Much of *Doctor Who* falls into a different category of camp which we'll come to later, but first it's worth stopping to giggle at some of *Doctor Who*'s moments of *conscious* campery. There aren't many, and given the series' need to appeal to both children and grannies it's also pretty 'safe' stuff.

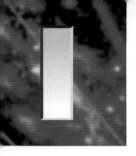

The year is 1966 and *Doctor Who* has just borne witness to the single most shocking change in its history. In the blink of an eye, and largely without warning, the partrician, grandfatherly figure of the First Doctor was replaced by the impish, playful Second. But the surprise of seeing a whimsical Doctor playing 'Mr Sludge the Snail' on his recorder while skipping around in an absurd hat in his first serial was as nothing compared to his actions in the second, *The Highlanders*.

Attempting to undermine a group of English slavers selling defeated Scots rebels into a life of hard labour after the battle of Culloden, the Doctor adopts a variety of disguises, including those of a German medic and an English soldier – complete with mysteriously sourced false moustache. Between these, and to great camp comic effect, he poses as a raddled old washerwoman. In pinafore frock and shawl, the Doctor totters round a crowded tavern, cackling in the voice of an old hag. Later, he is complimented by his assistant Polly. 'Those dresses really do suit you,' she says. 'Oh, you *saucy* girl!' the Doctor jokes back. It could be a Sid James or Peter Butterworth *Carry On* film performance.

Patrick Troughton isn't the only Doctor to drag up. Jon Pertwee dresses as an office cleaner, complete with comedy turban, in 1973's *The Green Death*. A mirthful Captain Yates of UNIT comments, 'I like your handbag', while the Doctor seems to enjoy the experience more than is strictly necessary.

This cross-dressing is, of course, a very simple form of camp humour. The subversion of gender characteristics is common to a wide range of comedy, from pantomime to Dame Edna. The conscious *exaggeration* of sexual characteristics has much the same effect – witness Shirley Bassey, Joan Collins or *Coronation Street*'s Bet Lynch – and was a formula celebrated by *Blake's 7* in its employment of the glamorous, homicidal and highly sexual female villain Servalan. In *Doctor Who*, the late 1970s was stuffed with similar characters – *The Stones of Blood*'s Vivien Fey, *The Androids of Tara*'s Madame Lamia, *The Creature from the Pit*'s Lady Adrasta – all, either through manner or dress, revelling in their sensuality. With this support, and with a confident and sexy Romana by his side, Tom Baker's Fourth Doctor spent 1978 and 1979 enjoying the series' most tongue-in-cheek and high camp of eras.

But, this *deliberate* archness aside, *Doctor Who* also stands as a prime example of the even more subjective form of *unintentional* camp, a territory it shares with such varied cultural 'phenomena' as *Space: 1999*, Rolf Harris, the novels of Jackie Collins and almost every American daytime soap opera.

In *Doctor Who*, this flavour of campness is a side effect of its often exaggerated style and stereotypical characters, sometimes trivialised moral issues and wild costume design. This is not to say that *Doctor Who* avoids 'big issues' of politics, emotion or morality. In many ways, that's just the point: the series *does* present storylines of threatened genocide or Fascist takeover, but it's the way such issues are confronted by an outraged and outrageous alien who lives in a telephone box with his robot dog that, in the end, inexorably renders the finished product camp.

The Doctor's own first accidental camp moment in the series comes from just such a clash of seriousness and triviality, at the end of 1964's *Inside the Spaceship*, *Doctor Who*'s third serial, when the TARDIS crew are recovering after a problem with the ship has had them, quite literally, at each other's throats (see Chapter F). The TARDIS lands on a snowy mountain and the Doctor, Ian, Barbara and Susan kiss and make up, recent accusations of attempted murder and Susan's near-homicidal rage instantly forgotten.

Ian has borrowed an Ulster from the Doctor and merrily pirouettes around the control room in it, to much chuckling from the Doctor, who tells him (in the first of the series' long parade of light-hearted name-drops) that it used to belong to Gilbert and Sullivan. 'I thought it was made for two,' quips Ian. Still laughing, the jolly gentlemen friends turn to leave the TARDIS arm in arm. Now *that's* camp.

Being first and foremost television entertainment, *Doctor Who* gives precedence to style, form and surface values. The majority of its supporting characters have little depth and few nuances of personality, existing only on the level of cliché – particularly the string of cursing villains and curmudgeonly figures of authority who are ranged against the Doctor. Visual and verbal shorthand is used in costume design and dialogue wherever possible. Any Fascist, such as Stahlmann in 1970's *Inferno* or Nyder in 1975's *Genesis of the Daleks*, will look as if he's goose-stepped straight from Hitler's SS. Policemen, from 1964's *Planet of Giants* to 1989's *Ghost Light*, are decent notepad-carrying chaps, dogged in the pursuit of their duties. Scientists wear glasses and clutch clipboards. Bureaucrats doff bowler hats and gesture with umbrellas. But, however simplistic these ciphers, it is still always the characters who form the absolute focus of *Doctor Who* stories – and one of the series' great strengths is that it allows its characters to drive the plot, rather than vice versa. With a good mix of clear-cut, neatly labelled friends and enemies, *Doctor Who* is thus able to embrace both parody and emotional identification at the same time. This is, perhaps, as neat a definition of camp as we might find – and one that just as easily describes the work of Victoria Wood and Kenneth Williams as it does the adventures of the Doctor.

Doctor Who's highly developed sense of warm self-parody, along with the series' habit of presenting life-or-death issues against a backdrop of playfulness and whimsy, makes it particularly prone to unintentional campery. And generally, the more stiff and pompous the Doctor, and the more simplistic and stooge-like his support, the more likely such a tone is to emerge.

Strong and sensual women...
Top: Vivien Fey (Susan Engel, right) with Romana (Mary Tamm). *The Stones of Blood* (1978)
Middle: Madame Lamia (Lois Baxter). *The Androids of Tara* (1978)
Bottom: Lady Adrasta (Myra Frances). *The Creature from the Pit* (1979)

Main: Kate O'Mara as the Rani in 1987's *Time and the Rani*

In both of William Hartnell's and Jon Pertwee's first years in the role, there is little room for camp. Their associates – whether Ian and Barbara, or the Brigadier and Liz Shaw – are carefully constructed characters who bring an adult perspective to their scenes and willingly engage in stern moral debate. As time passes and they are replaced by the likes of Vicki, Dodo, Jo Grant, or even just more trivial versions of themselves, camp begins to take hold. When Ian and Barbara first face the Daleks on Skaro, we are privy to their emotional responses: their fear of dying so far from home, their sense of injustice at the plight of the Thals. By the time of 1965's *The Chase*, the schoolteachers are written more simply, and we have no sense that they may genuinely fear for their lives. As the atmosphere of threat is reduced, the sense of fun and camp increases, particularly if the Doctor still oozes conviction and self-importance and insists on taking the threat posed by a robotic Frankenstein's monster terribly seriously.

From the early 1970s, it is easy to see that the character of Brigadier Lethbridge-Stewart is being softened and simplified by the show's production team as the years pass. There is little camp in 1970 *Doctor Who* as the Third Doctor, the Brigadier and Liz seriously discuss the deadly nature of any danger they find themselves in. A short time later, with the earnest Liz replaced by the giddy Jo, and the harder, intelligent Brigadier evolving into a warmer, blustering figure of fun, we're back in the realm of camp. The Brigadier can now confront a homicidal gargoyle with the unlikely order, 'Chap with wings... five round rapid', as he does in 1971's *The Dæmons*, or cause his friends' eyes to roll up in disbelief in *The Three Doctors* as he insists that the alien world he finds himself on is actually the beach at Cromer.

In her work *Against Interpretation,* media writer Susan Sontag comments that 'camp taste reponds to "instant character"… and, conversely, is not stirred by any sense of the development of character… the idea of a person being one, very intense thing'. This is why Jo Grant and the later Brigadier are found camp by viewers with such a sensibility, while Liz Shaw (her absurd hairstyles aside) and the early Brigadier are not.

Jolly larks in 1987...
Top: Mel (Bonnie Langford) at the mercy of the cardigan-clad cannibal Rezzies in *Paradise Towers*
Above: The Doctor (Sylvester McCoy) gets into the *Hi-de-Hi* spirit at a *Delta and the Bannermen* photocall

Main: A cleaning robot that takes no prisoners... another denizen of *Paradise Towers*

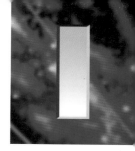

Funnily enough, Liz Shaw's ever-changing 1970s haircuts actually raise an important point, which is that any sense of camp is almost always heightened by the passage of time. *Doctor Who*, particularly those Jon Pertwee/UNIT years, represents a programme that has *become* camp. The series was never intended to be 'high' culture, merely colourful, disposable light entertainment, and it is 'instant' cultural forms such as this – along with pop music, advertising, TV sitcoms or mainstream movies – that are the most transient and therefore most susceptible to becoming camp. These things always remain a product of the moment of their creation, closely located within their cultural context and untranslatable outside that situation, being lost without the accompanying attitudes of the time. Susan Sontag noted, 'This is why so many of the objects prized as camp taste are old-fashioned, out-of-date, *démodé*. It's not a love of old as such. It's simply that the process of ageing or deterioration provides necessary sympathy... Time liberates the work of art from moral relevance, delivering it over to camp.' In *Doctor Who*, the sight of an off-duty UNIT soldier in swinging flares, or even Barbara's imposingly lacquered hair, offers a kitsch appeal that can cast even the most thought-provoking of plots into the realm of camp. Committed fans of the series – those who have made an emotional commitment to it – easily forgive such trivia, but in the eyes of most other modern viewers 1970s-style clothes, cars and even politics will instantly provoke a chuckle.

In his 1969 essay 'Anatomy of Rubbish', commentator Michael Thompson points out that cultural artefacts progress from 'transient' to 'valuable but decreasing in value' to becoming 'rubbish' – of no cultural or monetary value. Finally, however, the same objects can become 'durable', after 'discovery and restoration' their value increasing. 'The essential feature of camp taste,' says Thompson, 'is that things are lifted out of the rubbish category "before their time"', the attraction of camp being its 'quest for rubbish to discover and make durable'. This is a trend that could be said to apply equally accurately to *Doctor Who* as to repeats of the original *Star Trek* or *The Sweeney*, or a modern revival of the gameshow *Blankety Blank*.

As the years pass and we gradually lose sight of the context in which the *Doctor Who* episodes were made, much more of the series' style will begin to seem camp and absurd. It can only be hoped that the producer of any future revival will take time to figure out which aspects of that campness were deliberate, which happily unintentional and which just side effects of the passage of time. Camp remains an important part of the *Doctor Who* mix, but add too much or too little and the series lurches into either send-up or po-faced self-consciousness. Get it just right and the end results can be very enjoyable indeed. ◖

Love is a very special thing in the world of *Doctor Who*. The Doctor himself seems untouched by its charms, but his companions are often happy to shack up with the first prince or Nobel Laureate that comes along. This is their story...

If a friend told you they were planning to marry someone they had met just thirty-six hours before, you might at least take a few moments to sit them down and politely ask if they were sure they were doing the right thing. More likely, you would stare at them open-mouthed before throwing up your hands in disbelief and declaring them stark, staring mad.

When the Doctor's devoted assistant Jo Grant drops such a bombshell on her colleagues in 1973's *The Green Death*, no one so much as takes her to one side to point out that she met her fast-fiancé Professor Clifford Jones only the day before, and even then that he has spent most of the afternoon in a delirious fever before proposing marriage. Perhaps it would be someone's place to quietly suggest that Jo and Cliff might want to spend more than half an hour alone together before plighting their troth. Alas not. Instead, everyone just cheers, joins a rousing chorus of 'For They are Jolly Good Fellows' and sets out to party the night away. I don't know about you, but I would want my friends to be a wee bit more solicitous of my welfare than that.

Generally, there is little time for romantic love in the fast-moving, time-twisting world of *Doctor Who*. The Doctor seems to be entirely free of its unpredictable attentions – Cupid seemingly unable to spear both his hearts with one arrow – as, on the whole, does his succession of good-looking young companions. None of his shanghaied fellow travellers ever complained about being forcibly separated from a lover. Those who joined him willingly never seemed to worry about leaving a 'significant other' behind.

Sometimes, however, even in the midst of the most distracting and adrenalin-fuelled of adventures, one of the Doctor's friends can find their head turned by a passing rebel, soldier or scientist; and when true love strikes, it strikes fast. A chaste look is swiftly followed by a gentle kiss (no tongues). After that, their destiny is sealed and it can be but mere hours before a proposal of marriage is made or, at the very least, plans for cohabiting are announced to their nearest and dearest. If love is a drug, in *Doctor Who* it is an astonishingly fast-acting one.

The series' great difficulty in trying to offer a believable romance lies in the fact that its stories unfold over such a short space of time. Traditionally, any given alien invasion or genocidal masterplan is discovered and defeated within about forty-eight hours. When we visit the cinema or read a romantic novel, star-crossed lovers can still meet and marry within ninety minutes or three hundred pages, but at least the stories told in the great romances of literature or the movies take a little longer to unfold in their own fictional world. *Doctor Who* was never one for sprawling epics, so while the troubled courtships of Rhett and Scarlett in *Gone With the Wind* or Elizabeth Bennet and Mr Darcy in *Pride and Prejudice* unfold over a period of months, the young heroes of a two-day *Doctor Who* adventure are made to seem more sexually rapacious than hormone-fuelled teenagers at a school disco.

Despite this, a clever sleight-of-hand employed by those behind *The Green Death* helps even the supersonic courtship of Jo Grant and Cliff Jones to appear touching and believable. We'll come back to that particular happy couple later, but first it's worth taking a look at some of *Doctor Who*'s other fast-track romances...

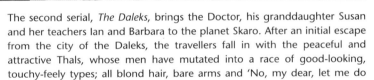

Will they, won't they?
Perhaps they have already...
Dubiously relaxed scenes of domestic
bliss for Ian and Barbara in *The Romans*
(1965)

The second serial, *The Daleks*, brings the Doctor, his granddaughter Susan and her teachers Ian and Barbara to the planet Skaro. After an initial escape from the city of the Daleks, the travellers fall in with the peaceful and attractive Thals, whose men have mutated into a race of good-looking, touchy-feely types; all blond hair, bare arms and 'No, my dear, let me do that.' Barbara catches the eye of the gentle Ganatus, and while Ian and the Doctor are busy plotting an attack on the Dalek city, Barbara and her admirer drift off into the forest, the teacher seemingly happy to have found herself a New Man thirty years before they will be invented.

At first, it seems to be an almost note-perfect seduction, as they sit together beneath a tree and Barbara wistfully comments on the ethereal glow in the sky above a nearby lake. Ganatus, however, nearly blows it. Rather than going for a traditional response, along the lines of, 'It pales beside *your* beauty, my dear', he instead looks longingly into her ear and plumps for the somewhat less romantic, 'There's horror down there in the swamp.' Barbara doesn't seem to mind much, but one would think that alarm bells should ring when a first date ends with a suitor apologising for being morbid.

Later, as the couple join an expedition to penetrate the Dalek city via a treacherous network of caves, Barbara rarely lets go of the Thal's hand. Significantly, Ian makes no comment and displays no sign of jealousy, happily sending them off together on a side mission rather than attempting to separate them.

When the Daleks are finally defeated, the TARDIS crew assemble outside the ship to bid farewell to their fair-headed friends. Barbara and Ganatus return from another stroll – having probably discussed their impossible future – and, somewhat self-consciously, stand slightly apart. Their final parting is touching. 'Well, Ganatus,' she says. 'Well, Barbara,' he replies, as they look at one another. Ganatus tries to make a final play, 'I wish we –', but is interrupted by an oblivious Susan calling for Barbara to hurry. Resigned, Ganatus takes Barbara's right hand in both of his and gently kisses it. Then she is gone.

Some time later, in 1964's *The Reign of Terror*, Barbara again catches the eye of a handsome stranger. Imprisoned in post-Revolution France, she is rescued from the guillotine by a group fighting to overthrow Robespierre's regime. One of them, the dashing Léon Colbert, is obviously entranced by beautiful Babs, who seems to enjoy the attention. When Susan later challenges Barbara on the subject ('You like Léon, don't you?'), her former history teacher just laughs and changes the subject – a dead giveaway.

Sadly, the blossoming affair is not to last. Colbert is revealed to be a double agent working for Robespierre and is killed after attempting to lure Ian into a deadly trap. Barbara expresses no immediate concern for Ian, instead becoming angry with him for Colbert's death, which has obviously affected her on a personal level. Happily, she soon comes to terms with the fact that this was one relationship that wasn't going to reach even the hand-holding stage, and apologises to Ian.

But if Barbara was the TARDIS's first man-magnet, she was soon overtaken by Susan, whose adolescent enthusiasm actually gave the series its first full-blown snog.

Battling the Daleks again, this time in twenty-second-century England, Susan meets and falls in love with freedom fighter David Campbell. To an untrained eye, they seem poorly matched. David appears to be about twenty-seven, while Susan is barely older than sixteen. He wants to be a farmer when the Earth has been liberated – something that hardly seems appropriate for his future wife, who has lived a life of constant action and adventure around the universes. If you've trekked across the Himalayas with Marco Polo and survived the murky jungles of the planet Quinnus, spreading fertiliser on a field of barley at five o'clock in the morning must be a bit of a comedown.

The most alarming thing about David and Susan's burgeoning relationship is the Doctor's reaction to it. When he sees the pain on his granddaughter's face as she tries to say goodbye to David, he takes the drastic step of locking her out of the TARDIS and leaving without her. This is passed off as some act of kindness: the Doctor forcing Susan to prioritise her feelings for David over her sense of duty to him. But why is the Doctor so sure he knows best? He may know that the youngsters are attracted to one another, and he may want to encourage Susan to assert herself and claim her freedom, but that's hardly enough to justify abandoning the girl on a ruined planet with only one shoe and a man who 'just wants to watch things grow' for company. Only a matter of days before he was treating Susan like a child, telling her that what she really needed was 'a jolly good smacked bottom'. Then as he locks the doors to the ship, he says, 'You should live normally like any woman should do.' Quite a turnaround.

So either the Doctor is an old and wise romantic who knows true and undying love when he sees it, or he has so little understanding of its subtleties that he falls into a flat panic and runs away at the first sniff of a seduction. Along with later evidence, his behaviour towards Susan would certainly suggest the latter was true.

Two eager young men rejected by Jo Grant...
Top: Latep from *Planet of the Daleks* (1973)
Bottom: King Peladon from *The Curse of Peladon* (1972)

Main picture: Jo with Professor Jones in *The Green Death* (1973)

'I WILL FEAST MY EYES ON HER DELICACY!'

Unwanted attention received by the Doctor's companions can be sincere, seedy or downright sinister. Here are some of the more memorable examples…

◯ **Barbara**
Barbara is menaced by the brutal Vasor in *The Keys of Marinus*, in a disturbing scene that almost suggests an impending rape. After sharing what looks for all the world to be a post-coital drink with Ian in *The Romans*, she is lustfully pursued by the emperor Nero through the corridors of the imperial palace. Later, in *The Crusade*, she finds herself trapped in the wicked El Akir's harem.

◯ **Ian**
A giant butterfly appears to take rather a shine to him in *The Web Planet*.

◯ **Polly**
The 'dolly-bird' secretary is seriously hit on by a London wide-boy in *The War Machines*.

◯ **Sarah**
Sarah is pursued by the gentle giant Tommy in *Planet of the Spiders* – unfortunately he has the mind of a five-year-old. In *The Masque of Mandagora*, she is gently courted by Prince Giuliano of San Martino, although she might have had to fight his 'close friend' Marco for him.

◯ **Leela**
The savage is one of a host of pretty young ladies who are lured to the lair of Magnus Greel to have their life juices drained in *The Talons of Weng-Chiang*. She eventually leaves the TARDIS after *The Invasion of Time* to set up home on Gallifrey with rat-faced guard captain Andred. Heaven alone knows why. [Main picture]

It soon becomes time for Barbara and Ian to leave the TARDIS as well. By this point, Barbara has lost her wandering eye, and one begins to wonder whether she and Ian might get together, having surely become firmly bonded by their shared experiences. There is no real evidence on screen for this, but it would be nice to think that after they returned to England in their own time, one of them proposed (probably Barbara, given past form) and they skipped off to Gretna Green or Las Vegas for a whistlestop wedding.

Keeping the Doctor company after the teachers' departure is Vicki, the Doctor's new young ward and surrogate Susan. And just as with Susan, he loses her to a younger man.

Vicki's first flirtation is with yet another hot-headed, hot-blooded young rebel – in this case the fey Tor, fighting to liberate a Space Museum from an oppresive regime. Eventually, however, she visits the ancient city of Troy at the time of its fall, adopts the name Cressida and is caught up by mythological destiny. Ancient Greek legend, medieval poetry and Shakespeare himself ordain that she must fall for the seventeen-year-old Troilus, Prince of Troy.

With great confidence, Vicki makes all the running, pestering King Priam of Troy with questions regarding Troilus: 'Is he your youngest son? He's very good-looking, isn't he? I thought he was rather nice!' Fellow traveller Steven is initially sceptical of the merits of Vicki's new romance. After she's told him how much she likes the young prince, Steven coldly replies, 'I doubt whether that will matter when the city starts to burn.' The story, 1965's *The Myth Makers*, ends with Vicki informing the Doctor that she is leaving the TARDIS to wed Troilus. The Doctor has little time to comment and raises no objections. Presumably he's seen *Troilus and Cressida* and knows what's going to happen next.

It wasn't until the Doctor was in his third body that he was once again called upon to bless the marriage of one of his young companions – which brings us back to where we started, with the life and loves of Josephine Grant.

Jo spent more than two years with the Doctor, and during this time she proved herself to be the most desired of his associates. Whether it was UNIT's Captain Yates taking her for 'a night on the town' or Latep – yet another eager young Thal – inviting her to join him on Skaro, Jo had to beat them off with a stick. One of her most ardent admirers was the young King Peladon of Peladon, whose advances she spurns despite the fact that he offers her a share of the throne of an entire planet. But then, perhaps Jo is also scared off by his worryingly Oedipal claim that she reminds him of his mother – never a healthy basis for a marriage.

So, having passed up the usual *Doctor Who* husbands – soldiers, freedom-fighters and royalty – what kind of man was going to be good enough for Jo? The answer was obvious: only the Doctor himself would do. Well, almost.

At the top of this chapter, Jo's great romance with Clifford Jones was singled out as *Doctor Who*'s best. It is just as amusingly hasty as all the others, but in this case the production team behind the serial took time to bring another layer to their story.

Jo is the first to say it, singing the praises of ardent environmentalist Professor Jones before she has even met the man. She tells the Doctor, 'Professor Jones is fighting for everything that's important, everything you've fought for... In a funny way, he reminds me of a sort of younger you.' And she's right. Cliff is a Nobel Prize-winning scientist who patronises Jo one minute and has her laughing at a joke the next. He wants to feed the world and eliminate poverty, crusading for what he believes to be 'logically, aesthetically and morally right' – words that could indeed describe the nature of everything the Doctor strives for. He's even setting out on an adventure into fearsome, unknown lands – in this case, the Amazon Basin.

So, with the added irony that Jo's first meeting with Cliff is almost identical to her first meeting with the Doctor – as she blunders into his lab and almost ruins his experiment – everything seems so charmingly neat that this romance doesn't feel rushed at all; it feels *right*. Logically, aesthetically and morally. Jo's friends also seem to recognise this – they dance and drink at her engagement party and not a single doubt is voiced. But as with his own granddaughter, the Doctor finds the whole business difficult to deal with. He slips quietly away from the party and into the night.

Why is the Doctor so dysfunctional around young lovers? Although there has been barely a hint of real romance in the Doctor's life, the fact that he has a granddaughter implies at least that he once had sex and presumably cared for a woman. So why the hang-ups? Was he spurned? Was there a painful divorce or bereavement? What secret pain does he carry?

These questions may never be answered, and perhaps it's better that way. As a series, *Doctor Who* has survived by offering us few insights into its hero's heart, helping to keep him a more intriguing and fascinating figure. When, in the 1996 Paul McGann TV movie, the Doctor reciprocated a kiss from the amorous Dr Grace Holloway, you could almost hear millions of viewers' toes curling. Not because of any particular distaste at his choice of partner, just because the idea that the Doctor might actually fall in love just seems so everyday, so *ordinary*. Love implies settling down, and settling down implies mortgages and other such mundanities. That's not who we want the Doctor to be. We don't want to be reminded of our own lives; we want to escape.

And so, as his friends slip away from him into marital bliss, we are happy that the Doctor doesn't know how to react, doesn't know where to put himself. And in this sense, it is better that the only kind of love in *Doctor Who* is true love – love uncluttered by guilt or confusion. The Doctor is spared the discomfort or emotional complication, and both he and we are free to head straight off on another adventure.

'I WILL FEAST MY EYES ON HER DELICACY!'

Jamie
Romance appears to bloom between the young Scot and the troubled Samantha Briggs in *The Faceless Ones*. But after a tender farewell snog, Jamie takes his leave of the Liverpudlian temptress.

Nyssa
The tender Traken is kidnapped by a shambling heavy-breather in *Black Orchid*, when the hideously scarred George Cranleigh mistakes her for his former fiancée, Ann.

Tegan
In *Enlightenment*, the abrasive Aussie is followed everywhere by Mariner, an empty-headed Eternal who claims to only want the former stewardess for her brain.

Peri
Peri is held captive by the dangerously unhinged Sharaz Jek, who, in *The Caves of Androzani*, wants to 'feast his eyes on her'. The slimy mortician Jobel harasses her in *Revelation of the Daleks* and the half-man, half-halibut Borad later seeks to mate with her in *Timelash*. We are told she marries the shouty warlord Yrcarnos after the events of *The Trial of a Time Lord*.

Ace
The aggressive Ace goes for soldiers: she is taken with Sergeant Mike Smith in *Remembrance of the Daleks* (until he is revealed to be a Mosley-ite) and fervent Stalinist Colonel Sorin in *The Curse of Fenric* (until he is possessed by a force of Evil from the Dawn of Time).

Grace
The cardiologist snogs the Doctor himself in the TV Movie *Doctor Who*, but later decides to leave him and return to a bare apartment and the dole queue. Perhaps the Time Lord is just a bad kisser...

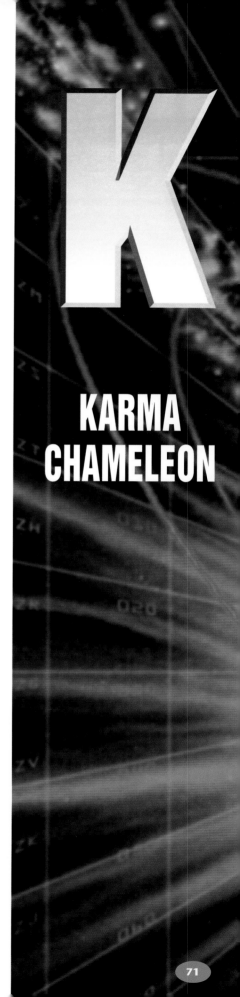

K

KARMA CHAMELEON

If you're of a religious frame of mind, be careful which god you decide to worship in the hard and rational universe of *Doctor Who* – they'll probably eat you.

'The old man must die, and the new man will discover, to his inescapable joy, that he never existed.'

The words of Cho-Je, assistant to the Abbot at a Buddhist retreat in southern England in 1974's *Planet of the Spiders*, not only prefigure the impending regeneration of the Doctor, from his third body (Jon Pertwee) to his fourth (Tom Baker), but also represent part of a rare investigation of the beliefs of a contemporary religion by a series that consistently shied away from such topics.

Although the meditation centre that forms the main location in this story is used as a base by a number of power-hungry, balding bachelors attempting to summon up the power of evil (or, as it turns out, achieve interplanetary and cross-time communion with a race of avaricious giant spiders) through the chanting of mantras, the faith and practices of the innocent acolytes at the retreat are actually accorded a great deal of respect. Admittedly, the script has Cho-Je responding aphoristically to every mundane question with what sometimes seems like so many Buddhist greetings-card *bon-mots*, but even this remains, at its heart, an honest presentation of the genuine beliefs of a real religion. When Cho-Je tells the Doctor's friend Sarah, 'A man must go inside himself and face his fears and hopes, his hates and his loves, and watch them wither away. Then he will find his true self, which is no self', he is actually explaining one of Buddhism's central tenets. No other religion has ever been afforded such an opportunity to set out its stall in *Doctor Who*, a series where belief in a god, or faith in anything other than science or the human spirit, is normally dismissed as silly superstition.

But while *Doctor Who* has rarely explored the ideologies of genuine, living religions, it has been happy to conjure up a wide variety of imaginary alien belief systems and visit several long-dead Earth religions just for the fun of knocking them down with the Doctor's decidedly unspiritual brand of scientific rationalism.

In such situations we are almost always introduced to a high priest who, in turn, is soon exposed as little more than a beleaguered politician struggling to protect his or her power base within a culture on the verge of embracing the 'civilising' effect of scientific enlightenment. As early as *Doctor Who*'s first serial, we find Old Mother – the 'wise woman' figure of a Palaeolithic tribe – attempting to stop the Doctor passing on the secret of making fire, afraid of the effect the possession of this skill will have on the status quo. Soon after, when visiting an Aztec city in fourteenth-century Mexico, the High Priest of Sacrifice is depicted as a machiavellian figure feeling undermined rather than ecstatic when the Doctor's companion Barbara is adopted as the reincarnation of one of his gods. When Barbara seeks to ban human sacrifice, he responds by attempting to have her unmasked or murdered – fearful of the erosion of his power over his superstitious subjects.

Away from Earth, the story is just the same. In 1972's *The Curse of Peladon*, we visit the feudal, 'dark age' planet of Peladon, where they worship the bear-like beast of Aggedor and only the reactionary high priest Hepesh stands in the way of the planet joining the technological Galactic Federation. His xenophobia motivated by a twisted form of patriotism, Hepesh strikes fear into others as he prophesies that the fearsome 'wrath of Aggedor' will sweep away this modernising regime, all the time cynically using the last of the surviving beasts to murder his political opponents. In the end, and with typical *Doctor Who* rough justice, he is killed when his own 'god' turns on him. In 1978's *The Power of Kroll*, the spear-waving 'Swampies' of a human-colonised moon of Delta Magna

False gods of Earth...
Top: Azal (Stephen Thorne), amoral alien scientist mistaken for the devil in prehistory. *The Dæmons* (1971)
Bottom: The Cailleach (Susan Engel), a Celtic goddess who proves to be intergalactic criminal Cessair of Diplos. *The Stones of Blood* (1978)

Main: Kronos the Chonovore, resident of the Time Vortex and part-time god of Atlantis. *The Time Monster* (1972)

Far right: Sutekh the Destroyer, also known as Set, Sados, Satan or the Typhonian Beast – dark god of Eygpt and would-be destroyer of the Earth. *Pyramids of Mars* (1975)

worship Kroll, a long-unseen but very real and very big squid who lives under the marsh. Kroll's high priest, Varlik, understands the political power he has over his people as the mouthpiece of his tentacled god, and is not adverse to forcing one of his assistants to dress as an octopus to spice up sacrificial ceremonies. When the real Kroll wakes from a long sleep to make a horizon-spanning reappearance, it's no coincidence that all Swampies who hold to their faith are casually eaten by their god, while those who recant and admit that their original religious beliefs were a bit silly – as the Doctor puts it, Kroll can't actually distinguish between Swampies, humans and 'half an acre of dandelion and burdock' – survive to live in the brave new world of the planet's scientifically minded alien settlers.

Similar territory had been explored two years earlier in another Tom Baker serial, *The Face of Evil*. Here, the savage Sevateem tribe were 'blessed' by a close relationship with their god, Xoanon (ancient Greek for an idol supposed to have fallen from heaven). Xoanon would talk directly to the Sevateem via his high priest, Neeva, guaranteeing his intermediary a position of great power in the tribe. In a crucial difference to the set-up on Peladon or Delta Three – where the faithful were made to look superstitious and backward for the worshipping of blithely uninterested bears and squid – Xoanon is exposed as a deranged computer deliberately manipulating the tribe via a long-distance transmitter. Neeva's already shaky faith crumbles and he dies in a suicide attack on his false god. In the standard *Doctor Who* pattern, all those who have ever questioned their saviour's supernatural credentials – including, perhaps in a dig at Christianity, a doubting tribesman called Tomas – live to see a new day, freed from the 'tyranny' of faith.

A very similar story is told in 1980's *Meglos*, where the local god is revealed to be little more than a giant battery (high priest Lexa is shot; scientist Zastor survives); and 1984's *Planet of Fire*, where the deity of the Planet Sarn turns out to be a man in a silver radiation suit (high priest Timanov holds to his faith and perishes in a volcano; young moderniser Amyand is rescued by science). Over and over, *Doctor Who* sends out a cautionary message that too much religion can kill you.

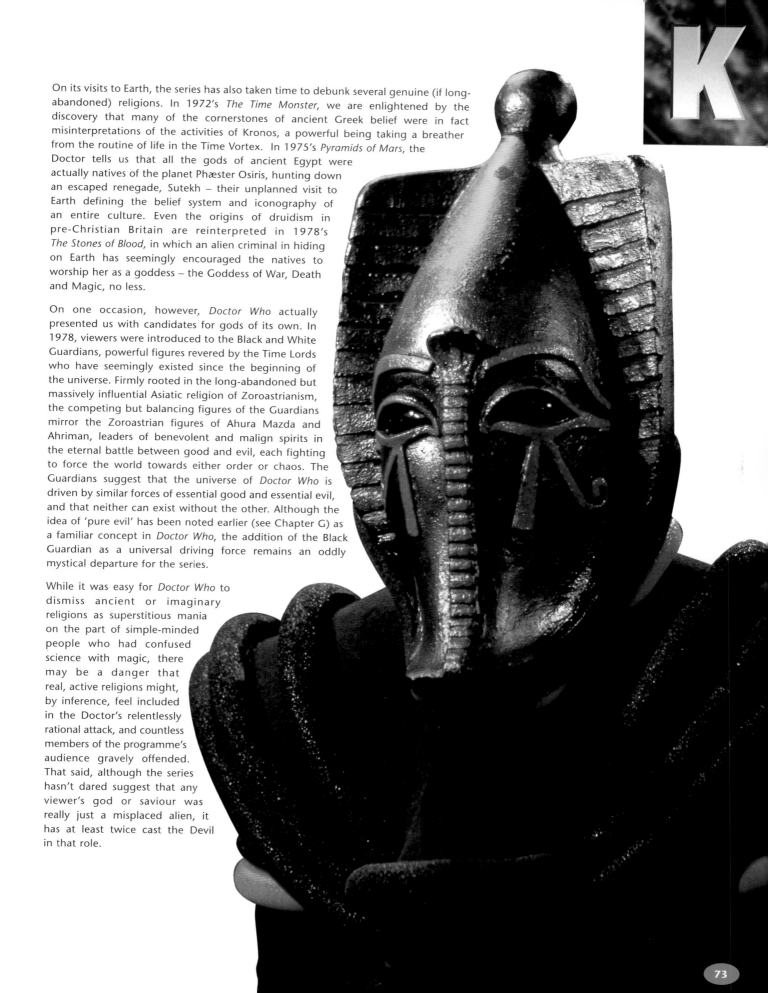

On its visits to Earth, the series has also taken time to debunk several genuine (if long-abandoned) religions. In 1972's *The Time Monster*, we are enlightened by the discovery that many of the cornerstones of ancient Greek belief were in fact misinterpretations of the activities of Kronos, a powerful being taking a breather from the routine of life in the Time Vortex. In 1975's *Pyramids of Mars*, the Doctor tells us that all the gods of ancient Egypt were actually natives of the planet Phæster Osiris, hunting down an escaped renegade, Sutekh – their unplanned visit to Earth defining the belief system and iconography of an entire culture. Even the origins of druidism in pre-Christian Britain are reinterpreted in 1978's *The Stones of Blood*, in which an alien criminal in hiding on Earth has seemingly encouraged the natives to worship her as a goddess – the Goddess of War, Death and Magic, no less.

On one occasion, however, *Doctor Who* actually presented us with candidates for gods of its own. In 1978, viewers were introduced to the Black and White Guardians, powerful figures revered by the Time Lords who have seemingly existed since the beginning of the universe. Firmly rooted in the long-abandoned but massively influential Asiatic religion of Zoroastrianism, the competing but balancing figures of the Guardians mirror the Zoroastrian figures of Ahura Mazda and Ahriman, leaders of benevolent and malign spirits in the eternal battle between good and evil, each fighting to force the world towards either order or chaos. The Guardians suggest that the universe of *Doctor Who* is driven by similar forces of essential good and essential evil, and that neither can exist without the other. Although the idea of 'pure evil' has been noted earlier (see Chapter G) as a familiar concept in *Doctor Who*, the addition of the Black Guardian as a universal driving force remains an oddly mystical departure for the series.

While it was easy for *Doctor Who* to dismiss ancient or imaginary religions as superstitious mania on the part of simple-minded people who had confused science with magic, there may be a danger that real, active religions might, by inference, feel included in the Doctor's relentlessly rational attack, and countless members of the programme's audience gravely offended. That said, although the series hasn't dared suggest that any viewer's god or saviour was really just a misplaced alien, it has at least twice cast the Devil in that role.

In one of these stories, 1971's *The Dæmons*, the Devil is a stereotypical horned and cloven-hoofed figure, Azal – a rather sulky scientist from across the galaxy – and the Doctor takes the opportunity to debunk all manner of paganist and occult rituals that had grown up around his early appearances on Earth. However, mainstream Christianity also takes a bit of a battering at the hands of writer 'Guy Leopold' (a pseudonym for Robert Sloman and series producer Barry Letts). The evil Master poses as the vicar of the troubled village of Devil's End and hosts black masses in a cavern under his church, while the figure of 'good' in the story takes the form of local white witch and unbeliever Miss Hawthorne. Sloman and Letts's original script went further still, but their plans to have the Master reciting the Lord's Prayer backwards in front of the altar as he invoked 'the Devil' in the church nave were quickly abandoned for reasons of taste.

It was the same writing team that took the series on its journey through the byways of Buddhism over the course of the following three years. The action of 1972's *The Time Monster* skids to a sudden halt in its final episode to allow the Doctor to share a moment of transcendental contemplation with Jo Grant. He tells of childhood visits to an old hermit who lived under a tree on a snow-capped mountain near his Gallifreyan home who had, according to hearsay, discovered the secret of life. The Doctor remembers a 'black day' when he sought the advice of the hermit to lift him from despair. The hermit, it seems, 'Just sat there silently, expressionless, and he listened while I poured out my troubles to him... When I finished, he lifted a skeletal hand and he pointed. Do you know what he pointed at?... A flower... Just like a daisy, it was.'

The Doctor continues, 'I looked at it for a moment, and suddenly I saw it through his eyes. It was simply glowing with life, like a perfectly cut jewel... Yes, that was the daisiest daisy I'd ever seen... So later I got up, ran down the mountain, and I found that the rocks weren't grey at all. They were red, brown, purple and gold!'

False gods born of superstition...
Top: Aggedor, innocent beast of the planet Peladon. *The Curse of Peladon* (1972)
Above: Logar, god of Sarn, but really just a man in a flame-proof suit. *Planet of Fire* (1984)

...and one fake believer
Main: Sarah (Elisabeth Sladen) disguised as a monk in 1973's *The Time Warrior*

Buddhist learning tells that the Hindu prince Siddharta Gautama, known as Buddha or 'Enlightened One', was distressed by human suffering and left his palace and beloved family to seek wisdom and a solution to the world's problems. It was when sitting under a tree on a mountainside, contemplating a flower, that he finally came to understand the cause of and a way to find release from suffering. As the Doctor later says of his hermit friend, 'He taught me how to look into my own mind.'

The result of Buddha's meditations are enshrined in the 'four noble truths', which are: 1) that all lives experience suffering; 2) that suffering is caused by desire; 3) that suffering ceases when desire is eradicated; 4) that desire can be eradicated by following the 'eightfold path', whose steps are right views, right thought, plain and truthful speech, right conduct (including abstinence from immorality and taking life, whether human or animal), right livelihood (harming no one), right effort (always pressing on), right awareness of the past, the present and the future, and, lastly, right contemplation or meditation.

Long-serving *Doctor Who* writer Terrance Dicks once described the Doctor as one 'always on the side of right and truth and justice... He is never cruel, never unkind. He always tries to make peace.' Although Dicks's use of the word 'always' is a trifle optimistic (see Chapter G), and the Doctor often lacks consistent moral motivation in some of the more sweeping life-and-death decisions he makes, it is also clear that he possesses a general code of ethical behaviour broadly analogous to Buddha's eightfold path. Always pressing on, moral, plain and truthful, and with a clear awareness of past, present and future, the Time Lord regularly demonstrates an understanding that suffering indeed stems from desire – desire for conquest, desire for power, desire for immortality – and it is the destructive nature of that desire in others that draws him into all his battles.

Within Buddhism, a follower acquires merit by following these rules in his or her 'chain of lives'. This is a concept rooted in Hinduism, in which life is seen as a cycle of lives (*samsara*) in which an individual's destiny is determined by his or her deeds (*karma*) and from which they may gain release during a cycle of continual reincarnation. In Buddhism, following the four noble truths offers release to nirvana, where individuality is lost – 'as the dewdrop slips into the shining sea' – by merging with universal life.

Writing *Planet of the Spiders*, Robert Sloman – still working closely with Barry Letts – clearly signposted his agenda as the Doctor moves towards the next stage in his cycle of lives. As Cho-Je says to a fretting acolyte, 'All things pass away... this world of samsara, this world of appearance, is the world of change... one day you will learn to walk in solitude amidst the traffic of the world.' Sloman was obviously attempting to add a more spiritual dimension to what has previously been the mere biological necessity of Time Lord regeneration in order to suggest that it can also be a time of – as the monk says – 'inescapable joy'.

In the story, the Doctor realises that the terrible situation he is trapped in – absurdly enough, battling a sixty-foot spider with designs on the universe, but the point is made – has been caused by his own 'greed for knowledge, for information'. The suffering around him is the terrible result of his own desire. Only by the 'right thought' of facing his fear – laying down his current life in the process – can he 'improve' his karma and pass to a worthy new life.

Buddhism's position as *Doctor Who*'s favoured religion is secured by the fact that it has no formal god – Buddha never claimed to be anything other than a man, although systems of worship have developed over the centuries – so it stands apart from the politics- and ritual-choked religions so often lampooned and debunked by the series.

Given that this religion offers what seems the most appropriate human label for our hero's ethics and beliefs – and those of the series as a whole, where bad things always happen to those who behave badly – perhaps even the Doctor, with his cycle of reincarnations and understanding of karma, would happily identify himself as a Buddhist.

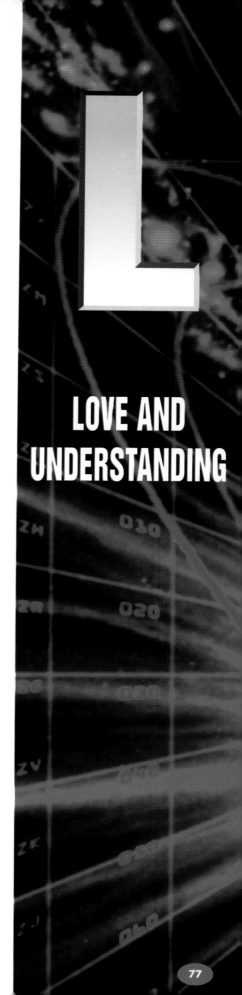

In 1974, regular *Doctor Who* writer Robert Holmes accepted the post of the series' full-time script editor. The skill, insight and enthusiasm he was to bring to the role would redefine audience expectation and catapult the series into its second golden age of popular appeal.

LOVE AND UNDERSTANDING

'If anyone decides that Doctor Who *is an art form, its death knell will be sounded. It is good, clean, escapist hokum – which is no small thing to be. When it's done well, it is the best thing of its kind around.'*

These are the words of Robert Colin Holmes, a writer credited on screen for fifteen *Doctor Who* serials between 1968 and 1986, uncredited for one more and who, in his role as the series' script editor between 1974 and 1977, had a massive input into seventeen others. In this latter period, he helped to guide the programme through its second great period of mass public acclaim – this time without the support of the Daleks – and establish a reputation among the series' fans as their undisputed favourite script writer.

Doctor Who may have been graced by the work of more erudite or more experienced writers than Holmes. It may have used scripts from those who crusaded to bring a 'higher purpose' to their storylines, rife with obscure commentary on politics, religion or the human condition. But what made Holmes's work on the programme so significant and so popular can be traced to this belief that 'good, clean, escapist hokum' was as worthy as the most complex and multi-layered adult drama. He also knew that it was as difficult to create, and he relished the challenge this presented. He carried an innate understanding of not just the strengths but also the key limitations of *Doctor Who*'s format, and he knew precisely how to play to the former without breaching the latter.

As a result of this faith, his work on *Doctor Who* displays not a trace of cynicism or laziness, and is instead marked out by its verve, style and wit – three qualities on which the series has always thrived. Holmes's enthusiasm for the programme shows through in every line of dialogue he wrote, every character he created. In turn, he inspired all those he worked with, earning their appreciation, respect and lasting friendship. Quite simply, he was the best kind of writer and editor *Doctor Who* could have had.

Robert Holmes had marked himself out as a dedicated and driven man at every stage of his varied and incident-packed life. Joining the Army as a fresh-faced youth of just sixteen, he soon earned himself an officer's commission from the Queen's Own Cameron Highlanders and, while serving in Burma during the Second World War, would be the youngest commissioned officer in the entire British Army. After the war, he left the forces, returned to England and began training for the police force at Hendon College. Typically, he graduated top of his year, finding himself earmarked for great things, and was posted to Bow Street police station in London.

However, Holmes soon found that the routine duties of a beat policeman offered little of the adventure and stimulation he had enjoyed during his time in the Army. On appearances in court to give evidence for the prosecution, he often watched and envied the scurrying, frantic reporters at work in the public gallery, fighting to add an entertaining or dramatic spin to their stories before racing to phone them back to their newspapers to meet their deadlines. With characteristic dedication, Holmes taught himself shorthand in his spare time before resigning from the police force to pursue a career in the more liberating field of journalism. The gamble paid off and he was soon on the payroll of a range of local and national papers, first in London and then in the Midlands, as well as filing syndicated reports for the Press Association.

Three popular companions introduced in Robert Holmes scripts
Top: Jo Grant in *Terror of the Autons* (1971)
Middle: Sarah Jane Smith in *The Time Warrior* (1973)
Bottom: Romanadvoratrelundar ('Romana') in *The Ribos Operation* (1978)

Following a spell writing and editing magazine short stories in the late 1950s, Holmes made his move into television, providing a number of scripts for the Granada adventure series *Knight Errant*, before taking the post of story editor on the series for a year from 1959. After completing five scripts for the Highland medical series *Doctor Finlay's Casebook*, Holmes went on to draw on his real-life police experience and secured writing work on a range of 1960s crime dramas, including *Ghost Squad* (Scotland Yard undercover agents), *Public Eye* (adventures of seedy detective) and *Intrigue* (industrial espionage). His first fantasy work was in 1965, when he provided the scripts for *Undermind*, an eleven-part *Invasion of the Body Snatchers*-style drama, and the storyline for *Invasion*, a British sci-fi B movie from the Merton Park studio. Well received by critics ('A modest but highly intelligent science fiction thriller,' said the *Financial Times*), the full script for *Invasion* came from Holmes's *Public Eye* colleague Roger Marshall, but the story bears many Holmes hallmarks, and includes many ideas and themes he would return to in his *Doctor Who* work.

Around this time, Holmes submitted to the BBC, on spec, an outline for a stand-alone science fiction drama entitled *The Trap*. The synopsis was swiftly returned to him by Head of Serials Shaun Sutton, who informed him that there was no longer an available slot for such a production, but encouraged the writer to resubmit the idea to the *Doctor Who* office. This Holmes duly did, meeting up with series' story editor Donald Tosh, who outlined the direction in which he and producer John Wiles wanted to take the series. Tosh encouraged Holmes to reshape his ideas to fit this planned new style. Holmes, however, appears to have been too busy at the time with his work on *Public Eye* and *Undermind*, and failed to capitalise on this initial interest in his work from the *Doctor Who* office.

ABC, the independent TV station behind *Public Eye*, lost its licence to broadcast during the 1968 round of regional commercial franchise renegotiation and renewal. The series was ultimately picked up by Thames, but it was perhaps with the future of one of his most steady sources of work under threat that Holmes decided to pitch his 1965 proposal, now titled *The Space Trap*, at the *Doctor Who* office once again. His timing couldn't have been better.

Doctor Who's uncredited assistant script editor at the time, Terrance Dicks, saw some worth in Holmes's storyline and, having time on his hands, set about developing the story as a 'spare' for the series' sixth year – a luxury rarely available to an overworked *Doctor Who* production team. 'I worked on it with Bob Holmes in a very leisurely fashion,' said Dicks later, 'and it became something of a hobby for me.'

But this 'leisurely' period of calm was not to last for long, as 1968 ultimately proved a fraught year for the programme, with a number of commissioned scripts falling by the wayside and others having to be frantically extended by the full-time production team to fill vacant slots. *The Space Trap* didn't stay on the shelf for long. Rechristened *The Krotons* before it went before the cameras, location filming for the story began on 10 November 1968, less than six months after Holmes had sent in his original synopsis 'on the off chance'.

The story takes the Second Doctor, Jamie and Zoe to the world of the Gonds, a gentle race who venerate unseen gods-cum-dictators, the Krotons. The Gonds believe the greatest honour that can be bestowed upon their young is to be summoned to become a 'companion' of the Krotons, an invitation extended to only their brightest students. But the Doctor discovers that these 'companions' are actually having their mental powers drained before being killed, the Krotons needing the energy to reanimate themselves and ultimately power their spaceship on its journey to rejoin their fleet.

Although the story lacks many of the later Holmes touches, it still features one of his most distinctive plot elements: the crippled villain trapped in an underground lair, kidnapping others and drawing on their strength, either intellectual or physical, to fuel a return to power. Later Holmes creations - Linx in 1973's *The Time Warrior*, Sutekh in 1975's *Pyramids of Mars*, Magnus Greel in 1977's *The Talons of Weng-Chiang* and the dying Master in 1976's *The Deadly Assassin* – also do more than their fair share of lurking and leaching.

Even surrounded by more original and dramatic material in the late 1968/early 1969 run of serials – the elliptical *The Mind Robber* and Patrick Troughton's epic, final adventure, *The War Games*, which revealed a great deal of the Doctor's alien background for the first time – *The Krotons* proved to be very popular with the viewing public, Holmes's first work on *Doctor Who* bringing the series its highest single episode rating since *The Daleks' Master Plan* two years earlier. This response, along with the establishment of an instant rapport with Terrance Dicks (now full-time script editor) served to guarantee Holmes a privileged place in *Doctor Who*'s then quite small repertory of writers.

Robert Holmes would go on to pen one more Patrick Troughton serial, *The Space Pirates*, at very short notice and four adventures for Jon Pertwee's Doctor. This early work on the series clearly demonstrates

Holmes's increasing confidence. While *The Krotons* was something of a stylistic throwback to *Doctor Who*'s early years – having much in common with William Hartnell's *The Sensorites*, *The Space Museum* and *The Savages*, for example – his second serial showed that Holmes was looking to take the show in a new, distinctive direction.

The Space Pirates displays the first use of one of Holmes's key story-telling tricks: the placing of an easily recognisable modern cultural stereotype into an absurdly inappropriate fantasy setting. Here we have Milo Clancey, every inch the clichéd American Wild West gold prospector – chewing baccy and cussing – recast as an independent space mining pioneer in the far future, his traditional well-loved stubborn mule becoming an equally fickle and unreliable spaceship. Holmes clearly recognised that this juxtaposition of images, language and iconography allowed viewers to more readily understand the motivation of his characters, drawing them into the action more easily. Holmes's scripts, with their characters driven by such seemingly simple motives as greed or revenge that viewers can, if not entirely empathise with, then at least recognise, actually seem more sophisticated than scripts relying on villains in search of a spurious sci-fi plot device, or global conquest for the sake of it. In all his serials from *The Space Pirates* on, Holmes offers viewers a helping hand, a familiar reference point, which not only helps to showcase a serial's more fantastic elements by throwing them into sharper relief, but also makes the whole situation easier to accept and understand.

When a Time Lord comes to Earth to relay a warning to the Doctor in Holmes's 1971 serial *Terror of the Autons*, he stands in mid-air disguised as a City businessman in pinstripes and bowler. In this scene, Holmes is working several tricks at once. We are presented with a pleasing visual gimmick and a useful iconic shorthand to help us understand the bossy, businesslike nature of the Time Lords, while the quirkiness of the image draws our attention to the crucial content of absurd visitor's message – all this and a hint of Surrealism too, with references to Magritte's bowler-hatted men in his painting *Golconda*.

This mixing of the familiar with the fantastic added a level of sophistication to Holmes's work that would keep it interesting and entertaining for older members of *Doctor Who*'s audience without confusing and alienating the youngsters. *The Deadly Assassin* (1976) tells, on one level, the simple story of a murderous monster stalking the Time Lord world of Gallifrey; on another level, it is a clever commentary on corruption in politics and modern media manipulation of the news; and on a third level, it is an intelligent pastiche of the 1962 film and political thriller *The Manchurian Candidate*. In writing such a story, Holmes almost contradicts his own comment that *Doctor Who* should not be treated as 'art', as, in common with great art, *The Deadly Assassin* shifts and changes depending on how much understanding and insight the observer brings to it. The story offers rewards for viewers of every age and background, with the important built-in protection that you are not obliged to 'get' every reference or metaphor to enjoy it. It is not surprising that *Doctor Who*'s ratings rose during Holmes's tenure as script editor, the series keeping its traditional viewer base of excitable ten-year-olds while simultaneously recapturing the attention of many of those who had long since grown up and away from the programme, thinking it had nothing new or interesting to offer them.

Holmes's greatest strength was that he seemed to bring with him no preconceptions regarding the kind of stories *Doctor Who* ought to tell or the manner in which they should be told. While many of his fellow writers would view the series as merely down-the-line science fiction and try to write within the narrow limitations of their perception of that genre – often all militaristic aliens and their unlikely invasions – Holmes accepted no such boundaries. He seemed to have little interest in the trappings of sci-fi – the technology and the gadgetry – beyond their use in establishing the basic fantasy gimmick of a plot. *The Caves of Androzani*, Peter Davison's final serial from 1984, tells a tale of gun-running and drug-smuggling that could quite easily be set in the jungles of modern-day Colombia rather than the arid planet of Androzani Minor. Soldiers fight with machine pistols and grenades while politicians fake righteous indignation at the loss of life in a war they manipulate themselves. The action of 1978's *The Ribos Operation*, while it claims to unfold on the ice world of Ribos at some point in the future, could be painlessly relocated to fifteenth-century Russia – a period from which Holmes's script actually invites the story's set and costume designers to take their visual cues.

Robert Holmes was playful in his 'borrowing' of familiar plots and characters from literature and film. He did it in his own work – the Sax Rohmer *Fu Manchu*-styling of *The Talons of Weng-Chiang* standing as a prime example – and encouraged it in others, be it Terrance Dicks's reworking of *Frankenstein* in *The Brain of Morbius*, Terry Nation's *Invasion of the Body Snatchers* moments in *The Android Invasion* or Robert Banks Stewart's co-opting of the setting and plot of *The Thing from Another World* in *The Seeds of Doom*.

This may seem like just so much plagiarism, but in many ways Robert Holmes was simply taking the series back to basics.

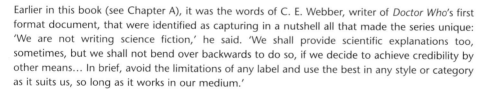

Faces of evil from Robert Holmes scripts...
Top: A robotic Mummy. *The Pyramids of Mars* (1975)
Middle: Mr Sin, a homocidal ventriloquist's doll. *The Talons of Weng-Chiang* (1977)
Bottom: Vengeful drug runner Sharaz Jek. *The Caves of Androzani* (1984)

Main: The Wirrn queen. *The Ark in Space* (1975)

Far left: Holmes's dream team of Fourth Doctor (Tom Baker) and Sarah (Elisabeth Sladen)

Earlier in this book (see Chapter A), it was the words of C. E. Webber, writer of *Doctor Who*'s first format document, that were identified as capturing in a nutshell all that made the series unique: 'We are not writing science fiction,' he said. 'We shall provide scientific explanations too, sometimes, but we shall not bend over backwards to do so, if we decide to achieve credibility by other means… In brief, avoid the limitations of any label and use the best in any style or category as it suits us, so long as it works in our medium.'

Although it is unlikely that Holmes ever read these words, he would surely have agreed with them. He rarely felt the need to provide rigorous scientific explanations, his use of thinly disguised modern characters in fictional settings was certainly a device to 'achieve credibility by other means' and his co-opting of ideas and moods from classic works of pulp fiction was simply making use of the 'best' from other genres.

Holmes understood, at the most fundamental of levels, what made *Doctor Who* work and employed this knowledge in every word he wrote. He knew the series wasn't created to be great art but a cheery, inexpensive tea-time entertainment – seeing that not as a barrier to creativity but a challenge to it. A high achiever in all areas of his life, he was determined to do his best by *Doctor Who*, and was willing to work and work and work to make it as good as it could possibly be.

Holmes's belief in the merits of *Doctor Who*'s 'good, clean, escapist hokum' remained undiminished by the passage of time. In a 1985 interview he said, 'I see no reason why I couldn't carry on writing one script a year if I satisfy them [the production team]… With any luck, though, I shall carry on writing for *Doctor Who* until its deathbed.'

Tragically, Robert Holmes died in May 1986 after a short illness. The series he believed in so strongly, and had enjoyed writing for for so long, followed him less than four years later.

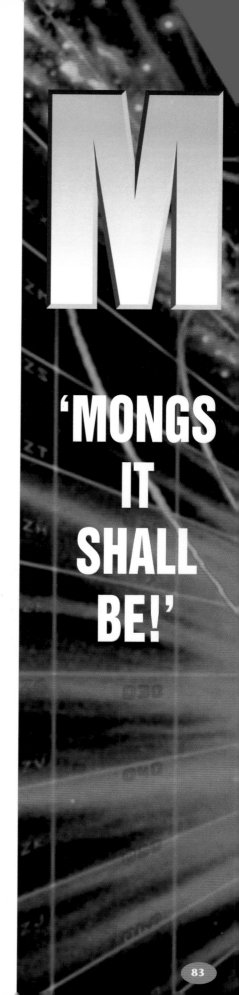

For twenty years the *Doctor Who Annual* was as much a part of a fan's Christmas as mince pies and *Morecambe and Wise*. For an audience starved of original *Doctor Who* fiction, it was the only place to turn. Or rather it would have been if only the stories had the slightest resemblance to the TV series they claimed to take as their inspiration...

'Oh, I don't know what we can do, Levi!' groaned the Doctor. 'There must be *some* way to escape the clutches of these clever, but unfeeling Medusians!'

It's enough to make you stop reading before the story has even begun, but there again, perseverance brings its own rewards. These are the opening words of *War on Aquatica*, a bizarre tale from the mad-as-you-like 1977 *Doctor Who Annual*.

Anyone looking for *Doctor Who* in a late 1970s *Doctor Who Annual* is in for a certain amount of disappointment – and never more so than in the 1977 edition. Sure, there is the odd glimpse of a chap with a long scarf among the disturbing, fractured illustrations. True, characters called Sarah and Harry are referred to in the text. However, these few familiar comforts do little to prepare you for the sinister lunacy that oozes from the book's eighty full-colour or duotone pages. The stories are obviously from the pen of someone who has never seen a single episode of the series but has had it described to them by someone whose language obviously lacks words for 'plot', 'logic' and 'self-control'. If Lewis Carroll had been kept in a dark room for six weeks, force-fed hallucinogenic drugs and then made to watch every episode of *Lost in Space* in one sitting, he would perhaps have struggled to his desk to scratch out the stories for this book before finally collapsing in a delirious fever. Lock up painter Francis Bacon with him and provide him much the same diet, and you would get yourself a useful collection of suitably disturbing illustrations at the same time.

Sadly, the identity of the writer of these tales remains unknown to this day. The drawings and paintings, however, are the work of Mancunian Paul Crompton, who years later would blame his then recent discovery of real ale for the surreal nature of his work on the annual. Crompton made this observation after noticing that the large illustration on the endpapers includes an image of a small bird perched on a severed hand. 'The state of my mind must have been warped!' he commented.

But all this still fails to quite capture the mind-expanding phantasmagoria that is the 1977 *Doctor Who Annual*. To help you to see more clearly, here's the 'plot' to the aforementioned *War on Aquatica*...

The Doctor, Sarah Jane and Professor Vittorio Levi – 'the Doctor's colleague and friend... zoologist, botanist, astronomer, anthropologist and amateur space traveller', in case you were wondering – are trapped in Medusia, one of the three kingdoms of the planet Aquatica (the others being Matterdom and Phyllosia). We don't know why Levi is with the Doctor and Sarah, but they don't seem to enjoy his company very much. Quote: '"... it is a wonder they did not-a turn the evil eye upon us!" the Professor had exclaimed monotonously, much to the annoyance of the Doctor and Sarah.' It remains a moot point whether it is actually possible to exclaim anything monotonously, not to mention what any Italian readers might have thought of Levi's hilariously presented accent. When the Doctor suggests that the dreary scientist might like to punch their guard insensible, Levi chimes back, 'Bump-a 'im one? He-he! Nothing-a would-a give me greater pleasure!' A comedy foreigner included for no discernible reason!

How enriching!

Back to that plot. The frustrated trio escape from the one-eyed, serpent-haired Medusians and meet up with two beautiful Phyllosians, whose 'eyes were sapphire-blue, from which rays shone like strobes from a cinema projector' no less. These telepathic creatures, Phyllos and Dyonne (can we hazard a guess that the unknown author had friends called Phyllis and Diane?), explain that they are seeking to stop a war between Medusia and Matterdom, for fear of being caught in the middle. Still with me? Good. The Medusians, you see, are 'filled with greed... are of a high intelligence, have telepathic powers and incredible magnetism'. This, it turns out, is not Phyllos suggesting that the Medusians have particularly engaging personalities; he means that they are quite literally magnetic. They have been using these powers to steal glyt ('a scintillating mineral of great value') from the Mattermonks of Matterdom. More damning still, they have also been kidnapping Phyllos's Lumidolphs – you guessed it, fluorescent dolphins – to which they attach warheads before rocketing the creatures towards the doubtless rather startled Mattermonks.

The Phyllosians, the Doctor and friends travel to Matterdom in Phyllos's motorboat and secure an audience with King Chympanzo, who, while scratching a blue armpit and picking blue fleas off himself, despairs: 'I am at my wit's end to know what to do!' Phyllos's suggestion – 'Then why not combat the Medusians by *using* your pets, the Mongs, Your Cleverness!' – is initially dismissed by Chympanzo as immoral. But, after further persuasion, the blue king perhaps comes to recognise that there can be no real morality in a war fought with Day-Glo thermonuclear dolphins. Chympanzo's final speech is worth noting for the record in full, as no true history of *Doctor Who* can possibly be complete without it...

'"Then – Mongs it shall be!" he said. "And tomorrow, Phyllos, I will arrange that they invade Medusia from the air. Our saucers shall transport them, and our newly-invented dissolving parachutes will drop them to the ground. They have a timing-device in the fabric, so that when the job is finished they disintegrate; then the Mongs shall be set free!"'

The parachute-trained Mongs, it turns out, are a type of mongoose that terrifies the Medusians by heartlessly tugging at their serpentine hair while they sleep. This new weapon in the increasingly surreal war eventually triggers a lasting peace, and all the races of Aquatica – Medusians, Mattermonks, Phyllosians, Lumidolphs, Mongs and Frug-frugs (they swarm in the rivers, apparently) – live together happily ever after.

The Doctor, who you'll note has played no part in this unfolding

Paul Crompton art work from the 1977
Doctor Who Annual
Above: The Doctor under attack in *The
Time Snatch*

Left: The Doctor, Harry and Sarah (the
latter seemingly in a wedding dress) at
the mercy of the *Menace on Metalupiter*

Far left above: The Doctor, Sarah and
the mysterious Vittorio Levi flee from
War on Aquatica

drama whatsoever – perhaps assuming that he's going to wake up sometime soon – makes his farewells. 'I could stay here forever!' Sarah exclaims, perhaps just out of politeness, as they leave, prompting the Doctor to rather rashly promise to return. Sadly, any second trip to Aquatica remains unrecorded.

Other stories in the 1977 annual offer fewer rewards to the discerning reader. In *The Time Snatch*, unnamed aliens attempt to steal 'Crystal Z' from UNIT. They fail. We don't even find out where the crystal is from or why it is important. In *Detour to Diamedes* the Doctor makes… well, a detour to the planet Diamedes.

The terrifyingly visceral comic strip *The Body Snatcher* serves up the disturbing sight of men with dog skulls where their heads should be, wearing no more than what appears to be a pair of leather briefs – like a David Hockney painting brought to life by Damien Hirst – and an unlikely exclamation from the Doctor when he shouts, 'Oh, my God!' Another comic strip, *Menace on Metalupiter*, is distinguished only by the Doctor's deathless line on examining a cheetah-shaped robot, 'My word! No wonder there was no response! His whole brain is made of rubber!' The robot later manages to stutteringly explain, 'We could not move… They came and stole our memories… replaced them with rubber.'

More satisfying – but no less bizarre – is the text story *The Eye Spiders of Pergross,* in which the Doctor, Sarah and Harry stumble across a group of enormous spiders each with bodies formed from a giant eye. Exactly which smoke-filled room just before dawn spawned this story is anyone's guess. As the travellers advance towards the spiders, they are lifted into the air 'as easily as pigeon feathers' and 'drawn gently but firmly by a powerful crimson magnetic ray, toward the biggest eye'. The tale goes on: 'Its pupil dilated enough to let them pass through with ease. The Doctor and his companions found themselves in a tunnel which propelled them along a psychedelic corkscrew, toward the centre of this unbelievable creature of the year 3872.' Psychedelic corkscrew? Heavy, man.

The annual was further bulked out by educational features on hot-air balloons, space travel and the charming career of rocket scientist Wernher von Braun, and a number of puzzles and mazes. One little test deserves a mention, namely 'Problem of the Painted Planet'. Here 'Dr Who' has to help the natives of the planet Jimorris to divide up the surface of their planet equally. Their problem, you see, is that 'their logic is limited and their natural intelligence is among the lowest in the cosmos' (although presumably not quite as low as that of the now insecure kids struggling to complete this irritating puzzle). This is all by the by, as the most important detail is that these natives of Jimorris happen, of course, to be called Jimorrisans – an amusing reference to the hallucinogen-addled 1960s rock star that's actually perfectly appropriate to a book that seems to have peered through a few too many doors of perception itself.

This annual was the eleventh published by World Distributors Ltd since 1965 in a series that would run until 1986. Often dismissed as one of the worst – if not the very worst – by fans of the *Doctor Who* TV series because of its only nodding acquaintance with the programme, or indeed with reality, it is

actually the most fascinating for the very same reasons. But this is not to say that the others don't have many points of interest.

The very first annual was reportedly written by *Doctor Who*'s first story editor, David Whitaker. His tales took the trouble to maintain closer links with the content of the parent programme. One story, *The Lair of Zarbi Supremo*, pits Dr Who once more against the giant bipedal ants from the 1965 serial *The Web Planet*, now rendered more threatening than ever through Whitaker's lurid prose: 'Their huge mandibles… could tear the limbs from a man just as a man might tear apart a roasted chicken.' There is even a distant prefiguring of the film *Aliens*: 'A great opening to one side revealed, in a lightning glimpse, what Dr Who had suspected from the beginning. Perhaps two or three hundred feet in length she lay, a bloated queen with a host of workers feeding her and stroking her.' Later, humans mount an attack on a mass army of the scuttling insects in a *Starship Troopers*-style scene that would be far beyond the humble resources of the BBC.

In another story, Dr Who meets the rather endearing-looking Fish Men of Kandalinga, who find themselves under threat from the alien Voord – the rubbery monsters of 1964's *The Keys of Marinus*. Here the Doctor finds out what has happened to the Voord since they were cast out from Marinus and stops to debate some of the moral issues arising from that earlier television adventure. He finally defeats the 'cruel and emotionless' Voord leader by destroying his mental control over his troops. The result is this simultaneously tragic and amusing moment: 'The Voord whom he had deformed was wandering about aimlessly on the causeway, mewing like a cat, apparently all his senses askew with the loss of his telepathic organ.'

As William Hartnell gave way to Patrick Troughton, the annuals lost some of their grip on the style of the TV series and dipped a first toe into the world of the strange. The Troughton annuals are distinctive for their attempts to bring a philosophical, almost spiritual twist to the Doctor's exploits, often reading like some mannered, would-be intellectual science fiction from the close of the last century.

In *The Celestial Toy-shop*, a story from the Patrick Troughton annual produced for Christmas 1968, the good ship 'Tardis' and its crew – the Doctor, Jamie and Victoria – land on a giant toy shelf, where they play on an oversize toy train and stroll through an enormous doll's house. The Doctor discovers another, correctly proportioned doll's house inside the one he is exploring. Somehow, he finds himself reduced and stepping inside this second house – where, of course, there is yet another tiny house. In a dream-like state, he makes this recursive trip over and over, with a sense of wonderment and joy growing all the time. Finally, he finds a last house that 'glows like a jewel' in a room of blinding light. 'But the light that shone out was quite unbearable to his human eyes and he closed them completely and turned blindly toward the door by which he had entered, away from that glittering small jewel which seemed to radiate all the Light in the Universe.' As the Doctor runs and runs, we discover: 'The first house in that enigmatic toy-shop had been the focus point or hinge of an infinite pivot, about which turned the multi-dimensions of the entire infinite cosmos… he had seen the Light – yes, that was it, the Light! It had drawn him and he had retreated. No human being could face the Light!'

Finding Jamie and Victoria again, the Doctor collapses into their arms, sobbing miserably after this almost religious experience. Back in the TARDIS, the Doctor retires and we are treated to an

Top: The Doctor seeks out *The Lair of Zarbi Supremo* in his first annual, published in 1965...
Middle: ...in which he also fails to enjoy a healthy plate of plankton, served by a shocked Voord in *The Fish Men of Kandalinga*
Above: The Doctor at his tiny TARDIS console in the 1968 annual story *Only a Matter of Time*

Main: The Doctor, Jo and the Brigadier ponder their recent adventure with the Breelians in *Dead on Arrival*, a strip story from the 1975 annual

extraordinary closing paragraph: 'The Doctor slept for hours and not a dream disturbed him. That strange and utterly unearthly place where the dimensions had overlapped, at last, ceased to trouble him. But it left a tiny, nebulous regret that he could never afterwards understand. Eden is lost every moment of our lives.' Perhaps a generation of eight-years-olds re-read this wistful observation several times, looking for meaning, before finally shrugging and opting to crayon a picture of a Dalek over the page instead.

In a similar manner to his spin-off comic strip adventures (see Chapter T), Jon Pertwee's annual adventures successfully aped the style and characterisation of the TV series, offering brief, traditional stories of UNIT versus aliens, although the pompous tone of the Troughton books survived. Liz Shaw and the Brigadier are captured particularly well, although the Doctor's attitude towards the supposed sanctity of all life was reinterpreted somewhat in passages such as this from the conclusion of the 1970 story *Caverns of Horror* (during which the Doctor discovers hideous insect creatures under England): 'Every last one of these foul things must be destroyed!... Liz, for the first time in my life I'm scared. Let us get out of here, now. These UNIT chaps know all about killing; they're trained to it. Let them get on with it. This time I've got to admit how welcome it is to have a few professional killers around.' Let 'em have it, Doctor!

The majority of the Tom Baker annuals were similar in style and tone to the 1977 edition celebrated above – dark, bizarre stories accompanied by disturbing illustrations – even if they did not quite scale the same heights of lunacy. With the arrival of the 1980s, relative normality was resumed, resulting in a few books fronted by Peter Davison and Colin Baker which were sadly neither as interesting nor as accidentally hilarious as their predecessors. It seems that fan writers had become involved by the time of two Colin Baker annuals, which presented a number of continuity cross-checked tales of Time Lords and UNIT, backed up with some token behind-the-scenes features on the production of the TV show.

The final World Distributor's *Doctor Who Annual* was published for Christmas 1985. Sales figures had dropped considerably during the 1980s, as fans opted to spend their money on more substantial factual fare from other publishers and the market for TV-based annuals as a whole slumped into recession.

So the annuals are gone, but they should not be forgotten. Sometimes thought-proving, sometimes wildly original and more often just stark staring mad, the *Doctor Who Annual* took the Time Lord on journeys to planets and civilisations undreamed of by the comparatively conservative TV series. As long as the reader has a broad mind and a strong stomach, these adventures can, in their own terrible way, be just as entertaining.

ANNUAL EVENTS

○ The first *Doctor Who*-related book in an annual format was *The Dalek Book*, published in June 1964 by Souvenier Press and Panther Books. The same company followed this up with *The Dalek World* in 1965 and *The Dalek Outer Space Book* in 1966.

○ World Distributors (Manchester) Ltd published their first *Dr Who Annual* in September 1965, with a cover price of 9/6d. The company would release one per year – except 1971 – until the 1986 edition in September 1985.

○ The second annual was the first to contain a comic strip alongside the text stories.

○ The 1968 edition was the first to feature companions alongside the Doctor in the stories, in this case Ben and Polly with the Second Doctor.

○ The 1975 annual included a story – *The House That Jack Built* – written by Keith Miller, then head of the small Doctor Who Fan Club. It would be the first piece of professionally published fiction from a *Doctor Who* fan. He was paid £9.

○ In 1982, *Doctor Who* producer John Nathan-Turner was so dissatisfied with World's output that he suggested their licence be withdrawn. World eventually persuaded the BBC that they should be allowed to continue.

○ World also published four editions of *The Dalek Annual* from Christmas 1975 onward – featuring the adventures of Mark Seven, Joel Shaw and the Anti-Dalek Force – and a *K9 Annual* in 1982. Two compilation books of World *Doctor Who* material were issued in 1981 and 1985, the first by World themselves, the latter by Galley Press.

Left: The Sixth Doctor returns to Gallifrey for *The Time Savers* story in the 1985 annual

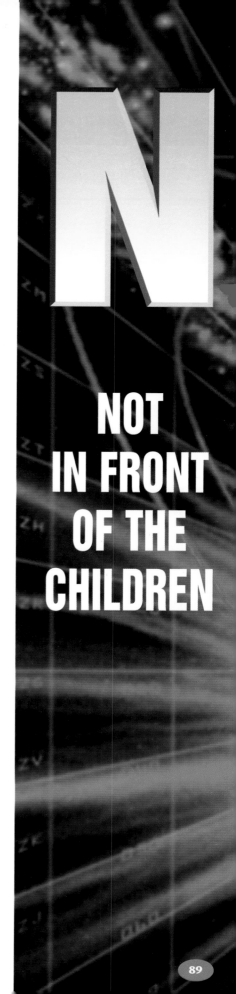

N

NOT IN FRONT OF THE CHILDREN

In the mid-1970s, the Doctor had to battle giant spiders, murderous Time Lords, deadly vegetables and robotic mummies. He was shot, strangled, crushed and drowned – but that's nothing compared to what one old lady from Birmingham wanted to do to him...

In retrospect, it was probably the freeze frame that did it.

It is 13 November 1976, and 13 million people are tuned in to Part Three of *The Deadly Assassin*. Throughout the episode, the Doctor's unconscious mind has been linked to a powerful computer on Gallifrey while he shares an all-too-real nightmare with a murderous rival Time Lord, Chancellor Goth. After a cat-and-mouse hunt through forest and marsh, the pair have reached a final confrontation in a shallow pool bubbling with methane. Goth leaps on the Doctor, forcing him beneath the water. The Doctor struggles, but to no avail, the grip on his shoulders too firm. Goth feels the life ebbing from his rival as the Doctor's body finally goes limp. 'You're finished, Doctor,' he snarls exultantly. 'Finished!'

As the scale-descending howl of the closing music crashed in, the last sight of the Doctor for those 13 million viewers until the following Saturday was a close-up freeze frame of his face, distorted and refracted under the water, all his adventures seemingly at an end. Many of those watching would have been on the edge of their seats, most enjoying the buzz of a well-orchestrated and masterfully executed cliffhanger, a few perhaps genuinely distressed by the apparent death of their hero. One viewer, however, was incandescent with rage, and by the end of the following week she had put pen to paper to express her feelings to Sir Charles Curran, Director-General of the BBC. Her name was Mrs Mary Whitehouse.

Whitehouse, a staunch Christian, was fifty-three when she launched her 'Clean-up TV' campaign in 1964. A part-time schoolmistress, she had taken charge of sex-education classes at a girls' secondary school, where her lessons had been as much about chastity and virtue as the nature and consequences of intercourse. She was on a hiding to nothing, however – this was, after all, the 1960s, a time for free-living and free-loving, and all her 'gels' wanted to talk about were the romantic exploits of the dashing TV medic Dr Kildare. Whitehouse would later recall, 'It was then I realised that, in a few brief words in a television programme, they had been won over to a sub-Christian concept of living.' Mary believed that God had given her a mission to halt the corrupting influence of television and to help those in control of the medium, who were stumbling blind, to see the light.

At first she took her message to Harman Grisewood, Assistant Director-General of the BBC, but she was certain that he didn't take her seriously. Feeling her impotence as a lone voice in the wilderness, she gathered various apostles to her cause – her MP, her close friends. On 5 May 1964, she booked Birmingham town hall to deliver her first sermon on the mounting levels of sex and violence on television. An audience of 250 was expected, but nearly 2,000 made the pilgrimage to hear her speak. Soon after, the National Viewers' and Listeners' Association was formed and Whitehouse appointed honorary general secretary; she became president in 1980, a post she would hold until the mid-1990s. Her name became synonymous with the NVLA's campaign to remove sex, violence and bad language from British TV, as she proved always ready to offer immensely quotable words of condemnation to the newspapers – generally to the right-wing *Daily Mail* and *Daily Telegraph*, which would frequently seek out her opinions – about whatever she judged to be sordid, gratuitous or blasphemous on television. To some, she was a noble and heroic figure, spearheading a campaign for 'basic decency and good Christian values'. To others, she was little more than a whining killjoy or a barely tolerated busybody. But, however the woman herself was viewed, there is no doubting the immense influence wielded by the NVLA throughout the 1970s and into the early 1980s. Although much of the Association's time during this period was spent fighting the 'sex-mad' writers and producers of *Play for Today* and its ilk, as the Association grew in strength it would turn its critical eye towards everything from the news to sitcoms, from Desmond Morris to *Doctor Who*.

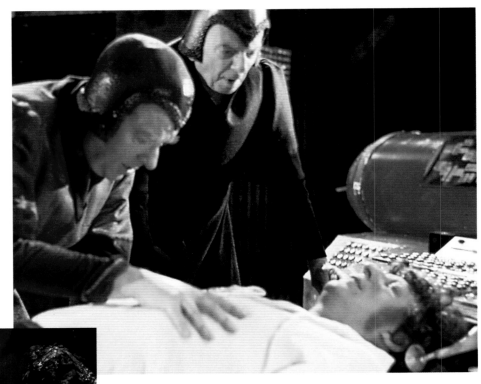

The NVLA's first major intervention came in the aftermath of the final Jon Pertwee adventure, *Planet of the Spiders*. Mrs Whitehouse was dragged into the fray by the ever-moral *Daily Mail*, which had spotted a likely story in the medical magazine the *General Practitioner*. 'Who's afraid of Dr Who's spiders?' the paper asked on 28 February 1975. 'A recent series of the TV science fiction show created large hairy spiders as Dr Who's monster opponents. Dr Michael Hennison, consultant psychiatrist to the Church of England's Children's Society, says that "Fears and phobias are almost universal among young children… a recent *Dr Who* series was probably responsible for an epidemic of spider phobia among young children."' The mention of the Church probably had the *Mail* reporter on the phone to Whitehouse in an instant, and although any campaign to be tough on arachnophobia – and tough on the causes of arachnophobia – had hardly been at the centre of the NVLA's launch manifesto, the Christian soldier was happy to pontificate. 'This psychiatrist precisely underlines the warnings we have been giving about the effect of *Dr Who* on the very small child,' she said. 'We intend to ask the BBC as a matter of urgency to finance independent research into the effect of *Dr Who* on the under-fives, and, in the meantime, ask it to switch the programme to 6.30.' *Planet of the Spiders* had originally been shown at around 5.40 p.m. in the summer of 1974, but had seen a compilation repeat as early as 2.45 p.m. the following Christmas.

Mrs Whitehouse would continue to chip away at *Doctor Who* for the next couple of years, with serials such as *Genesis of the Daleks* and *The Seeds of Doom* coming in for particular criticism for their 'horrific content'. But this running commentary would have little effect upon the attitude of the *Doctor Who* production team, or the BBC as a whole. Until, that is, the Doctor drowned.

The Deadly Assassin's drowning scene, Whitehouse noted, was in direct breach of the BBC's own house rules for the depiction of violent material. The notes concerned, published in 1972 as 'The Portrayal of Violence in Television Programmes – A Note of Guidance', had been the result of two years of study on the subject by the Corporation's own Advisory Group on the Social Effects of Television. 'Small children in particular work in much shorter dimensions of time than adults,' they read. 'Next week is an eternity away. In drama serials divided into several episodes, the dramatic effect of violent "cliffhangers" at the end of individual instalments should be treated with caution… For young children even a week may be too long to wait for reassurance that the characters with whom they identify are safe… care must be taken with the selection of images with which a child

may not be able to come to terms.' Furthermore, the guidelines expressly warned against 'frightening close-ups' and any 'over-detailed portrayal of death'.

Mrs Whitehouse could also invoke seemingly real-life witnesses for the prosecution. 'What finally persuaded me to write to you,' she explained to Curran, 'was a story I heard from a young mother who lives nearby. During the week following the programme, her son of five said to her, apparently apropos of nothing in particular, "Mummy, I know what to do with [his younger brother] when he makes me cross. I shall hold his head under the bathwater until he's still, like the man did with Doctor Who."' It is obviously the idea that children might imitate the action of the cliffhanger in their own home that troubled Whitehouse the most.

The BBC had already trimmed the sequence prior to transmission. The scene had been recut on the instructions of Bill Slater, Head of Serials, who was apparently *au fait* with the guidelines on violence and was troubled by the impact the scene would have on children over the course of the seven days between episodes. Producer Philip Hinchcliffe had been less willing to compromise: 'I thought [Bill's decision] was bull, but we had to cut it down.'

Curran wrote Whitehouse a letter obviously designed to appease by giving some ground, while not actually admitting any mistake had been made. 'With hindsight [the BBC] does accept that one or two people other than your panellists may have imagined that Dr Who's dreams were reality. What actually happened was that the head of department responsible felt, before these episodes were transmitted, that some of the sequences were a little too realistic for a science fiction series. Accordingly, several of them were edited out before transmission. The result was what you saw on screen which I myself think was reasonably acceptable although, as I say – with hindsight – the head of department responsible would have liked to have cut out just a few more frames of action than he did.'

No one had behaved too badly then and the scene was 'reasonable' according to Curran, whose strongest statement would be only that 'the television service was not particularly satisfied [with the episodes]'. But if they were only 'not particularly satisfied', then it stands by implication that they were not particularly dissatisfied either.

Whitehouse would reply via the pages of the *Daily Telegraph* a little after Christmas, 'I am very pleased with this acknowledgement that a mistake of judgement has been made.' But the only mistake that had been admitted by Curran was that Slater would maybe have liked to trim a few frames. There was no admission of a breach of guidelines and no comment on the suggestion that the scene in question might have led to toddlers up and down the country standing trial for manslaughter by drowning.

Below: The Doctor (Tom Baker) and Sarah (Elisabeth Sladen) flee from a Krynoid in *The Seeds of Doom* (1976), another story to attract the ire of Mary Whitehouse. 'Strangulation – by hand, by claw, by obscene vegetable matter – is the latest gimmick,' she would observe

Right: Leela (Louise Jameson) is savaged by a giant rat in a London sewer in 1977's *The Talons of Weng-Chiang*
Below: The villain of the piece, the masked Magnus Greel

Moreover, there was no hint that any further action would be taken to ensure that this kind of thing never happened again – but then, the BBC has always been disinclined to wash its dirty linen in public. Curran may not have wanted to give Whitehouse or the NVLA the satisfaction of knowing that they had provoked change – that they had 'won' – but action was to be taken to curb the perceived excesses of the *Doctor Who* production team. Other changes were afoot, meanwhile, as just a matter of weeks after the broadcast of *The Deadly Assassin*, *Doctor Who* found itself assigned a new Saturday evening slot of 6.30 p.m. – the very scheduling requested by Whitehouse in 1975.

But any changes in the programme's style and content were to take a little time to filter through the system; for while Whitehouse and Curran exchanged missives that December, the *Doctor Who* team were lurking in the dark back streets and alleyways of Southwark, re-creating the Victorian London of Jack the Ripper for the filming of *The Talons of Weng-Chiang*, the six-part serial that would conclude the 1976–7 season for which *The Deadly Assassin* had more or less marked the half-way point. Down by the docks in Wapping, cameras lined up for a shot of a corpse floating in the Thames as police officers struggled to hook it out of the water. A raddled ghoul is hopping from foot to foot nearby. 'It's a floater orl right!' she drools. 'On my oath, you wouldn't want that served up with onions! Never seen anyfin' like it in all my puff… Make an 'orse sick, that would!'

When the story was broadcast in January and February 1977, viewers were to discover that the 'floater' was a victim of a fifteen-feet-long rat lurking in the sewers of old London town. The outsized rodent was to provoke a response in the pages of the *Daily Express* on 11 February from Jean Rook, who, it turned out, also hadn't seen anything like it in all her puff. The article was entitled 'Who do you think you are, scaring my innocent child?'

'What has gone wrong with the innocent tea-time thrill of watching *Dr Who*?' bemoaned Rook. 'Aged three, my son used to watch *Dr Who* at mother's knee. At four he squinted from behind my back. Five, he was under the armchair. Now he is pushing six. And when, last Saturday, he told me three times, before noon, that he didn't want to watch *Dr Who* at 6.20 p.m., I accepted that psychologically he'd come across something slimy and monstrous… I blame myself for not noticing the extremely nasty turn which this cult, 14-million-viewer programme has taken since, I gauge, last year's Sutekh episode. In which, your scalp may stir to remember, Dr Who's assistant was stalked through a snapping, crackling autumn wood by two 7-ft, grey-bandaged Egyptian mummies. Twin

Frankensteins that would have put the wind of heaven up Peter Cushing… What has gone wrong is in not realising that *Dr Who* is no longer for children. And that it has grown out of a rubber monster show into a full, scaly, unknown horror programme.'

It was script editor Robert Holmes who was called upon to reply to Rook's accusations. At first, it seems, he is allowed to speak freely. 'Of course it's no longer a children's programme,' he is quoted as saying. 'Parents would be terribly irresponsible to leave a six-year-old to watch it alone… I wouldn't let any child under ten see it. A certain amount of fear is healthy under strict parental supervision… We are not in the business to harm children.'

Having received this measured response, Rook attempted to undercut Holmes's credibility by describing the writer and editor as 'tall, grey-haired, and bloodless, in a cape-shaped fawn mac. He looks like Sherlock Holmes playing Dracula. He reads Poe, Arlen and Bradbury in bed.' In short, Rook was trying to suggest, rather offensively, that Robert Holmes himself wasn't the sort of person you would want to let near your children, let alone any of his more scary creations. Perhaps the title of her article was aimed at him personally.

The journalist then took the last word. 'Watching Saturday's episode, I accept that *Dr Who* is nerve-wrenching, spine-gripping, and now totally grown up. I find I have 40-year-old friends who can't watch it… It's a great TV achievement. But I wonder if this inflated, ex-children's programme is over-stretching itself to 15-ft rats. And worshipping its own, uninhibited cult.'

Strong words from Rook which, combined with Whitehouse's sustained attack, obviously began to make a difference at the BBC. The Corporation was already troubled by some of the more gruesome violence that had begun to sneak into the series. Blood was beginning to be regularly on show in a programme that had very rarely shown any before. *The Brain of Morbius* (1976) featured a scene in which a character is shot in the stomach (his stomach blowing outward in a shockingly sensational way) which uses the same style of special effect and a remarkably similar framing of camera shot as the murder of General Mapache in Sam Peckinpah's ultra-violent 1969 Western *The Wild Bunch* – inappropriately strong reference material for a children's series.

Although such scenes were rare at the time, and nowhere near as sadistic as material to feature later in the series' life (see Chapter V), it was nevertheless understandably far too much for the Beeb. This, coupled with the wider complaints about horror (as opposed to violence), meant that change was in the air. *The Talons of Weng-Chiang* would be the last serial to be produced by Philip Hinchcliffe, who had guided the series through this most controversial of phases. He found himself reassigned to another series – the adult thriller *Target* – without warning. He would comment later, 'I didn't know I was being replaced until Graham Williams walked in the door.'

Williams would be Hinchcliffe's successor, and he arrived with clear instructions as to the direction in which he should take *Doctor Who*. 'I was happy to tone down the realistic horror,' he would remember some years later on. 'But then the BBC told me to go further and actually clean it up. It was an over-reaction, of that I am sure.' So out went horror, in came humour, and *Doctor Who* made one of its regular tonal shifts.

It's very rare that a single viewer can affect the development of a whole television series, or wield such influence that decisions on programme content will be made based upon their tastes alone. Although Mary Whitehouse had the backing of the NVLA in almost everything she did, it was her name, and her name alone, at the bottom of the letter to Sir Charles Curran. And it was that letter – one letter – that changed the direction of *Doctor Who* for some years to follow. Curran was the right person to hit at the right time – his replying to Whitehouse's charges under his own name, rather than passing the responsibility to, say, the Head of Serials, only goes to prove that he felt there was a case to be answered, and for all his perhapses and maybes, it was clear that changes would be ordered. Although Curran had to be seen to be backing his 'troops', he had been put in a compromising position by Whitehouse's brilliantly targeted complaint. And if anything can be guaranteed in a large company, it is that the Director must not be compromised under any circumstances.

The fact that *Doctor Who* was still pulling in an audience of around 13 million guaranteed that change would not be too sweeping – it would surely be unwise to tinker too much with a reliable and popular formula. But change breeds change, and the new producer brought with him ideas of his own. One of these was that it would be a constructive move to unshackle the creative input of the show's star, Tom Baker.

Williams, *Doctor Who* and its audience would soon not know what had hit them…

Too scary by half?
Top: *Planet of the Spiders* (1974)
Middle: *Genesis of the Daleks* (1975)
Above: *Pyramids of Mars* (1975)

O f the eight actors to play *Doctor Who* on television, none had as much of an input into the scripting and production of episodes as Tom Baker. He also cared passionately for the Doctor – which is just as well, since the Doctor contained more than a little of himself...

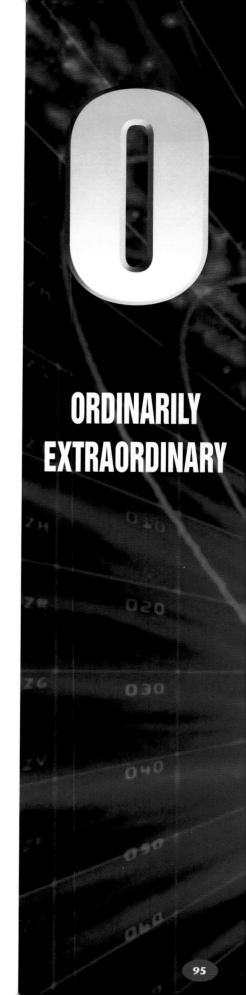

ORDINARILY EXTRAORDINARY

Despite the fact that each of the Doctor's incarnations tends to be viewed as identifiably individual, they are all, under a veneer of eccentricities, much the same. One might be seen as uniquely 'crotchety', 'whimsical', 'bombastic' or 'manipulative'; one might play a recorder, another drive lots of fast cars, a third enjoy a good game of cricket. But these are just small distractions from the basic truth that, no matter what he looks like or what little hobbies he takes on, the Doctor is... well, just the Doctor.

In many ways, he is not really a 'character' in the true sense of the word. Free of responsibilities, he travels from one time to another, from one world to the next, completely unaffected and unchanged by his experiences. He doesn't grow old, he doesn't mature emotionally, he rarely stops to ponder the mistakes of his past and he never has to plan for his future. The real acts of creativity on the part of *Doctor Who*'s writers come in the form of their supporting characters, their new monsters and their carefully contrived alien worlds – little attention is paid to the Doctor at all. He stands in opposition to each week's foul scheme or fiendish villain, but his motives for doing so are rarely explored. For each new serial, he fulfils the function of hero as required and is defined only by his reactions to whatever has been sent to oppose him. The Doctor doesn't drive the plots of *Doctor Who*; that role is undertaken by a largely unalterable four-act story structure of 'mystery', 'investigation', 'exposition' and 'confrontation'.

As a television series, *Doctor Who* is far removed from the realm of the soap opera, where, if the characters have been fully thought through by their creators, the writers simply have to ask themselves such questions as, 'What would alcoholic X do if he found out wife Y has slept with vicar Z?' and the storylines will begin to develop by themselves. The inhabitants of their fictional world can be wound up like clockwork toys and set off to bump into one another and interact in every possible way, and the unfolding consequences will seem perfectly credible as long as the characters are consistently played by the actors concerned and aren't bent out of shape by the writers. When this rule is broken, soaps find themselves condemned as 'unrealistic'. If a *deus ex machina* plot device is imposed – a previously unmentioned first-born son returns to the family home; a random air crash wipes out half a dozen unpopular characters; a series of dramatic events is revealed to be no more than a dream – then the hand of the writer can be seen at work and the illusion of realism is lost. The relatively common employment of such external manipulations of plot is why *Dynasty* is seen as less realistic than *Brookside*, which in turn is less realistic than *EastEnders*.

Doctor Who was never written or presented like this. Characters were shaped by the needs of the plot, not vice versa – and this was especially true of the Doctor. He was rarely given an agenda of his own, and on the few occasions he was, it could seem so incongruous that he was often said to be acting 'out of character'. The Second Doctor's manipulation of events in 1967's *The Tomb of the Cybermen* – as he helps a group of archaeologists gain access to the resting place of the cybernetic monsters, thus engineering their downfall – is a prime example. This uncommonly proactive approach seems strange because we are so used to seeing the Doctor playing only a *reactive* role in such situations. Only in the series' last few years was there any ongoing attempt to make the Doctor the initiator of his adventures and this, tellingly, was part of a broader scheme to redefine the character (see Chapter X).

For this reason, actors playing the Doctor have very little raw material to work with. They cannot get inside the Doctor's head, as they might with King Lear or even any of the denizens of *Coronation Street*, because they will find next to nothing in there. In this sense, it can be said that the character of the Doctor is almost 'actor-proof', that the Time Lord is a blank canvas and that as long as a given actor can remember his lines and not bump into the monsters, anyone can play him – provided, of course, that a few novelty quirks and ticks are employed to differentiate the new 'version' from those that have gone before.

Eight actors have played *bona fide* incarnations of the Doctor on television, each in his own way and each to varying degrees of popular acclaim. Several tackled the role as they would any other acting job, learning their script, delivering the lines in the right order and with due conviction, pocketing their pay cheque and heading off home. One or two took things much more seriously, reading around the subject, studying the performances of their predecessors and taking time to argue – as best they could with the inconsistent material with which they were provided – points of characterisation and plotting with their script editors or producers.

One alone of those gentlemen transcended this mundane, workaday approach. He found there was no need to ponder his character's motivation in a given situation – he just responded as he would himself. He didn't need to don his costume to mentally centre himself for his performance – he dressed like that anyway. There was no careful preparation required to play this aphorism-spouting, unpredictable outsider of quixotic mood, because that's who he was seven days a week *outside* the studio. Put baldly, Tom Baker *was* the Doctor.

This is not to suggest that Tom Baker ever thought he was *really* a Time Lord, decided to playfully adopt wholesale the mannerisms of his character for himself, or was in any way lazy by opting to play the Doctor just as some space-faring version of himself. The truth is more complicated than that.

In his seven years in the role, the boundaries between Tom Baker the actor and the time traveller called the Doctor became so blurred that it was eventually almost impossible to separate one from the other. The two would certainly find themselves in very different situations – the Doctor would never be seen falling drunk out of a Soho private club, Tom Baker never had to fight the Daleks on the other side of the galaxy – but they seemed to approach life in much the same manner, Baker arguing with a belligerent barman as animatedly and amusingly as he might with Davros himself. The impression one has of Tom Baker during his time in *Doctor Who*, gleaned from assorted interviews and his own autobiography, is of a somewhat bewildered individual swept along by events around him. At the time of his casting, he had few real possessions and was of no fixed abode, finding it difficult to put down roots. Instead, he would soak up all that any new environment had to offer in an instant, put on his best show for a dumbstruck and appreciative audience and then sweep off to some new challenge. Which is about as good a definition of the Doctor as one might find.

Interviewed in 1978 for the *Sunday Express*, Baker commented, 'Some actors get a bit neurotic when they are approached by people and are called by the name of the character they play. I don't mind being called Doctor Who – which I am all the time. I can't tell you how dull life was when I was just Tom Baker… I must always remember that I don't have an existence as Tom Baker. Apart from close friends and colleagues, everyone calls me Doctor Who. Even children in pushchairs point at me in the street… It is important to me, therefore, that I never disappoint people, especially children. I would never be seen raucous in the street, or plastered, or smoking cigars.'

Baker took his responsibilities as a children's hero terribly seriously, finding it easier – and certainly more fun – to stay in character when he was out in public. He would tell people where his TARDIS was if they asked, inform them that K9 was quite happy in his kennel today and even sign autographs 'Doctor Who'. He knew that's what his fans – especially his youngest followers – really wanted.

In the same interview, Baker told the now famous story of stopping off at the house of a member of the public to watch an episode of *Doctor Who* he had a particular desire to see. 'Two children,' he remembered, 'were glued to the programme, which had just started. I sat down quietly. Suddenly one of the children looked across at me. Then he looked back at the set. Then he looked back at me. He couldn't believe his eyes.' It is difficult to imagine any other actor feeling confident enough to sit in the house of a complete stranger watching their own work on television. This is surely because, in such a situation, Baker was still playing the Doctor. During the late 1970s, as he strode around the streets of London, Baker regularly wore a long coat and scarf and a floppy hat, and carried a bag of jelly babies in his pocket, brightening the day of assorted tramps and down-and-outs by offering them a sweet and a couple of ten-pound notes – a generous gesture worthy of the Doctor – so it's easy to imagine the effect he must have had on those two small children into whose lives he passed so briefly. And Baker *loved* it.

Even when 'off duty', away from impressionable youngsters or moralising parents, Tom Baker never seemed to stop playing Doctor Who. Shortly after he stepped down from the role, he was accompanied by writer William Marshall around central London for an evening. The long night for Marshall, Baker and his ragtag female followers began in an art gallery: 'Tom, with his flock of wild, bouncing hair, stood before one painting and boomed in that fat, rolling voice, "Just look at that arse, how it goes with the sweep of the scenery in the background." He looked it up in his catalogue – he happened to be carrying three of these, each as thick as a Bible – and found they were for an exhibition next door.' So there Baker was, loping past pictures, taking charge of all around and expounding his eccentric theories, while all the time in the wrong gallery. It could have been the Doctor himself, admiring acolytes at hand, lost in Soho when he should have been on Skaro, talking as confidently about a magnificent arse as he might about an awe-inspiring alien city.

Discussing his decision to leave the series with Marshall, Baker said, 'Finishing with *Doctor Who* is a great emotional jolt after playing it for so long, but we need these emotional jolts in our lives, they are good for us.' By 1984, he was more forthcoming regarding his thought processes at the time in an interview with *Doctor Who Magazine*. 'It was in the works for months before,' he remembered. 'I struggled with all the arguments for and against staying, but seven years is a long time. I'd given the show all I felt I could give it, but I loved it so much in other ways I didn't want ever to go… I had the happiest days of my life with *Doctor Who* – it was such a thrill to be the Doctor.' In another interview with the same magazine eight years later, Baker would add, 'There was a kind of slight fatigue. And also I was becoming neurotically proprietorial about it… the signs were that it was entirely mine, so in other words it was really time to go because that meant that I couldn't be influenced… [In those circumstances] you're not going to have a jolly time.'

Four ages of Tom Baker on *Doctor Who*…
Far left: Relaxed on set for *The Ark in Space* (1975)

Left: Sombre during the recording of *Horror of Fang Rock* (1977)

Top: Having a fine time with Beatrix Lehmann on location for *The Stones of Blood* (1978)
Above: Subdued while shooting *State of Decay* with future wife Lalla Ward in 1980

Those who worked alongside Tom Baker in his later years on the series fall into two distinct camps: those who found him an inspiring creative force and those who thought he was an egotistical fool who tried his damnedest to make their lives harder. Paddy Russell, director of 1977's *Horror of Fang Rock*, recalled, 'In rehearsals, Tom Baker was uncontainable, quite prone to walk out the door and go get a cup of tea. He was utterly convinced he *was* the programme… The fact that nobody wanted to work with him by then made no difference to him… If Tom forgot his lines or missed an entrance he blamed his fellow actors, or he blamed the crew. And vocally – are you kidding?'

Ken Grieve, director of 1979's *Destiny of the Daleks*, tells a very different story: 'Tom Baker was a consummate professional. He was word-perfect and totally familiar with the scene he was about to do. He would help inexperienced actors, was spot on with his marks, knew his lenses. He'd thought through his character progression for the story and the scene. He never threw a wobbly on set. There was never any delay because of him, though because he knew the business so well himself, he would pick up when someone else didn't. You would get 50 per cent more work out of a day because you weren't hanging around waiting for the lead actor to get his act together.'

One area of production to which Baker paid a great deal of attention was the scripts. He certainly appreciated that the Doctor was not a very complex character. Speaking again in 1984, he said, '*Doctor Who* was not an acting part. By acting I mean an actor's definition of an acting job, which is when a character actually develops and discovers something so amazing there is actually a transformation… But there's an utter predictability about playing heroic parts. With heroes, you know which side they'll come down on. Doctor Who isn't suddenly going to become obsessed with sex or money or gratuitous violence – he's predictably good, like an innocent child. Within that predictability, within all that certainty, the fun of doing it was, "How do you surprise the audience and hold them and make them want to watch again and again?"'

Baker really *cared* about *Doctor Who*. It wasn't just his job, it was his life – all that defined him. His own need in the outside world to surprise, to entertain, to amaze, made him constantly strive to bring these characteristics to the role he was playing. His response to this challenge is what ultimately set him apart from all the other actors to play the Doctor. He continually pestered his writers, his directors, his producers for the chance to innovate and embroider. He railed against the predictability of the Doctor-as-hero and, as he was living the life of the Doctor himself, was perfectly placed to bring a consistency to the character, smoothing out the changes in mood and attitude that were forced upon the Time Lord as a result of being defined only through the eyes and responses of an ever-changing rota of guest characters. Tom Baker had a far greater creative input into the role than any other actor before or since.

He would recall in 1984, 'I always felt that the series gave you such free rein, such scope for imaginative plots, that our writers were throwing the chance away with dramatic stereotypes. So I was shamefacedly badly behaved with the scripts – I maltreated our writers' reputations in rehearsal more than anything else, I found it so frustrating… I was always suggesting this or that – maybe an extra line or a different situation – and the director would say yes or no. Generally they were very kind to me. They humoured some of my extravagances but took me seriously as well.'

As Baker points out, not everyone responded to his interference with enthusiasm or even equanimity. Some were under so much pressure to get the job done that they had no time to listen, and then the actor would go into a suitably Doctor-like sulk if he didn't feel he was being heard. But those who were happy to indulge him would often come to value and even encourage his input – and Baker in turn would work harder on their behalf. This helps to explain the wildly different perceptions of the actor and his attitude offered by directors Russell and Grieve.

It was this complete immersion in the role that would, however, be Baker's downfall. Although he constantly strove to find and suggest different ways to play repetitive stock situations – escaping from a cell, walking down a corridor, confronting a villain, even just coming through a door – Baker eventually found himself banging up against the limitations of the format. The odd joke or moment of physical comedy would, at first, be enough to keep him interested and entertained but, like an addict, in time even this would fail to satisfy his craving for innovation. In his later years, he needed more and more of these 'hits', and with the like-minded producer and script editor team of Graham Williams and Douglas Adams at the end of the 1970s, he binged on an increasing number of one-liners and goofy double-takes to camera. But finally, this approach could be taken no further without shattering *Doctor Who*'s already strained dramatic credibility and tipping the series into the realm of full-blown farce.

In 1980, Williams and Adams moved on and the more strait-laced John Nathan-Turner and Christopher H. Bidmead took over their positions. Both agreed that *Doctor Who* needed to be played straight, and focused dramatic conflict rather than comedic by-play would be the hallmarks of their new order. Tom had to play to the rules and he found his stream of increasingly wild ideas falling on deaf ears.

In his final year, it is a subdued and often apparently uninterested Baker on display – an actor addicted to the 'highs' of working in a driven and creative environment forced to go cold-turkey. The series had moved on and there seemed to be no place for him any longer. Recognising that his work was done, that he was no longer valued or loved in the way he had once been, he put on his hat, coat and scarf and slipped quietly away.

Baker did, however, remember to take his companion with him on this new journey into unknown, demonstrating the strange blurring of his real and fictional lives by marry actress Lalla Ward, who played the second incarnation of Romana. The wedding was he on 13 December 1980 – predictably, a Saturday afternoon. Sadly the marriage didn't hor and in a matter of months Baker found himself looking for a new companion.

How very like the Doctor. ◑

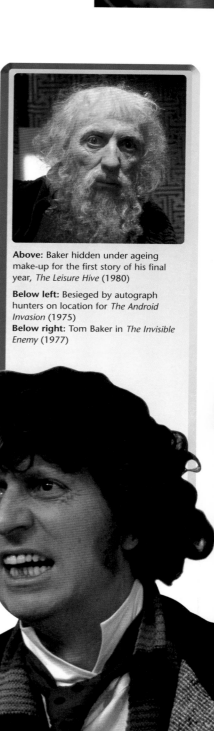

Above: Baker hidden under ageing make-up for the first story of his final year, *The Leisure Hive* (1980)

Below left: Besieged by autograph hunters on location for *The Android Invasion* (1975)
Below right: Tom Baker in *The Invisible Enemy* (1977)

PERHAPS NOT...

For every *Doctor Who* serial that made it to the screen, several other storylines were considered and rejected by the production team. The limited details that have 'leaked out' regarding ideas that didn't make it have long fascinated fans, and can often tell us as much about what *Doctor Who* is as those ideas that did...

At two o'clock on the afternoon of Monday 19 November 1979, the cast and crew of the Tom Baker serial *Shada* finished their lunch in the BBC canteen and returned to Studio Six at Television Centre to resume camera rehearsals for block two of the recording. The cast were ready to continue their walk-through of the material due to be committed to videotape later that evening.

Location filming for the serial had already been disrupted by an ongoing industrial dispute within the BBC regarding the demarcation of duties of various technical personnel – electricians, production assistants and so forth. A planned night-time session of filming on Thursday 18 October in the chief location, Cambridge, had been cancelled when technical manager Tony Bate was recalled to London by his union. Two lighting crews had stood idle as director Pennant Roberts struggled to reschedule a complex chase sequence for the following day without the use of lights and Tom Baker had retired to the Baron of Beef pub for a lengthy session of double gins and increasingly rowdy bar-room philosophy. The team had returned to London at the weekend with the requisite work in the can, even if not in the form that had been originally anticipated.

However, by 19 November the dispute had become a full-blown strike and orders came down for the main studios of Television Centre to be sealed. So, on one side of the bolted doors of Studio Six were the already assembled sets for block two – the interiors of a spaceship and a Cambridge laboratory – and on the other a freshly fed but confused production team willing but unable to continue work on a serial that had already been in development for almost six months and would require only five more days of main-studio recording to see it through to completion. Internal prioritisation by a desperate BBC management meant that most of this time would be claimed by the BBC comedy department for various Christmas specials. After a spirited fight by new producer John Nathan-Turner to salvage the serial, *Shada* was finally written off by the BBC the following June.

Shada was scheduled to stand as the climax to what would prove to be Tom Baker's penultimate year as the Doctor. It was essentially a simple tale of yet another mad scientist seeking to bend the peoples of the universe to his will, but one enlivened by a droll script from *Hitch-Hiker's Guide to the Galaxy* creator Douglas Adams, much interstellar to-ing and fro-ing, and the aforementioned lavish location shoot in Cambridge. Cancellation rendered *Shada* the only *Doctor Who* serial ever to be abandoned part-way through recording and conferred upon it an aura of mystery and fascination that would leave the series' fans pondering, for years to follow, what might have been. The 1979–80 run of serials had, broadly speaking, been poorly received by the fan press of the time, with stories such as *The Horns of Nimon* and *Nightmare of Eden* standing as targets for virulent criticism of their necessarily on-the-cheap alien settings and unconvincing monsters. *Shada*, however, was rumoured to offer exiled Time Lords, terrifying creatures seemingly made of glowing rock and even guest appearances by a Zygon and a Cyberman. By default, it became the repository for all their fannish hopes, a dream end-of-season epic that could have redeemed what was generally seen as an otherwise disappointing year.

Top: Jackie Lane on location for 1966's *The Massacre of St Bartholomew's Eve*, a story wiped by the BBC and which remains lost to this day
Above: William Hartnell in 1965's *The Rescue*. Although a copy of this story was discovered in the vaults of BBC Enterprises, 47 of Hartnell's episodes are still missing

Far right: Christopher Neame and Lalla Ward recording material for the ultimately aborted *Shada*
Far right inset: Tom Baker on set for the same serial. In 1992, the actor would record a special linking narration to allow the half-completed story to be released on video

In the early 1980s, even Douglas Adams attempted to cool these impassioned believers. 'I think it's not such a great story,' he commented. 'It has only gained the notoriety it has got because no one's ever seen it. If it had been finished and broadcast, it would never have aroused so much interest.'

Shada, of course, is not the only *Doctor Who* serial to have been hyped by fans into becoming something it wasn't, and never could have been. Many other adventures have been 'lost' in one way or another, and have found themselves accorded an almost unseemly, quasi-religious degree of respect simply because they can no longer be called upon to speak for themselves. In the 1970s the BBC junked many of the monochrome William Hartnell and Patrick Troughton serials from their archive, judging them to be of no further commercial value – this being, of course, a number of years before the explosive expansion of the home video market. Although copies of episodes from the majority of these serials found their way back to the BBC in the 1980s from overseas broadcasters, there remain eleven serials for which no complete episodes are known to exist – with only audio recordings and the rosy memories of older fans standing as evidence of their quality. Just as, in the wider world, conspiracy theories tend to develop to add a level of drama to political events about which there seems to be a deficit of information – *vis-à-vis* the assassination of President Kennedy or supposed government suppression of 'facts' regarding UFOs – in the world of *Doctor Who* fans, endless 'talking up' of these lost stories allows them to assume often unjustified majesty. In the 1995 book *Doctor Who: The Discontinuity Guide*, one such serial, 1966's *The Massacre of St Bartholomew's Eve* is claimed by the book's young authors to be 'arguably the best ever *Doctor Who* story' – a really rather facile statement that is difficult to refute in the circumstances.

But another type of 'lost' story that is prone to deification by *Doctor Who* fans comprises those commissioned and developed by a production team but then abandoned – for whatever reason – before reaching the studio.

It is impossible to estimate how many hundreds of ideas for *Doctor Who* stories were considered and rejected throughout the series' twenty-six years on air. The majority probably took the form of unsolicited proposals from members of the viewing public – endless tales featuring the Daleks and the Cybermen uniting to destroy Gallifrey – each of which would have received a polite 'thanks, but no thanks' letter from the BBC. An equally healthy number doubtless got no further than a freewheeling conversation between an established writer and a script editor over a pint of bitter in the BBC Club or the Bush pub near the *Doctor Who* production office on Shepherd's Bush Green after both had concluded a formal meeting or retired in embarrassment from a cast rehearsal. A few of these writers would, if either party could remember the discussion the next morning, be invited to submit a written story outline to the production office. It is impossible to estimate how many such storylines were considered by the series' front office, as official records – and the memories of those involved – are patchy at best. Many of these ideas, particularly those from popular writers, or people famous for work on other series or in other fields of writing entirely, have gained a certain notoriety in *Doctor Who* fan circles and become the focus for endless *Shada*-style discussion over their likely content, despite the fact that they didn't, in any real sense, get any closer to production than the craziest ideas thrown up at those beery, post-rehearsal drinks sessions. When controversial writer Dennis Potter – of *Blue Remembered Hills* and *Singing Detective* fame – reportedly recalled, many years after the event, that he submitted a storyline to the *Doctor Who* office in the series' early days, the resultant fevered fan imaginings of what it might have contained undoubtedly far exceeded in vision and eccentricity what the inexperienced Potter probably pitched at the time.

But if a story outline *did* prove to be of interest to a production team, the writer would generally be asked to provide a detailed scene-by-scene breakdown of each episode, for which he or she would receive a fee. If confidence in the material remained high, then full scripts would be commissioned, but this was no guarantee that the writer's work would make it to the screen. During the three years of Peter Davison's tenure as the Doctor, for example, enough ultimately unused scripts were commissioned and paid for to fill a whole further year-and-a-half's worth of story slots.

During *Doctor Who*'s first year, beyond the eight serials that made it to the screen, a further seventeen are known to have been considered, either briefly or seriously, by the production team. For ten of these, contemporary documentation reveals little more than the names of their prospective authors and perhaps the date upon which storylines were submitted to the production office. Two more – *Nothing at the End of the Lane* and *The Giants* – were no more than loose proposals for a possible pilot serial that formed part of C. E. Webber's initial background notes for the series (see Chapter A). The central plot device of the latter – a tale of the TARDIS crew reduced to a mere inch in height – would also form the basis of an

undeveloped storyline from writer Robert Gould, before finally being successfully employed by Louis Marks in *Planet of Giants*, the 1964 serial that would kick off *Doctor Who*'s second year.

Each of the remaining four had one or more scripts commissioned, if not actually delivered. *The Living World* by Alan Wakeman was written off at an early stage, and was possibly another aborted pilot script. *The Red Fort*, by soon-to-be comfortably well-off Dalek creator Terry Nation, was planned as a seven-episode historical tale exploring a nineteenth-century uprising in India and was commissioned two months before *Doctor Who*'s first episode aired on the BBC. Later bounced into the series' second year, it was eventually abandoned and its BBC project codes reallocated to what became the third Dalek serial, *The Chase*; presumably the phenomenal success of Nation's exterminators obliged him to continue providing scripts for them, thus denying him the chance to explore the darker side of the British Empire. Most interesting are our final two 'lost' story ideas, the abandonment of each of which does as much to illustrate the thought processes of *Doctor Who*'s first production team as the work that ultimately aired from November 1963 onward.

As early as 12 July that year, story editor David Whitaker suggested that *Doctor Who* would essentially offer three types of story, the Doctor's 'ship' taking its occupants either into the past, into the future or 'sideways' into other dimensions distinctly different from our own. From the off, Whitaker is woolly about which locations such 'sideways' material might explore, airily mentioning only 'transport... into non-gravitational existence or invisibility et cetera'. This breadth of ambition, tempered by a lack of conviction, later caused problems for the editor as he sought likely 'sideways' storylines. The troubled 'minuscule' story idea of a vertically challenged Doctor and team has already been mentioned, and so fraught was its extended journey to the screen that it even saw its third and fourth recorded episodes cut down and edited together before transmission, in order to strengthen its climax. Another 'sideways' tale, *The Hidden Planet* by Malcolm Hulke, was long considered a contender for *Doctor Who*'s first, and briefly for its second, year of production. What little is known about this storyline suggests that the team had no real sense of what these 'dimension-hopping' serials might offer. In an early briefing document, the cliffhanger lead-in to this serial (from *Marco Polo*) is described as showing the TARDIS landing 'in a country which at first sight could well be England. The cycling policeman they see on their scanner screen, however, once out of sight, behaves in a most extraordinary fashion, a way which leaves no doubt that wherever the Tardis has landed, it is certainly not 20th Century England.' One is left wondering what particular 'extraordinary' behaviour an out-of-sight policeman could have exhibited on a family TV show – not to mention what disciplinary action would have been taken against him if he was caught doing it in public!

The synopsis of *The Hidden Planet* goes on to read: 'Without knowing it, the Space and Time Travellers have landed on a planet identical to Earth, the Tenth Planet on the other side of Earth's Sun. The glass of fashion has a different reflection, the mould of form a different pattern, yet both have sprung from the same roots as their counterparts on Earth. Doctor Who and his friends find themselves in a world where every parallel is in fact a paradox that comforts while it mocks.' It is hard to imagine the attraction to a bunch of shuffling, hyperactive eight-year-olds of an adventure that hangs on the thrilling premise of the 'glass of fashion' having a different reflection. In its favour, however, the outline does develop a more dramatic-sounding if somewhat hackneyed central plot. The hidden planet in question is ruled by women, while men are fighting for the right to vote. Male rebels kidnap Barbara, who happens to be a dead ringer for the female leader, and force the schoolmistress to assume her identity, 'while Doctor Who, Ian and Susan find themselves caught up not only in the violent struggle for male suffrage but in a web of intrigue and suspicion'. Some years later, Patrick Troughton's Doctor would be forced to pose as Salamander, a murderous dictator and exact *doppelgänger* for the time traveller, in 1967's *The Enemy of the World*, and the idea of a planet ruled by women would form the basis of Dick Sharples's commissioned but unproduced Troughton *Doctor Who* comedy *The Prison in Space*, proving that sometimes bad ideas have just as much staying power as good ones. The only further details available regarding *The Hidden Planet* come from a 1970s interview with Malcolm Hulke, in which he indicated that the TARDIS would have landed in a field full of four-leaf clovers and the crew would have seen birds, with two sets of wings, flying backwards. (Perhaps the oddly behaving copper from the cliffhanger was merely struggling to dodge the bewildered wild fowl as they hurtled blindly across the countryside.) With such ideas as these, it is not difficult to see why *Doctor Who*'s production team dropped the serial soon after the delivery of the script to episode one.

Coming even closer to production than Hulke's effort was Anthony Coburn's *The Masters of Luxor*, ostensibly one of Whitaker's 'future' storylines when commissioned as an adventure set on thirtieth-century Earth, but in many ways becoming another 'sideways' proposal when the setting was later changed to a moon of the planet Luxor and the script opted to focus on a number of sophisticated moral and spiritual issues rather than being a straightforward aliens-with-guns adventure. *The Masters of Luxor* tells a *Frankenstein*-like parable of a human being's attempt to play God and produce a race of sentient robots. The time travellers encounter a series of ever more creepy mechanoids, including their self-created 'Perfect One', before meeting Tabon, the robot's own misguided ultra-modern Prometheus, whom they ultimately help to destroy the planet. Top-heavy with moral theology ('Why are you Earth people so afraid of the word God?' asks Suzanne [Susan] of Ian at one point. 'Perhaps because it is no longer scientific,' replies the teacher) and low on action (no one so much as breaks into a run until episode three), *The Masters of Luxor* lost its planned position as second in the running order of *Doctor Who*'s first season to Terry Nation's more knockabout Dalek debut serial to allow time for rewrites. It was briefly reconsidered for the series' second year, before finally being cancelled outright by the summer of 1964.

As *Doctor Who* began to define its own limitations, very few scripts were abandoned at a late stage in development simply because the script editor or producer got cold feet about the appropriateness or feasibility of its planned content, although a host of scripts would be certainly discarded by various production teams for any number of more prosaic reasons. A typical example is William Emm's *The Imps*, a tale of deadly plants germinating in a futuristic spaceport, which was initially scheduled to run as the third Patrick Troughton adventure but was abandoned at a late stage when the writer reportedly became too ill to finish the full set of scripts. In 1985, when Controller of BBC1 Michael Grade pulled the plug on the planned early 1986 run of serials (see Chapter W), a number of commissioned but composted serials became the focus of much fan speculation regarding their content, most notably the work of two former script editors, Robert Holmes's *Yellow Fever and How to Cure It* and Christopher H. Bidmead's *Pinacotheca*.

Of course, those stories that *were* abandoned after significant investment for reasons of suitability shed as much light upon what *Doctor Who* is and can be as those that actually made it to the screen. Dick Sharples's *The Prison in Space*, mentioned earlier, even had a director assigned and some preliminary casting decisions made before producer Peter Bryant voiced concern that the proposed comedy serial wasn't actually *that* funny, and that perhaps a planet of leather-clad, jackbooted female guards was perhaps just a little too exploitative for even his 'dolly-bird'-stuffed take on *Doctor Who*.

In 1977, David Weir's *The Killer Cats of Geng Singh*, scheduled to run as the final serial of Tom Baker's fourth year, was kicked into touch almost as soon as the completed scripts hit the desk of producer Graham Williams, despite the fact that a director was about to join the production and some key costumes had already been designed. The story, which told of a race of warrior cat people indigenous to the Time Lord planet, reportedly called for scenes to be filmed in Wembley Stadium featuring tens of thousands of extras in cat costumes – something well beyond the budget or capabilities of the BBC at the time, and possibly even today. Williams was later to comment, 'It is textbook proof that some writers are more suited to *Doctor Who* than others, irrespective of their background or work on other shows.'

Accepting that truth, it is a tribute to all those who worked full-time on *Doctor Who* that so few scripts had to be written off at the eleventh hour, and that unsuitable writers and material were generally weeded out early in the production process. It requires special insight from a scriptwriter to realise that *Doctor Who* cannot be anything they want it to be and that, although the series has been sketched on the broadest possible canvas, some limitations always apply, and it takes a special kind of writer to realise that key practical and structural restrictions must be respected, and can even be used to focus the mind and drive creativity, rather than simply stifle it.

So, much as we may regret the fact that some of the strangest story outlines were never fully realised as episodes – be they Donald Cotton's 1966 submission *The Herdsmen of Aquarius*, which featured a flock of Loch Ness Monsters, or Pennant Roberts's aborted 1979 dragon-packed sword-and-sorcery tale *Erinella* – we should also be relieved that we were spared what may very well have become just a series of over-reaching failures.

That said, Robert Holmes's 1978 story *The Power of Kroll*, also commissioned by Graham Williams, still bravely offers viewers the spectacle of a gigantic octopus spread-eagled along the horizon of an alien world. Just where the producer would draw the line of 'suitability' remained rather uncertain – somewhere between a host of humanoid cats and a five-mile-wide squid, one would imagine – but that uncertainty, and the resultant unpredictability of what might reach screen from one week to the next, were undoubtedly the fuel that drove *Doctor Who*'s popular appeal for so many years.

Above and **below:** Two scenes from 1978's *The Power of Kroll*. Advances in visual effects made the *Doctor Who* team confident that this story's big ideas could be realised on screen

Far left: William Russell in 1963's popular *The Daleks*, the success of which changed the priorities of *Doctor Who*'s production team
Far left inset: The epic ten-episode tale *The War Games* (1969) was a last-minute addition to a season that had seen several other storylines abandoned as unworkable, most notably *The Prison in Space*

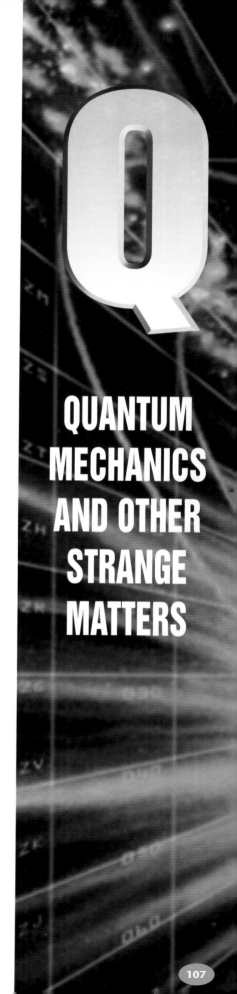

If *Doctor Who* can be referred to as a science fiction series, it's fair to say that the programme has always put the accent firmly on the 'fiction' rather than the 'science'. But once or twice, *Doctor Who* employed writers who had rather different priorities.

In late 1979, when incoming *Doctor Who* producer John Nathan-Turner was looking for a new script editor to work on the following year's run of stories, one of those from whom he sought advice was Robert Banks Stewart, a former *Doctor Who* writer then working as producer on one of his own creations, the BBC detective drama *Shoestring*.

Stewart had just received a letter of congratulation for his work on *Shoestring* from one Christopher H. Bidmead, a writer whose own work Stewart had edited on the now-forgotten 1970s daytime comedy series *Harriet's Back in Town*. Bidmead's letter arrived just as Nathan-Turner popped his head around the office door, asking for any recommendations. Bidmead was duly invited along for an interview the week before Christmas 1979. He listened politely to Nathan-Turner and executive producer Barry Letts, smiled, nodded indulgently and then told them he wasn't interested in the job. Bidmead had no great desire to return to television, having carved out a perfectly comfortable and lucrative career for himself as a writer of industrial films, and certainly had little interest in the idea of working on *Doctor Who* – a series he considered somewhat childish and trivial.

However, the producers were unwilling to take 'no' for an answer. They were very impressed by Bidmead's forthright and deeply held opinions regarding the recent 'silliness' of *Doctor Who* – opinions they broadly agreed with. They formally offered Bidmead the job and invited him back to the *Doctor Who* office so they could explain why they thought he was just the man they needed to champion their crusade to bring a sense of scientific realism to *Doctor Who*.

Bidmead was to recall later, 'Barry and John explained to me that the original premise of *Doctor Who* back in 1963 was to get children excited about the idea of science... that science was a way of looking at the world through which you could achieve things. I'd studied science at school and got diverted into the arts world, and I'd just come to the realisation at the age of thirty-six that I was getting a bit fed up with arty people and wanted the discipline of science back... The revelation of this basic premise of *Doctor Who* surprised me. I could only remember when the series went to the reverse in the 1970s, with hippie-style fantasy. It was a show about how you could achieve anything by waving a magic wand. I now saw striking possibilities with *Doctor Who*, not as a format but as an engine for generating ideas and stories using this unique character of the Doctor within a disciplined landscape.'

As we've seen in earlier chapters, there is some truth in Bidmead's comment that the series had made its home in the realm of fantasy rather than exploiting more traditional, technological science fiction concepts, but whether this approach was in breach of some higher original ambition is doubtful. Back in March 1963, when the BBC were first beginning to consider possible formats for their as-yet-unnamed Saturday adventure series, one of the first ideas mooted focused on a firm of scientific consultants called 'The Troubleshooters'. 'Each of [our characters] is a specialist in a certain field,' contemporary notes explain, 'so that each can bring a different approach to the problem. But they are all acutely conscious of the social or human implications of any case, and if the two men sometimes become pure scientist and forget, the woman always reminds them that, finally, they are dealing with human beings.'

QUANTUM MECHANICS AND OTHER STRANGE MATTERS

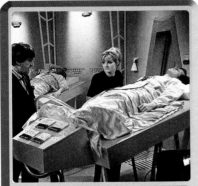

Top: The Doctor, Polly and Jamie visit *The Moonbase* (1967)

Above: Dodgy astrophysics from the Doctor in *The Twin Dilemma* (1984)

Far right: Writer David Fisher sought advice from physicists at Cambridge University before starting work on *The Creature from the Pit* (1979). The story formed part of a season commended by *New Scientist* magazine for its 'sophistication'

On receipt of these notes, Head of Drama Sydney Newman calmly wrote the word 'No' beside the 'Troubleshooters' idea. If the BBC had really been looking for a series that could educate children about the possibilities of science, why did they reject a proposal involving a group of modern-day scientific investigators in favour of one based around an alien travelling through time in a telephone box? Of course, you might point out that this decision was the very measure of the BBC's genius – Newman understanding that children know when they are being manipulated, and entertainment and innovation needed to be prioritised in the format of the new series, thereby suckering the kids into watching something that contained insightful comment on scientific and technological issues by sugaring the pill with a dimension-defying time machine. It's a reasonable argument, and one that might just be felt to hold water if *Doctor Who* hadn't pitched itself into the realm of pseudo-science with such alacrity in its very first serials. Once one discovers that the Daleks are powered by static electricity, that the Doctor has a machine which can make food bars that taste of eggs in one bite and slightly too salty bacon the next, and that his craft has some spooky, telepathic sentience of its own, it is difficult to suggest that the series ever really tried to avoid playing as down-the-line fantasy. By serial five, *The Keys of Marinus* (1964), viewers were offered the sight of an island of glass in the middle of an ocean of acid, on which could be found a mind-controlling computer whose four all-important micro-circuits had to be located by the Doctor and friends-one of which was being held by a race of disembodied brains with eyes on stalks who lived in bell jars. Such stories were far more likely to inspire school essays receiving the comment of 'You must try to be more grown up in your approach, Terry' than to fire Britain's next generation of scientific thinkers.

While a few of the early 1960s *Doctor Who* serials made an attempt to work current scientific issues into their storylines – most notably 1964's *Planet of Giants*, which looked at the effect of insecticides on the environment, a story element inspired by Rachel Carson's provocative and controversial 1962 book *Silent Spring*, which postulated that species the entire length of the food chain could be wiped out if man tampered with its lower reaches – it would not be until 1966 that a production team made concerted efforts to ground their scripts in scientific fact rather than easy-on-the-brain fantasy.

In the spring of that year, script editor Gerry Davis and producer Innes Lloyd decided that *Doctor Who* needed the part-inspirational, part-stabilising influence of a real-life scientific adviser – someone who could bring matters of scientific interest to the attention of Davis and have enough imagination to convert such material into the sensational form more suited to the programme's needs. Among the candidates considered by Davis was portly TV astronomer and xylophonist Patrick Moore, who, one would imagine, politely made it clear that he was far too busy mapping the surface of the Moon for the Apollo space programme to waste time discussing deranged computers and killer robots with Davis.

The man for the job turned out to be Dr Kit Pedler of the University of London. Although Pedler's Ph.D. thesis, on the causes of retinal diseases, might not at first glance have seemed to qualify him to postulate on the nature of life on the planet Mondas, the cheery ophthalmologist brought with him a great enthusiasm for science fiction and quickly struck up an easygoing and productive working relationship with Davis.

Pedler's first discussions with the script editor led to the development of *The War Machines* (1966), whose final script – from Ian Stuart Black – postulated that a sentient computer installed in the Post Office Tower might well use hypnotic signals sent via telephones to control human slaves, forcing them to build killer robots which it could use to take over, today, West Kensington and, tomorrow, the world. Whether this kind of idea actually required the input of a 'real' scientist is open to question, as no one in the story ever stops to consider the key scientific point – how said computer gained the power of self-determination in the first place. Over the next year or so, Pedler's place in the order of things became a little clearer, as he found himself rolled out by the production team on regular occasions to add a little gravitas to press coverage about the series. In an interview with the BBC in-house newspaper *Ariel* in February 1967, Pedler took time to outline how even the early Patrick Troughton serial *The Underwater Menace* (1967) was grounded in scientific fact, and that scientists *really were* looking for ways to provide deep-sea divers with a set of working gills. If this had been said by Davis himself, the reaction might well have been along the lines of 'Thanks, Gerry, now just slip on this jacket will you – yes, the sleeves are a bit tight around the back, aren't they?' Pedler, with his impressive Ph.D., could get away with a little more. Everyone would nod sagely at his insights and coo about how sophisticated *Doctor Who* was these days.

Where Pedler and Davies did score a notable success was in the creation of the Cybermen for 1966's *The Tenth Planet*. As Pedler outlined to *Radio Times* in 1968: 'I was talking to my wife – she's a doctor too – in the garden. We were discussing spare-part surgery and conceived the idea of someone with so many mechanical replacements that he didn't know whether he was human or machine.'

The Cybermen were the first of *Doctor Who*'s monsters to come close to capturing the public imagination in the same way as the Daleks, and this is often put down to the 'terrifying plausibility' and 'originality' of the Cybermen. That's right, the Cybermen – a once humanoid race who were on the verge of extinction and so added machine parts to their bodies. In the process, they sacrificed emotions, compassion and morality and found themselves driven only by a need to multiply and conquer. Oh no, sorry, that's the Daleks, isn't it?

Such crude sarcasm is merely employed to demonstrate that Terry Nation had long since proved that *Doctor Who* thrived on good, simple ideas. If Pedler's name on the credits to *The Tenth Planet* allowed the production team to say, 'It could actually happen, you know!' then that was all very well, but it didn't make the serial plausible in any real sense. How could it when its hero was able to change his face and travel through time in a large cupboard? While Pedler could probably help to bring a touch of verisimilitude to *The Tenth Planet*'s mission control sequences, ensure that the production team realised that the Moon's gravity was one-sixth that of Earth for 1967's *The Moonbase* and even justify the same year's Fish People in *The Underwater Menace*, the series was never more than a few minutes away from another piece of mumbled cod-science. In 1967's *The Evil of the Daleks*, fictional Victorian scientist Theodore Maxtible explains how he came to invent a form of time travel: 'A mirror reflects an image... so you may be standing there but appear to be fifty feet away! Following the new investigations twelve years ago by J. Clark Maxwell, and experiments by Faraday into static electricity... [we] attempted to first define the image in the mirror and then project it.' He goes on to outline how, with 144 polished mirrors and a supply of static electricity, they managed to bring back a Dalek from the future. Exactly how many successful school science projects such nonsense inspired is open to question, but it's interesting to note that in the midst of such airy waffle, writer David Whitaker drops in the names of real scientists as justification in much the same way as the *Doctor Who* production team were doing around this time with Kit Pedler.

Their duties on *Doctor Who* at an end, Gerry Davis and Kit Pedler pooled their creative resources again to create the hit 1970s science fiction drama *Doomwatch*, which told stories of the exploits of a special British government department set up to deal with threats to humanity from scientific research gone mad. With its stories of plastic-eating viruses and two-headed chickens, *Doomwatch* struck a chord with viewers in the early 1970s – a time that always seemed in the shadow of one kind of technological apocalypse or another – and was a more natural home for Pedler's 'plausible' extrapolations from current scientific theory. Interestingly, the series' basic structure is almost identical to the BBC's less-fantastical original 'Troubleshooters' idea mooted as a format for what would become *Doctor Who*.

The producers of early 1970s *Doctor Who* – which Bidmead would dismiss as 'hippie-style fantasy' – seemed to feel the same need as their 1960s predecessors to suggest that even their wildest storylines were scientifically plausible. When *Radio Times* visited producer Barry Letts and script editor Terrance Dicks at work for a behind-the-scenes feature on the show, a special photo session was held. Among the carefully placed props in the artfully posed pictures of Letts, Dicks and their secretary is an issue of the respected weekly journal *New Scientist*. It's a rather sweet and ingenuous gesture really, sending out all the right 'credibility' signals, although attentive viewers may have wondered which particular issue of the magazine had inspired such contemporary *Doctor Who* highlights as murderous telephone cables and alien mind parasites.

Even if we can't estimate the attention the *Doctor Who* team paid to the content of *New Scientist*, we certainly know that *New Scientist* paid a lot of attention to *Doctor Who*. In a 1979 issue, writer Tim Robinson compared and contrasted Tom Baker's penultimate year as the Doctor with the *Quatermass* serial, starring John Mills, that had just been broadcast on ITV. *Quatermass*, a tale of an alien intelligence harvesting mankind but ultimately defeated by game scientists, applied physics and a large radio telescope, was, according to Robinson, 'depressing and pessimistic'. *Doctor Who*, on the other hand, had 'taken on a new lease of life', being witty, sophisticated and set against a fascinating 'mind-bending technical backcloth'.

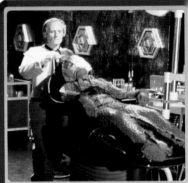

Top: Evolution and vivisection were key themes in 1980's *Full Circle*

Above: The Tractators, the monsters in Christopher H. Bidmead's 1984 serial *Frontios*, used gravity as a weapon

Main: A lecture on tachyonics in *The Leisure Hive* (1980)

Main right: The Monitor (John Fraser), whose mathematical powers could restructure the universe in *Logopolis* (1981)
Far right: In the same story, Tegan (Janet Fielding) finds a TARDIS inside *the* TARDIS. Recursion was a theme Bidmead returned to in 1982's *Castrovalva*

Only a matter of weeks after this vote of confidence for his 'silly' series from a spokesman of the scientific community, Christopher H. Bidmead took the job as *Doctor Who*'s script editor and set about tying the series into a more 'realistic' scientific rationale. One of his first duties was to sign the production office up for a subscription to *New Scientist*. The seven serials from Bidmead's year in charge all received a significant amount of input from him – some, he claims, were 'rewritten from top to bottom'. But for all his clearly voiced ambition to drag *Doctor Who* away from the 'arty' world of fantasy and into the more 'disciplined' arena of science, are these episodes radically different from what has gone before?

And the short answer is no, not really. The season opener, *The Leisure Hive* (1980), pays lip service to the 'science' of tachyonics – a study of the theoretical tachyon particle, which, it is thought by modern scientists, may have imaginary mass, zero energy and move at infinite speed. A product of purest quantum and relativistic mechanics, little is truly understood about the possible properties of the mysterious tachyon, but in *The Leisure Hive* it serves precisely the purpose of the 'magic wand' that Bidmead claimed to so detest in earlier *Doctor Who* episodes. It can bring life to a sterile race, duplicate people, make them older, make them younger, even duplicate them and make them younger at the same time. Very few other *Doctor Who* stories have employed such a multi-function plot device so shamelessly.

The following serial, *Meglos* (1980), features a villain seemingly trapped in the form of a cactus but who can 'modulate himself on a particular wavelength of light' (whatever that might mean) to possess other bodies and reshape them at will. There's also an old-fashioned *Doctor Who* time-loop (rechristened from the Greek by Bidmead as a chronic hysteresis – 'chronic' in its true sense of 'time') which the Doctor breaks by the most humorous but unscientific means possible.

Full Circle (1980) makes interesting use of evolutionary theory, but only after plunging the TARDIS through a Charged Vacuum Emboitment (CVE) into another universe. In his production notes, Bidmead explains the origin of the CVE: 'Experimental observation shows that matter and anti-matter can be created inside a vacuum subjected to a strong electromagnetic field. Twenty-first-century physics has also discovered that in some extremely rare circumstances the same conditions can create a charged vacuum within a charged vacuum, and that, theoretically at least, an almost infinite regression of charged vacuums can be nested inside each other like Chinese boxes. This "emboitment" leads through to an independent universe that is in all other respects completely isolated from the one we know.' How strange that Bidmead felt the need to call upon so much jargon to create such a simple plot twist, even calling upon the discoveries of 'twenty-first-century physics' to explain his reasoning. The CVE is clever, creative and certainly grounded in electrostatic theory, but it still seems a rather misguided prioritisation of effort for just another science fiction 'hole in space'.

The complexities of CVEs are no more significant to the plot when invoked once more in Bidmead's *Logopolis* (1981), where we discover that these voids are artificial in origin, having been created by a race of alien mathematicians to prolong the life of the universe. *Logopolis* is rooted in a number of areas of physics that fascinated Bidmead and is the only story of the year that can really be said to employ intelligently explored, genuine scientific principles as the focus of its script.

The planet Logopolis (the name derived from the Greek for 'city of words') is a vast, human-powered computer. Its inhabitants are arranged into 'registers' (computer components that hold a small amount of information) controlled by a being called the Monitor (the computer unit which compiles instructions from a computer program and passes appropriate coding to the output units). It is the chanting of the Logopolitan calculations that passes information across their world and forms their program. When the Monitor explains to the Doctor, 'Structure is the essence of matter, and the essence of structure is mathematics,' he is voicing a reductionist theory that all science can be reduced to the study of sub-atomic interactions and – if these processes are expressed as equations – pure mathematics. On the Monitor's planet-sized computer, this mathematics can actually alter the state of the physical universe.

The Logopolitans are battling to reduce the level of entropy – useless waste energy – in the universe and, via the Doctor, Bidmead even paraphrases the Second Law of Thermodynamics as 'entropy increases' – a statement that the universe can only ever run down to a point of 'heat death' through the loss of usable energy to entropy. But the evil Master is nearby and up to no good, his curiosity regarding the 'single great secret' of Logopolis leading to a fatal disturbance in the work of the mathematicians. His interference, according to the Monitor, will 'unravel the whole causal nexus' – the link between the cause of an action and its effect.

Bidmead employs big scientific and philosophical ideas in *Logopolis*, all of which proved perfect mental fuel for the series' many young academic followers at the time. The serial stands as the only really clear statement of his agenda as script editor – there are no monsters, no touchy-feely hippie fantasy and the universe is saved through the application of science and technology. Sadly, however, the material proved perhaps a little too cold and esoteric to the viewing public at large, and to at least one journalist on an important national magazine in particular.

Discussing *Logopolis* and 1982's *Castrovalva* (the first Peter Davison serial, which was also penned by Bidmead) in the context of a recent series of repeats of older *Doctor Who* serials, writer Malcolm Peltu observed that this new-style *Doctor Who* was an 'awful show' suffering from 'boring' scripts. 'The scientific jargon is too mundane,' Peltu continued. 'There are too many references to today's technology... to make the futuristic tone believable.'

Ironically, Peltu was reviewing *Doctor Who* for *New Scientist*.

READ ALL ABOUT IT!

Over *Doctor Who*'s first eighteen years on screen, only the Daleks and the pretty girls ever really caught the attention of the popular press. But in 1980, the series gained a thrusting new producer who was determined to make *Doctor Who* the most talked-about show in town...

On 23 October 1980, *Doctor Who* producer John Nathan-Turner hastily organised a press conference to announce that Tom Baker was giving up the role of the Doctor after almost seven years. The news had somehow leaked to the *Daily Mirror*, and Nathan-Turner reasoned that if it was already too late to keep things quiet, he might as well capitalise on the opportunity and let every paper run the story.

Baker was in a mournful mood as he outlined the reasons for his departure. 'I'm quitting while I'm at the top,' he said. 'I felt this year that things were beginning to drag.' But the assembled reporters were eager to find a juicier story, fishing for a hint of behind-the-scenes disagreement or ill-will. Had Tom jumped or was he pushed? Realising this, Baker made a joke which threw them off the scent completely. Smiling, he wished his as yet unknown successor well: 'I hope whoever gets the part will have as happy a time as I've had. I wish him, or her, luck.'

'Her? HER?' the pack clamoured, the fortunes of Tom Baker instantly forgotten. 'But surely you can't mean...' Baker just smiled again, refusing to say any more.

The next morning, the newspapers were in frenzy. 'The new Who could be a woman!' shouted the *Daily Mail* in 36-point type, with its competitors all taking a similar tack. But it had just been a joke. The possibility of the Doctor changing gender had never been seriously considered by the production team – nor would it ever – but even the barest suggestion of such a metamorphosis made great copy, the popular press always being the first to throw up their hands in shock at the idea of a beloved British institution being tinkered with. John Nathan-Turner certainly recognised this and was more than happy to propagate the rumour. He was almost certainly the 'BBC source' later quoted as saying, 'The part has not been offered to anyone, but we've spoken to various people and some of them have been ladies.' All evidence suggests that this statement was completely untrue.

This playful piece of misinformation would mark a sea change in the relationship between *Doctor Who* and the press. Whereas the majority of his predecessors in the producer's chair had shied away from a life in the public eye, one-time actor Nathan-Turner was still a showman at heart and was determined that *Doctor Who* should be promoted by the dailies as frequently and favourably as possible.

Before this point, any press interest in *Doctor Who* had followed naturally from day-to-day decisions made by the production office. If a new companion was cast or a new monster wheeled out on to the studio floor, the BBC press office would dutifully organise a photo call and issue a press release. For a new female sidekick, this would generally require the young actress concerned to stand wistfully in a garden wearing only the briefest of dresses and a coquettish smile as the camera shutters winked. For a monster, the PR material would take care to point out how this latest creation was 'set to terrify children everywhere' and 'undoubtedly threaten the Daleks for the title of Favourite Foe'. The tabloids would equally dutifully report these matters of import to their readers.

Of course, any producer worth their salt would recognise the need to create a splash every now and again, and throughout the series' history this would normally signify the re-employment of the Daleks. The creatures' regular resurrections were always guaranteed to attract attention, albeit to a steadily dwindling degree as the years passed and their shock stock declined in value.

If the Dalek ploy failed and there were no new companions around to flash some thigh for the camera, then a BBC staff photographer, or even representatives of the dailies, would be called to studio or location to snap some glossy ten by eights of the latest 'leggy lovelies' drafted in for supporting roles: Isobel Watkins from *The Invasion*, the leggy but not-so-lovely jackbooted Drahvins of *Galaxy 4* and even the rather plain-Jane girls from *The Ark* were typical targets of this special attention. For three decades, the associated headlines would, almost without fail, be either 'Who's That Girl?', 'Who's a Lucky Boy Then?' or 'Who-la-la!' It was all *very* predictable.

The remarkable response to the 'female Doctor' wheeze of 1980 changed all that. The story was untrue, but it didn't seem to matter – it was still reported in almost every newspaper. Indeed, so much fun was had that the trick was tried again in 1983, when Peter Davison announced his intention to move on. 'The next Doctor will be older and a little more eccentric,' John Nathan-Turner told the *Sun*. 'And I'm not ruling out the choice of a lady Doctor.' This type of rumour-mongering always served to guarantee weeks of speculation in the papers and a bigger splash when the selected actor was finally named. Even when off-air during its long summer break between series, Nathan-Turner ensured that *Doctor Who* was rarely out of the news.

The spring and summer of 1984 saw another great piece of Nathan-Turner manipulation when he suggested that he was again willing to think the previously unthinkable. The *Sun* was the first to break the news, as reporter Charles Catchpole – a friend

Top: The gentlemen of the press gather on the set of 1966's *The Ark* to photograph…
Above: …the serial's guest stars: a Monoid (centre) and his eager groupies

Main: The amoral Maaga (Stephanie Bidmead, front) and her beehived clones. 'Four for the Dads' from 1965's *Galaxy 4*

of Nathan-Turner's – announced, 'Dr Who's famous police-box time machine is set to fade away for ever. BBC chiefs plan to axe the battered blue box which has housed the TARDIS for twenty years... Producer John Nathan-Turner said yesterday, "Police boxes are a thing of the past... a whole generation of children has grown up believing the box to be a TARDIS and nothing else." He plans to phase out the police box during the next series of Doctor Who.'

The Daily Mail took things further, canvassing incoming Doctor Colin Baker for his opinion. 'It's a crying shame,' said the actor, rising to the spirit of the stunt. 'We ought to have a campaign to save the police box.' The Daily Star and the London Evening Standard were the first of a series of papers to seek a suitable replacement, with a post box, a photo booth, a workman's tent and a portable chemical toilet standing as the unlikely front-runners in this phoney poll.

Surprise, surprise! On 17 November 1984 the paper that broke the story also put it to rest in typical style: 'Sun readers have saved Doctor Who's famous police box from the scrap heap!' It was Charles Catchpole again, and Nathan-Turner was happy to play the game. 'Sun readers made me change my mind,' said the producer, cleverly managing to simultaneously schmooze those millions of readers and confirm his own generosity of spirit.

As Nathan-Turner later said of that time, 'I am a great believer in publicity. I wouldn't go quite as far as to say there is no such thing as bad publicity... but I would do whatever I could to keep the show in the public eye.' Anything but shy, Nathan-Turner was always happy to provide a useful quote for any interested journalist. A search of key national and regional newspapers in 1983 – the year the Sixth Doctor was cast – reveals that Colin Baker's name was used in association with the words 'Doctor Who' on thirty-eight occasions. Nathan-Turner's was used on forty-five.

As well as planting such stories, Nathan-Turner also instructed his directors to cast household-name actors and entertainers in lead roles throughout his tenure, mindful of the publicity their presence would generate. While the series had always employed its fair share of familiar faces in somewhat unlikely roles – the casting of Max Adrian as King Priam of Troy in 1965's The Myth Makers being little different in approach from the use of Beryl Reid as a bitter spaceship captain in 1982's Earthshock – Nathan-Turner could perhaps be said to have employed the technique as much to capitalise on the resultant press coverage as to enrich the production on screen. When model Koo Stark – famous in the early 1980s for being romantically linked with Prince Andrew – accepted the role of the Cryon Varne in 1985's Attack of the Cybermen, she attempted to impose what Nathan-Turner later referred to as 'unacceptable restrictions on publicity'. Tellingly, Stark was soon dropped in favour of the more amenable TV presenter Sarah Greene.

'GIBBERISH AND GARBAGE'

Some of Doctor Who's less positive newspaper reviews . . .

○ 'The heroes are the dullest quartet in fiction, and so remarkably incompetent that it would take their combined intellectual resourses to toast a slice of bread... I can understand how it catches the imagination of very young children, though I wish they had something better to feed on. As usual, television is cheating them.'
Peter Black on The Web Planet for the Daily Mail. February 1965

○ 'The stories are gibberish. So is the action. Little effort is made to make the thing believable; or, failing that, amusing. My children think it is gibberish too. The real fans of Doctor Who are middle-aged men who enjoy watching half-naked girls being chased by space monsters... Baker's interpretation of the Doctor is simply annoying – I sometimes wish that, with that long, silly scarf, he suffer an Isadora Duncan-style fate in the engines of a passing space cruiser.'
Peter McKay on The Pirate Planet for the London Evening Standard. August 1979

○ 'The plots are on another planet and the latest Doctor – Sylvester McCoy – should be struck off. Twenty-five years is a long time, even by TARDIS, and someone at the Beeb should have had the courage of their convictions and pulled the plug on this programme. The Doctor peaked with Jon Pertwee in command. Ever since, the series has been a load of intergalactic garbage.'
Jim Taylor on Remembrance of the Daleks for the Sun. October 1988

Left: Nicola Bryant as companion Peri in 1985's The Two Doctors

R

Some of *Doctor Who*'s less negative press notices . . .

○ 'An imaginative Christmas pudding script, taut direction, lavish filming and even a trendy ecological theme all contributed to the overall effect, but what makes this venerable series tick is the complete conviction of all concerned. They believe in the ubiquitous Doctor and so, for the moment, do we.'
Richard Last on *The Green Death* for the *Daily Telegraph*. December 1973

○ 'In Tom Baker the BBC has the almost perfect Dr Who; witty and humane, self-controlled, but with flashes of righteous anger when confronted by evil. Yet lurking under the surface of his assurance is a capacity for self-criticism and an ability to laugh at himself. All these abilities are invaluable to children as they grow up to face the problems of the world.'
Alan Thompson writing in the *Sunday Times*. March 1976

○ 'Not only is the Doctor a modern mega-Merlin, smarter than a wardrobe full of Nobel Laureates and capable of vaulting Einstein's theory across limitless time and space, but the scrapes into which he gets himself are the scrapes of the imminent now. They could just happen, and the fringe of believability is where magic is most potent. If you can bend relativity and set once-upon-a-time in a time that has not yet happened then the possibilities are, literally, endless.'
Alan Coren on *Silver Nemesis* for the *Mail on Sunday*. November 1988

Above right: Tickling stick at the ready, the 'tattifilarious' Ken Dodd helps to drum up some publicity for his appearance in 1987's *Delta and the Bannermen*. Dodd was third choice for the cameo role of Tollkeeper after Christopher Biggins and Bob Monkhouse
Below right: *Sale of the Century* and *Just a Minute* host Nicholas Parsons as Wainwright in 1989's *The Curse of Fenric*

Through the 1980s such popular actors and personalities as Ken Dodd, Nicholas Parsons, Richard Briers, Rula Lenska and Nerys Hughes turned up to do their bit. Fans of the series criticised much of this casting – they claimed that it was inappropriate and distracting – but few of the resulting performances can actually be identified as being below normal *Doctor Who* standard. And if the success of such a policy can be judged by the column inches of coverage secured in the newspapers, then it was certainly successful. Even famous faces who were *not* actually appearing found themselves fed to the publicity machine. For 1988's *Silver Nemesis*, a story set largely in the environs of Windsor Castle, the *Doctor Who* production office invited Prince Edward to take a non-speaking walk-on part. The prince politely declined to appear – even with the lure of a £50 fee – but that became a story in itself – 'Edward's too grand for a part in *Doctor Who*,' sniped the *Today* newspaper in the June before the serial's transmission. *Doctor Who*'s response was to cheekily place a lookalike for the Queen herself into one scene, managing to provide both a great photo opportunity and the chance for the papers to run the Prince Edward story again the following November. Although a perfectly reasonable gag in itself, exactly how many new viewers this kind of publicity pulled in is open to question.

In August 1984, during an interview with a *Doctor Who* fan magazine, John Nathan-Turner tempted fate by asserting confidently, 'No programme that keeps getting publicity like that can ever get the chop. The only show I can think of which gets repeated publicity like ours is *Coronation Street*, and look how secure that is as a programme.' Five years later, it was after falling before the staunchest of competition from *Coronation Street* that production of *Doctor Who* was suspended by the BBC.

During Nathan-Turner's producership, *Doctor Who* received the highest volume of press coverage it had seen since the heyday of the Daleks. At the same time, the series shed around 7 million viewers. Ironically enough, the period when the programme received the least mainstream publicity – if that can be gauged from the very limited number of on-set press calls which took place – covered Tom Baker's first two seasons; exactly when ratings were at their highest since 1964.

But in this respect, at least the 1980s were a fun time for *Doctor Who*. Almost every week a newspaper offered up some titbit of casting news or a teasing photo of a companion's new costume. Everyone seemed so busy, busy, busy – celebrating this, previewing that. It is only in retrospect that one wonders whether this energy could have been expended more productively elsewhere.

Above: Sophie Aldred at her first press call following her casting as Ace

Main: Sylvester McCoy with Dolores Gray, guest star of *Silver Nemesis* (1988). The national press seemed singularly unimpressed with her casting as an American tourist

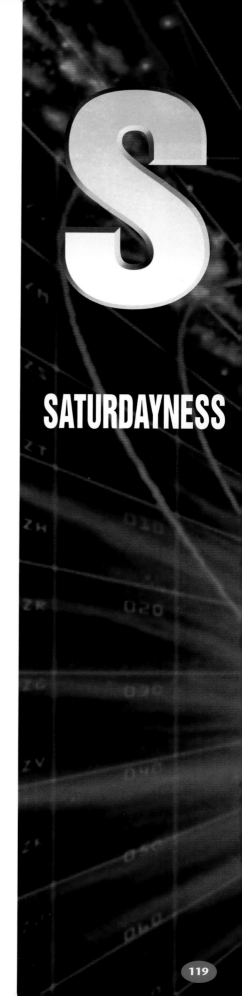

I n 1982, *Doctor Who* was cut loose from its familiar Saturday tea-time slot and served up instead as a form of twice-a-week fantastical soap opera. Depite the warnings of nay-sayers in the press, the move gave the nineteen-year-old series a fresh boost. All things being equal, in this new position *Doctor Who* could have gone on for ever...

For viewers in England, Scotland and Northern Ireland, Peter Davison made his debut as the Doctor in the first episode of *Castrovalva* at 6.55 p.m. on the evening of Monday 4 January 1982, with his second episode broadcast the following day. Did you catch that? *Doctor Who* on *Monday* and *Tuesday nights*, ladies and gentlemen. How absolutely shocking!

You don't think so? Funny, because the press at the time were appalled. That Monday's *Guardian* led the attack, suggesting that there was 'an extraordinary failure somewhere in the BBC hierarchy to understand the whole essential Saturdayishness of the operation'.

An only marginally less ugly new adjective was ultimately invoked by the *Daily Mail* a month later, when it tried to find someone to blame for this heresy. 'For 19 light entertainment years,' reporter Joe Steeples began drolly, 'and an infinity of intergalactic miles, Dr Who has survived the fiendish ministrations of Cybermen, Dalek, Voc and Wala. [For the record, Steeple appears to have made up the Wala.] But now the intrepid time lord has been laid low by a new enemy in the TV Centre. I refer to the fearsome Dirgendes, the Director-General Designate, otherwise known as Alisdair Milne... it was he who was ultimately responsible for the mindless sacrilege which moved Dr Who from his traditional Saturday slot into the dismal wastes of Monday and Tuesday. Now twice a week and adrift from his Saturday base, the fifth face of the Tardis-travelling Doctor (Peter Davison) is struggling against insuperable odds... Doesn't he realise that a vital ingredient in the appeal of the eccentric 900-year-old in the blue police box is the serial's essential Saturdayness?'

Extraordinary failure? Sacrilege? A struggle against insuperable odds? From the tone of these reports, one might imagine that the Doctor's day was already over. Perhaps the Time Lord, cast out of his Saturday tea-time paradise, was destined now to die, alone and unloved, in those 'dismal wastes' somewhere to the east of his weekend Eden. After nineteen years, it turned out that the major ingredient in *Doctor Who*'s success had just been a dollop of 'Saturdayness' all along – any of the series' other claims to fame were, by implication, insignificant.

But what exactly was this 'Saturdayness' the press so casually invoked? Well, presumably the term was being used as shorthand for the feeling of security and continuity offered by the line-up of programmes being provided by the BBC on that particular evening on winter weekends throughout the 1970s.

A 'classic' Saturday evening line-up might have started with a cartoon – perhaps *The Pink Panther Show* – and then the news and sports round-up. Half an hour of the light-hearted and sometimes rather risqué antics of Basil Brush would prime a young audience for *Doctor Who*. Parents, who had perhaps sat and enjoyed the Doctor's latest adventure alongside their excitable brood, would maybe let their very youngest stay up with a glass of milk and a biscuit to watch Bruce Forsyth and Anthea Redfern (or Larry Grayson and Isla St Clair) marshal the spirited high jinks of *The Generation Game*. By 8 p.m. perhaps *The Duchess of Duke Street*, *The Onedin Line* or *All Creatures Great and Small* would be in full swing – a prime slice of popular costume drama for the mums. Any older kids would probably be sent to bed after *The Two Ronnies* or *The Dick Emery Show* at 9 p.m.,

while the adults enjoyed the latest *Starsky and Hutch* before Dad slipped deeper into his armchair during *Match of the Day*. For those with the staying power, Michael Parkinson would be there to introduce the evening's guests on his chat show a little after 11 p.m.

By the late 1970s, *Doctor Who* was still in the role it had always been designed for, acting as a bridge between the children's programmes and the more adult material on Saturday night. The schedule had crystallised into perhaps the most perfectly tailored evening of programmes the BBC has ever offered – one that is spoken of in hushed and reverential tones at Television Centre to this day. As a measure of this success, it should be noted that during the 1996 Auntie Awards for all-time great BBC programming – a moment described in the Introduction – every single home-grown series mentioned above, bar *The Basil Brush Show*, was nominated for at least one award.

This clever scheduling meant that the BBC's stranglehold on the Saturday ratings remained unbroken until the end of the decade. *Doctor Who* was a small part of an invincible whole, fed, and in turn sustained by, the other programmes around it.

When many figures in the press – not to mention countless disapproving fans – suggested that *Doctor Who* couldn't survive away from its Saturday-night, fish-fingers-and-chips, feet-up-in-front-of-the-fire time slot, they were, in a sense, displaying a remarkable lack of trust in the series' ability to stand alone, to survive without the help of the perhaps equally camp Basil Brush and Larry Grayson. Luckily, the BBC itself had more faith in the series than that. When challenged by viewers via the letters page of *Radio Times*, Alan Hart – the Controller of BBC1 responsible for *Doctor Who*'s midweek redeployment – defended his actions: 'The decision to move the Doctor from his Saturday slot was not taken lightly. We thought carefully about it and decided that he needed new times; and the hope is that more people will be able to follow his adventures. In addition, we all felt the need to give him a new lease of life. A new Doctor, a new placing, a new challenge. Time will tell whether the TARDIS has landed on the right day.'

Main: In late August 1980, the Doctor (Tom Baker), Romana (Lalla Ward) and K9 returned to TV for the first episode of *The Leisure Hive*. It was the series' lowest rated season premiere since 1966, with only 5.9 million viewers tuning in
Inset: Conversely, part two of *The Creature from the Pit* the previous year, was watched by 10.8 million viewers

Time did indeed prove Hart and his mysterious 'we' right. By the end of Peter Davison's first fortnight as the Doctor, the series' ratings had reached 10.4 million. The previous year, *Doctor Who* had struggled to a 'high' of only 7.7 million and touched a low of 3.7 million – the series' most disastrous rating for a first-run episode in over ten years. Tom Baker's final season had also seen *Doctor Who* almost consistently outside the Top 100 most-watched programmes of the week for the first time since 1966. By contrast, episode one of *Time-Flight*, the final serial of Peter Davison's first year, was the twenty-sixth most popular programme on its week of broadcast.

Obviously, 'Mondayness' had appeals of its own, and while the *Guardian* and the *Daily Mail* berated the BBC for its lack of respect for tradition, the Corporation could take comfort from the fact that they had saved a series that, in 1980, seemed to have shed half of its regular audience overnight. *Doctor Who*'s presence on the BBC Saturday evening schedules may have been considered 'essential' by Joe Steeples and his ilk; it had just proved to be anything but to the public at large.

Taking a broader view, it would be fair to say that *Doctor Who* had never really been a phenomenal hit in terms of ratings. There were times, certainly, when the series had found and held a place in the Top 20 programmes of the week – chiefly during its second year, before the Dalek's novelty value had worn off, and during Tom Baker's second and third years in the lead role – but generally it had settled in the lower two-thirds of the Top 100. After the early days of Dalek glory, when *Doctor Who* had become an established part of the Saturday evening TV furniture, its audience rating was more often a function of the popularity or otherwise of the competition. As soon as *Doctor Who* became 'familiar', it was certain to fall victim to whatever was 'unfamiliar'. Regularly throughout its long run a sizeable portion of *Doctor Who*'s audience would casually turn away from the series when captivated by some glittering new jewel on the independent channel. However, for the most part, the series' intrinsic strengths held it firmly in the hearts of a loyal majority, and soon enough a fresh new audience would discover the programme for the first time, claiming it as their own.

Plotting a ratings chart for the series from 1963 to 1979, one can clearly observe this rise and fall in favour, both on a broad year-by-year scale and sometimes even from week to week – it's the steady in-out respiration of a generally healthy series. But by 1980, *Doctor Who* found itself gasping for viewers in the claustrophobic, competitive climate of its now over-played Saturday evening slot; the oxygen of popularity and publicity all but burnt up by the series' most energetic rival yet. ITV had taken a trip to the USA and brought back a surprise present for its viewers in the form of the flash-trash pulp science fiction series *Buck Rogers in the 25th Century*.

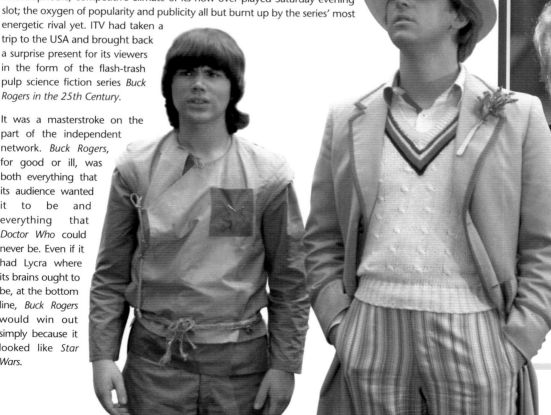

It was a masterstroke on the part of the independent network. *Buck Rogers*, for good or ill, was both everything that its audience wanted it to be and everything that *Doctor Who* could never be. Even if it had Lycra where its brains ought to be, at the bottom line, *Buck Rogers* would win out simply because it looked like *Star Wars*.

Doctor Who's 1982 season offered added value for its weekday viewers with a host of well-known guest stars...
Top: Nerys Hughes in *Kinda*
Middle: Michael Robbins in *The Visitation*
Above: Beryl Reid in *Earthshock*

Main: Peter Davison made his debut the same year, here with Adric (Matthew Waterhouse) in *The Visitation*

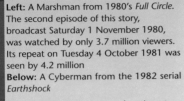

Left: A Marshman from 1980's *Full Circle*. The second episode of this story, broadcast Saturday 1 November 1980, was watched by only 3.7 million viewers. Its repeat on Tuesday 4 October 1981 was seen by 4.2 million

Below: A Cyberman from the 1982 serial *Earthshock*

Far right: Peter Davison on location at Heathrow Airport for 1982's *Time-Flight*, part one of which was the 26th most-watched programme of its week of broadcast. No other Davison serial achieved a higher chart position

It is impossible to overestimate the effect that *Star Wars* had upon TV and film science fiction – even *Doctor Who*'s distinctively quirky interpretation of the genre. To this day, *Star Wars* stands as the benchmark by which all similar productions are judged, consciously or unconsciously. It offered a universe so fully imagined and so stylishly brought to life that it actually came to define a form of *reality* for science fiction adventure. It was the first mass-appeal space opera to be produced after the 1969 moon landings and early 1970s space walks, and it was the first to convincingly re-create the true splendour of space for the cinema screen. Watching just the film's opening few seconds, as Darth Vader's sleek Cinemascope Star Destroyer rolled overhead, a whole generation of moviegoers sat up in their seats, gasped and collectively thought, 'Yes! *That's* what it would *really* be like!' From that point on, neither the guppy-like Starship Enterprise inching its way around a tomato moon nor the TARDIS dancing on its string before a backlit board, lovingly pin-pricked with holes to represent stars, could possibly compete. Kids now *knew* the sound that fast little spaceships made as they zinged past, they *knew* that the really cool space stations were the size of a planet. An unshakeable sense of reality for even the blatantly unreal was set in the summer of 1977, and although *Doctor Who* tried valiantly to evoke a little of that *Star Wars* magic in the years that immediately followed, it never, in all honesty, came within an imperial mile of doing so.

But *Buck Rogers* did. Over on ITV in the late autumn of 1980, you could find valiant humans zipping between

the planets in their ion-engined fighter craft. The forces of evil were dispatched week after week by the handsome hero, his attractive, lofty female sidekick, his wise mentor and his cute, beeping robot. *Buck Rogers* was shiny, thrilling and, for an all-important few weeks, utterly captivating. For the generation of kids for whom *Star Wars* was the very pinacle of entertainment, the arrival of *Buck Rogers* was like the Pied Piper coming to town. Over the hill to ITV the young viewers skipped, eyes alight, held in the thrall of a handsome stranger from a foreign land. Five million children and straggling parents were lost to *Doctor Who* that year.

But just as the venerable Doctor had been further empowered by standing four-square at the head of that juggernaut BBC Saturday of the 1970s, so the clean-cut Buck Rogers also had his own help from outside. In 1980 it was ITV, not the Beeb, wielding that mystical power of 'Saturdayness'. And it was all the fault of football.

That year, for the first time, ITV had outbid the BBC for the rights to screen league football on Saturday evenings. This banished the BBC's *Match of the Day* to a journey around various midweek and Sunday time slots, and allowed the commercial network to launch its own Saturday replacement, *The Big Match*, ready for the autumn 1980 season.

Before this time, it had been rare for the ITV network to show the same programmes, at the same time, across all its regional stations. On a Saturday night in 1979, for example, Granada in the north-west of England might have offered the amphibious adventures of *The Man from Atlantis* opposite *Doctor Who*, while London Weekend Television (LWT) plumped for the adventures of the Californian Highway Patrol in *CHiPs* – and both would have been knocked half-way into the following week by the sledgehammer punches of the Doctor and the BBC's assorted light-entertainment heavyweights. But in 1980, a thrusting young programming executive at LWT (who we'll meet properly in Chapter W) led the call for a fully networked, rationalised schedule for ITV on Saturday evenings, based around the football. The network tentatively agreed, and so ITV stole the rest of the BBC's clothes at the same time. Or rather ran off its own set of cut-price, no-frills copies.

This was a turning point not just for *Doctor Who* but for the BBC as a whole. Up till then, its ratings battles with ITV had been civilised affairs, the Corporation certainly trying its very best but always, deep in its heart, knowing that its licence-fee funding was inviolate and it had no need to surrender its dignity to a pell-mell chase for ratings in order to guarantee advertising revenue. In the 1980s, a new Conservative government put this state funding under increasing threat, and the BBC had to fight to jusify its existence alongside an increasingly successful independent network. For more than half a decade, the BBC battled to restore a steadily diminishing audience share, constantly re-evaluating and rearranging its schedules for maximum effect.

In many ways, the move of *Doctor Who* from Saturday to the middle of the week was little more than a symptom of insecure times at a rattled BBC1. The happy side effect was that the first year after the move gave *Doctor Who* its last great ratings boost, proving that as long the programme was offering what the public wanted to see – as long as it continued to innovate and entertain – it didn't matter on which day of the week the series was shown. ◖

TIDES OF TIME

In the 1960s, ray-guns, utility belts, rubber spaceships and Santa Claus were all staple elements of a *Doctor Who* comic strip. By the 1980s, the readers had all grown up – so the strips had no choice but to do the same...

In mid-July 1982, a fortunate group of *Doctor Who* fans were held engrossed by the seventh and final episode of one of the greatest *Doctor Who* stories ever told. In the tiny English village of Stockbridge, the fate of the whole universe, the whole of Time, hinged on a single ball in a game of cricket.

For six months, loyal followers had seen the Doctor battling the evil of the demon Melanicus, who had seized control of the Event Sythesiser – the massive instrument which has brought order to the universe since the beginning of Time – and was determined to plunge all life into a new realm of fear, destruction and chaos. The Doctor's quest to defeat the demon had taken him from a game of cricket in sleepy Stockbridge to the majestic towers of his home planet of Gallifrey. He had stumbled through a phantasmagoric funfair and ridden a fiery roller-coaster into the very mouth of hell. He had seen the worlds of Althrace: an entire solar system bolted together and set spinning in the heart of a white hole. He had witnessed the terrible Millennium Wars: a thousand worlds in bloody conflict for a thousand years.

After meeting Merlin, Dracula and a twenty-foot-high rubber duck, after the reversal of Time itself, the Doctor reached a final showdown with Melanicus in a ravaged Stockbridge of the future. At the top of the church tower, a magnificent act of self-sacrifice from the Doctor's new companion, the medieval knight Sir Justin, had seen the demon apparently perish.

Finally, back at the wicket on the village green, the Doctor waits for his first ball to be bowled again. Only then will he know if Time has been set back on its proper path. He adjusts his stance, raises the bat and braces himself for the delivery...

To this day, *The Tides of Time*, a *Doctor Who* comic strip published in issues 61–8 of Marvel Comics' *Doctor Who Monthly*, retains pride of place as perhaps the most sweeping and poetic *Doctor Who* story ever told. With the salvation of all civilisation as his mission, and the devil himself as his enemy, it took the Doctor on a journey across a universe of unparalleled vision, drama and beauty.

Sadly, however, on its first publication this story reached perhaps a maximum of 30,000 readers. Meanwhile, the other 8 million loyal followers of the Doctor's adventures that year had been forced to put up with some slightly more anorexic fare. The nineteenth series of *Doctor Who* – the first to star Peter Davison – had aired between January and March, and even though it showcased the atmospheric, abstruse *Kinda* and the crowd-pleasing, Cyberman-slaughtering *Earthshock*, it also coughed up the lacklustre *Four to Doomsday* (large frog stages a celebration of ethnic dance in spaceship) and *Time-Flight* (fey British Airways cabin crew battle grey Plasticine in the Pleistocene). *The Tides of Time* had run alongside and above all of these hits and misses and set a benchmark of its own: it was the first time that *Doctor Who* in a secondary medium had set a consistently higher standard than the TV series that spawned it.

It's fair to say, however, that it had taken the *Doctor Who* comic strip a long time to get there.

The Doctor made his first appearance in strip form back in November 1964. TV Publications Ltd (a subsidiary of *News of the World*) purchased the rights to the series' central character, and little else, for their weekly *TV Comic*. The title had been in print for a little over thirteen years, providing an eager young audience with such innocent delights as the illustrated adventures of BBC TV's whittled children's celebrity *Muffin the Mule* and the further exploits of the more gung-ho but equally highly strung stars of *Fireball XL5* and *Supercar*.

TV Comic opted to tailor their *Doctor Who* stories to suit their pre-pubescent readership. Simplifying the central concept, the Doctor (actually 'Doctor Who' for the majority of the run) was to be a whimsical human inventor, rather than the unpredictable and unreliable alien of the TV show's first year. Our first sight of the Doctor comes when his offensively precocious grandchildren, John and Gillian, stroll into his unlikely police box home. Finding themselves inside an amazing control room, there is barely time for a 'No! Don't touch that button whatever you do!' before they blunder outside again into the clutches of the Kleptons, a parasitic menace of the twenty-ninth century.

A series of light-hearted escapades with this first 'Doctor Who' were to follow over the next two years, almost all of which would in some way spurn common sense, flaunt the laws of physics or see the Doctor and his progeny engaging in some act of physical violence to achieve an often dubiously amoral victory over ugliness. The strip shunned one of the key moral niceties of the TV series – which generally sees the Doctor gently aid some subjugated and brutalised band of victims to overthrow a murderous regime – by simply having the Doctor blow up or gun down the villain of the piece. Similarly, a paucity of ideas would see the intrepid inventor producing all manner of useful weapons or other *deus ex machina* devices from the TARDIS or his trusty black leather bag which would hasten the destruction or humiliation of a foe. A good example can be found in 1965–6's *A Christmas Story*, when the evil Demon Magician is defeated using what the Doctor refers to only as his 'magic box'. But then, it can be justifiably claimed that the highly regarded Tom Baker TV adventure *Pyramids of Mars* is brought to an end in much the same way.

This catalogue of divergences from the style of the television series did not make the *TV Comic* strip bad in itself. Very much the product of a simpler time, and with no need, unlike the television episodes, to hold the more sophisticated attentions of an adult audience, many of its stories were enormous fun, high-spirited and adventurous, and its first few black-and-white months were certainly successful enough to see it move to full colour in the prestigious centre-page slot for much of its second year.

During this time, the comic had sat on newsagents' shelves alongside a more glamorous rival, City Magazines' *TV Century 21*. City had independently nabbed the right to the Daleks in late 1964, and developed a colour strip featuring the planet Skaro's finest to help launch this new title. Over the 104 episodes of *The Daleks*, eager readers followed the rise of the race from the aftermath of a neutron war in 2003, through the development of space flight, to a final cliffhanger which saw them pledging to invade and plunder the Earth. Equally independent of the continuity of the TV series, the greatest strength of the *TV Century 21* strip lay in its creation of the Daleks' Golden Emperor. This wise and wily leader was no less destructive or vengeful than his troops but, mainly due to the use of 'thinks' balloons on the strip, also had an endearing tendency to sink into introspection and philosophical pondering between his more usual declamatory dialogue. In one episode, with his home world threatened by collision with a rogue planet that has dropped out of orbit, the Emperor slips away into a dimly lit chamber to contemplate a new plan. 'A meteorite storm,' he ruminates. 'A last hope, perhaps?'

© BBC tv 1968

Largely scripted by *Doctor Who*'s early TV guru David Whitaker, and painted by some of the finest artists working in the field at the time, *The Daleks* is one of the definitive comic strips of the 1960s. A triumph in every department.

The week after the Daleks abandoned the pages of *TV Century 21*, a licence renegotiation allowed *TV Comic* to pit them against their Doctor, now drawn to loosely resemble Patrick Troughton. Typically, only the face had changed and not his manners – a fact quickly confirmed when he deals with a Dalek by smashing in its dome with a large rock ('Prepare for a nasty shock, my hideous metal friend!').

Then things started to get really surreal, and it's at this point that due tribute must be paid to semi-regular *TV Comic Doctor Who* scriptwriter Roger Noel Cook. Looking back, it's fair to say that Cook's Troughton stories represent some of the most bizarre – or perhaps simply some of the bravest – material ever passed off under the title of *Doctor Who* in any medium. With few concessions made to the philosophy and styling of the TV series, Cook's Doctor was a multi-purpose eccentric genius with a gadget for any occasion – there was absolutely nothing he couldn't or wouldn't turn his hand to... Need someone to manage a top pop band? No problem, the Doctor will even save them from bombs planted at their gigs by vengeful ex-managers! Looking for a mechanical housemaid? The Doctor will invent and market one without you having to ask. He'll even help you to celebrate 'hitting the big time' with the ensuing profits! You're a millionaire whose son has been kidnapped by alien dwarfs? Have no fear, the Doctor will assemble a hand-picked rescue team! He'll even ask Professor Frankel to bring his rubber spaceship – everyone knows that dwarfs can't detect them!

Strangely, in the midst of this inspired lunacy, some new continuity links were formed between the comic strip and its small-screen progenitor. As well as the Daleks, TV enemies the Cybermen and the Quarks made regular appearances. Happily, however, the supposedly emotionless Cybermen seemed to enjoy skiing, bickering with their comrades and waving their arms in the air if they think they've seen off an enemy. The Quarks, meanwhile, who only ever droned a few words and giggled until their batteries went flat in their single 1968 TV appearance, would happily turn their 'hands' to car-jacking and high-speed pursuit if the plot demanded.

IT IS DONE! THE STATUE IS UPRIGHT!

Above: The emotionless Cybermen get into a party mood as they raise a giant statue in honour of their Controller. From *The Cyber Empire! TV Comic* 1968

Below: The chatty Quarks swear vengence upon the Doctor and Jamie at the conclusion of *Invasion of the Quarks! TV Comic* 1968

MAKE A MENTAL NOTE OF THESE EARTHLINGS, IF THEY EVER CROSS YOUR PATH.. DESTROY THEM!

WE WILL SEARCH THE UNIVERSE... THEY WILL DIE!

THE INVASION FORCE WILL BE AVENGED! DEATH TO THE EARTHLINGS!

Drama plus next week when the Quarks send giant wasps against the Doctor !

Top: A typical issue of *TV Action + Countdown* from 1972

Bottom: *Mighty Midget – Doctor Who Comic*, a free gift with the first issue of the revamped, tabloid *Mighty TV Comic* in 1976. It featured a reprint of an old Jon Pertwee strip with Tom Baker's head drawn over Pertwee's

Right: A scene from the first episode of *Voyager*, one of Steve Parkhouse's most popular *Doctor Who* strips from 1984

Particularly worthy of note are the final five Troughton *TV Comic* stories. It seems that after the events of the second Doctor's final adventure, *The War Games* – in which the Time Lords decide to exile him to Earth with a different TV appearance – our hero managed to escape that second part of his sentence and happily took up residence in the 'swanky' Carlton Grange Hotel in London, while he continued to fight his good fight against anyone alien, fat or with a vaguely sinister moustache. Not noted for being shy ('Time and Space Traveller Residing in London' screams the headline of the *Daily Record* at one point), he even pitches up as a panellist on the TV game show *Explain My Mystery*. Sadly, this final bid for fame proves his undoing, as an investigation of farmer Glenlock-Hogan's walking scarecrows leads him into the middle of a Time Lord sting; for they are animating the straw stooges, who then nab the Doctor and finally force his regeneration. It all served as a perfect if somewhat off-the-wall bridge into the first Jon Pertwee TV serial, *Spearhead from Space*.

Spearhead from Space brought the Doctor down to Earth, and between the broadcast of its second and third episodes in January 1970 he and his UNIT friends, Brigadier Lethbridge-Stewart and Liz Shaw, took over as the stars of the *TV Comic* strip. For the first half of the year, the stories were still consciously aimed at a market of eight- and nine-year-olds, and the Roger Noel Cook mayhem continued.

But things slowly began to change. First, the experienced Alan Fennell (who had worked on the *TV Century 21* Dalek epic) briefly took over the scripting chores, and an ever-increasing dialogue between *TV Comic* and the *Doctor Who* production office ensured that the strip stuck more closely to the tone of the television series – probably a good thing, given that Cook's Doctor had recently both learned how to levitate and taken to holidaying on the Brigadier's private yacht! However, more sweeping changes were in the works...

In February 1971 the *Who* strip transferred to Polystyle's glamorous and sophisticated new comic, *Countdown*. The title's editor, Dennis Hooper, became the pen-and-ink Doctor's new regular scriptwriter and the links with the production office became stronger. Overall, the Third Doctor's two and a half years at *Countdown* and *TV Action* (the title into which *Countdown* gradually metamorphosed) represented the first time that a *Doctor Who* strip had come close to capturing the spirit and tone of the series itself. Certainly, the Doctor seemed to regularly remember and then forget how to pilot the TARDIS. Admittedly, there was no sign of Jo Grant, and precious few appearances by the Brigadier and the Master. And yes, he did rent a cottage in the country and drive a little car called Betsy. Nevertheless, these strips cleverly captured the attitude and moral tone of Jon Pertwee's TV episodes, and his Doctor's particular mix of the charmer and the bully.

Some even offered central story ideas that, with suitable embellishment, could easily have been made into a broadcast-worthy serial, especially *The Celluloid Midas* (cast of TV soap found turned into plastic) and *Back to the Sun* (possessed scientist wants to turn the Earth into a fiery home for his alien masters).

TV Action folded in 1973 and the *Doctor Who* strip returned to its ancestral home of *TV Comic*. Two years later, after taking over the lead role on TV, Tom Baker's features came to the pages.

The late 1970s represent one of bleakest periods in the history of *Doctor Who* comic strips. Neither as charmingly 'gung-ho' as the Hartnell and Troughton flights of fancy, nor as stylish and sophisticated as the potted Pertwee epics, the Tom Baker adventures instead adopted the worst inaccuracies and excesses of both – placing a pompous, patronising and somewhat misogynistic Doctor within a series of bleak and derivative storylines. There were notable exceptions of course, such as the entertaining *Return of the Daleks!*, *The Space Ghost!* and *The Emperors Spy!*, but even the addition of assistant Sarah Jane Smith, who weathered two years of the Doctor's mental cruelty and smug bullying, failed to imbue the strip with much of the charm of the TV series. (Even when Sarah Jane makes a perfectly reasonable inquiry, a typical response from this Doctor is, 'Ask any more of your infernal journalist questions and I'll personally brain you!'). Later, savage companion Leela would be captured a little more faithfully, aside from an uncharacteristic tendency to faint that is. By this point the whole of *TV Comic* seemed bereft of both cash and ideas. After several desperate format changes, the magazine finally closed in May 1979. It was the end of an era, but from the ashes...

In October of the same year, Marvel Comics UK launched *Doctor Who Weekly*, a new comic devoted entirely to the exploits of the Time Lord. Marvel's lead strip immediately captured the personality of both the TV series – then very relaxed and anarchic – and its lead character, who would now find his constant quest for a holiday in Benidorm interrupted by all manner of clever and stylish adventures. *Doctor Who Weekly* benefited from a team of writers who had not only grown up with *Doctor Who* but were also highly experienced in the special skills required to translate a story into the comic-strip medium. A secondary strip in the comic related Doctor-less tales concerning the Time Lord's foes. These more adult stories often played upon themes of greed, xenophobia and the tyranny of self-doubt, and inhabited a universe of few moral certainties and much ironic tragedy.

With the appointment of Steve Parkhouse as scripter on the lead strip in issue 53 of what was now *Doctor Who Monthly*, this tone of moral ambiguity was further developed in the adventures of the Doctor. Moving into a darker realm than that inhabited by the TV series at the time, Parkhouse's stories had a strong and independent identity of their own. While the Pertwee years had seen the strips come close to matching the energy and excitement of the television series, Parkhouse's award-winning work actually began to outreach and outpace it. *The Tides of Time* was to be his greatest triumph, but by no means his last.

Over his forty-seven issues at the helm, each of Parkhouse's comic strips was to be linked, either narratively or thematically, with the next. One- or two-part stories formed ambiguous preludes to later epics, which in turn stood as mere warm-ups to magnificent sequels.

Finally, in issue 99, after the ten-issue *Voyager* cycle of stories, Parkhouse actually decided to write himself out of his own strip. For some time, the Sixth Doctor had been plagued by the sinister Nostradamus – an arch-manipulator who toys with the Time Lord for his own inscrutable ends. At first, Nostradamus seems to have complete power over the Doctor, plaguing him with visions and at one point even directly scripting his actions in a Rupert Bear-like story. But when Nostradamus is exposed as a fake by the all-powerful Voyager, the hollow man cracks. Near death, he says, 'Ah, Doctor, how can you know how long I have been writing your life? What will you do now that I'm gone?'

While the years that followed Parkhouse's all-too-brief time with the *Doctor Who* strip offered a massive variety of material – some very good, some very, very bad – it never quite reached the same heights of confidence and creativity.

By the end of 1998, there will have been a *Doctor Who* comic strip in regular publication in the United Kingdom for thirty-four years: an astounding record which means that the comic strip has been in longer continuous production than the television show it took as its inspiration. With Paul McGann's version of the Time Lord running at full strength in the witty and stylish strip still offered by Marvel's *Doctor Who Magazine*, that record stands as a testament to the flexibility and longevity of the concepts central to the universe of *Doctor Who*. ◯

"I AM A LORD OF TIME!" I SCREAMED.

"AND I AM A LORD OF *LIFE!*" HE THUNDERED IN REPLY... AND HIS WORDS SOARED ALOFT AND WERE ONE WITH THE WIND.

THEN THERE WAS ONLY THE VOID... AND THE WIND-WRAITHS HOWLING LIKE A THOUSAND LOST SOULS...

STOCKBRIDGE AND SQUIDGE

Five other essential Doctor Who comic strips:

◯ *Challenge of the Piper* (*TV Comic*, 1965)
The Doctor defeats the challenges of the Pied Piper to rescue the children of Hamelin.
A great set-up for TV Comic's brand of junior Doctor Who, but it would have had Robert Browning spinning in his grave.

◯ *The Sabre-Toothed Gorillas!* (*TV Comic*, 1967)
The Second Doctor as action hero, as the team wallop monsters with a baseball bat made from 'Squidge' – a special material that 'bounces ten times as high as rubber and you can do anything with it'.
Absolute nonsense, but enormous fun nonetheless.

◯ *The Planet of the Daleks* (*Countdown*, 1972)
The metal meanies attempt to transform the Doctor into a humanoid Dalek. Surprisingly, he outwits them...
The styling and sophistication of the TV Century 21 Dalek stories come to a straight Doctor Who strip for the first time. Unmissable.

◯ *End of the Line* (*Doctor Who Monthly*, 1980)
The Doctor tries to aid the beleaguered survivors of a heavily polluted, cannibal-infested inner-city wasteland, but learns that he can't always save everyone.
The comic strip's great coming of age. A brief, sensitive and ultimately tragic tale.

◯ *Endgame* (*Doctor Who Magazine*, 1996)
The Celestial Toymaker visits his wrath upon the Eighth Doctor by creating a more powerful version of the Time Lord to be his champion.
Revisiting Parkhouse's Stockbridge, this story also recaptures the hectic pace and surreal tone of Marvel's finest hour.

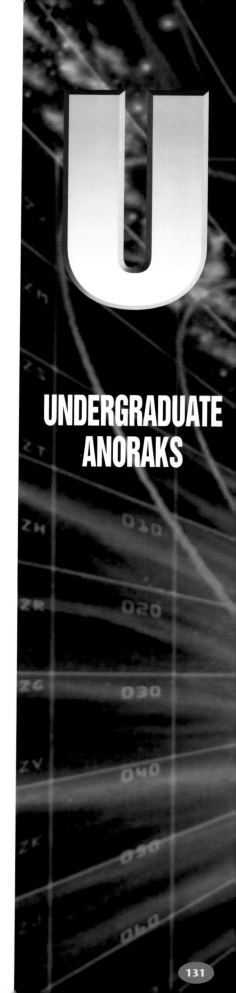

UNDERGRADUATE ANORAKS

Through the 1980s, *Doctor Who* turned ever more frequently to its own past to find inspiration for new stories. Soon, twenty-something fans who had grown up with the series found a new buzz word: 'continuity'. But then, so did the rest of the world. Theirs was 'anorak'.

'It collected together, in one neat demonstration package… all that had become gimcrack and silly about the serial over the years: hollow Daleks, Cybermen in baggy suits and latter-day Time Lords in comic hats. They were all there.'

This is respected TV critic Philip Purser's opinion of *The Five Doctors*, published in the first edition of *Halliwell's Television Companion* in 1984. *The Five Doctors* was a specially commissioned ninety-minute special, produced to celebrate the twentieth anniversary of *Doctor Who* and first shown in the UK amid the BBC's *Children in Need* frenzy of 25 November 1983.

The initial concept of such a celebration must have seemed a good one in the production office. Ten years earlier, the four-part serial *The Three Doctors* united William Hartnell and Patrick Troughton with incumbent Jon Pertwee in an entertaining adventure where the presence of the early Doctors was a nice bonus, but didn't get in the way of telling a solid *Doctor Who* story. 1980s producer John Nathan-Turner and his team brought together not only five Doctors but also ten companions, four old enemies, two other recurring Time Lord characters, the Doctor's old car and even Rassilon – a figure from Time Lord legend referred to in passing in a handful of earlier serials – for good measure.

It was as if the programme's makers, in attempting to sum up the content and worth of twenty years of *Doctor Who*, compiled a list of nouns rather than adjectives. The brief to scriptwriter Terrance Dicks would have contained such words as 'Cybermen, Time Lords, Liz Shaw, Bessie', rather than, say, 'original, brave, engaging, witty'.

Of course, given that they were making a fast and funny anniversary romp, a birthday reunion and knees-up, this approach can be forgiven. However, it is indicative of a shift in style and priorities undertaken by *Doctor Who* in the early 1980s. It was certainly the shift noted by Philip Purser in that review, and one which would have far-reaching consequences for the future of the series. *Doctor Who* had begun to turn inward and feed off its own history, to retread old ground, and so, inevitably, failed to surprise in the way it used to.

Through the 1960s and 1970s, *Doctor Who* did little in the way of self-referencing. At various times separate serials were linked by ongoing themes – such as the desire of companions Ian and Barbara to get home in that first year, or the Third Doctor's attempts to escape his exile on Earth – but these devices were used chiefly to set up a dramatic context for a new adventure, making the characters seem more isolated and vulnerable, and not as central plots in themselves.

Indeed, for much of *Doctor Who*'s first decade it was very rare for the series to go over old ground, and the concept of a sequel was largely unknown. Certainly, during this time the Daleks popped up every few months, but after their first resurrection in *The Dalek Invasion of Earth*, no one stopped to remark upon their continuing survival. Ian's first amazed comment, 'Doctor, I don't understand this at all. We saw the Daleks destroyed on Skaro. We were there!' and his friend's reply, 'My dear boy, what we saw on Skaro was a million years ahead of us in the future!' would more or less cover things for the Daleks' next half-dozen or so appearances. Later, after the Doctor helped to destroy the home planet of the Cybermen in their debut serial, the popular foes made a comeback with an excuse broadly along the lines of, 'Oh dear, didn't we tell you, we've got another home planet by the way. Sorry.' This, essentially, was the level of *Doctor Who*'s internal continuity for many years.

Below: The Silurians, left for dead in 1970's *Doctor Who and the Silurians*

Right: Their latter-day resurrection in *Warriors of the Deep* (1984), was not judged a success by fans of the series

The Jon Pertwee years provided the series with something of a continuing narrative once again, based mainly around the Master's many attempts to rule the world, and the sci-fi soap set-up of the Doctor having fallen in with UNIT. Even then, few demands were made on the general viewer to keep up with detailed continuity.

Early 1972 saw the return of the Ice Warriors in *The Curse of Peladon*, their most recent previous appearance having been in 1969's *The Seeds of Death*. This was something of a minor turning point, as aside from the Daleks – whose massive popular impact ensured that different rules applied to them – this was the first time a monster or character had returned to the series after more than a year away. Up to this point, each revival – be it that of the 'Meddling Monk', the Cybermen, the Yeti or the first comeback of the Ice Warriors themselves – had been mere months after their previous outing. No producer had really bothered to look back any further, and even in this case it would be fair to assume that the reheating of the Ice Warriors three years 'out of time' was chiefly due to the fact that it was really their creator, writer Brian Hayles, who was making a return to the series, and the Ice Warriors were what he knew. The same would later apply to writer Gerry Davis, who brought the Cybermen back from the dead in 1975, after more than five years away from the TV screen. Fundamentally, old ideas and settings would rarely be reused unless the original writer was lobbying to do so. The other chief exception to this rule was the Time Lords, who were employed by a variety of scriptwriters for a variety of purposes. This meant that in each of their appearances in the 1960s and 1970s they would often be

presented differently. Terrance Dicks, their co-creator, would, in their introductory serial, *The War Games* (co-written with Malcolm Hulke), and in his script-editing influence upon *Colony in Space* and *The Three Doctors*, treat them as grand and otherworldly, with essentially supernatural powers over time and technology. Robert Holmes, meanwhile, would add a note of comedy and humanity when they appeared in his own stories. So when Holmes's 1976 serial *The Deadly Assassin* showcased his complete new vision of what the Time Lords should be – with all their vanities and insecurities on display – long-term viewers of *Doctor Who* were somewhat taken aback – or even angry – being, as they were, completely unused to such contradictions.

Around this time, the first sizeable organised network of individuals who would identify themselves as *Doctor Who* 'fans' was forming. Memories and notes were swapped among these devotees, further research undertaken and detailed lists drawn up for the first time: lists of planets the Doctor had visited, lists of scriptwriters, lists of companions. To this point, the only real reference works for would-be *Doctor Who* fans were Terrance Dicks and Malcolm Hulke's 1972 volume *The Making of Doctor Who* and the glossy *Radio Times Doctor Who* Anniversary Special from 1973. Both contained potted synopses of all the Doctors' adventures to date, but were short on detail. The new world of organised *Doctor Who* 'fandom' wanted much more; they felt they needed a complete, consistent story of the Doctor's life, and were more than happy to compile it themselves. Little did they know that the very act of collecting all this 'fictional' information together in one place, and in such detail, would have major consequences for the nature of the television series itself.

In the 1960s, popular alien races generally made return apperances within a year of their debuts...
Above: A Dalek in *The Dalek Invasion of Earth* (1964)
Below: The Cybermen from *The Moonbase* (1967)

For much of *Doctor Who*'s first fifteen years, in the absence of a large-scale or particularly vocal fan club, the series' production teams received only the most general of feedback. They would have certainly known that the series attracted a loyal audience, and they would have read and perhaps responded to individual letters. Overall, however, their creative decisions would have been made based on their own skill, insight and intuition, tempered by whatever qualitative and quantitative BBC audience research data was available. The show regularly shifted in tone and content under the influence of different production teams, each of which had their own agenda. In this environment, no one really worried in the slightest about whether the overall fictional history of the show was consistent; whether, for example, the 'D' in TARDIS stood for 'Dimension' or 'Dimensions', or if a 1975 serial gave a different name to the Daleks' ancestors from that given in a 1964 adventure. They didn't even have any real way of checking. A production office file provided brief synopses of stories, but this was largely just to ensure that, say, no one in 1972 commissioned a script that had the Cybermen invading a base on the moon, a story that had been told perfectly adequately in 1967.

While fans welcomed the return of old foes in the 1980s, the serials featuring them would often be very poorly received...

Top: *Attack of the Cybermen* (1985)
Above: A Sea Devil from *Warriors of the Deep* (1984)

Right: The Ice Warriors were one of the few popular monsters to not see a 1980s revival. Here, Lord Izlyr (Alan Bennion) argues with the Doctor (Jon Pertwee) in 1972's *The Curse of Peladon*

In the early 1980s, however, two important things happened. First, whereas *Doctor Who* had been the product of a variety of regimes, and had effectively been made as several different programmes, its fans now wished to derive an overall history and universe for the Doctor's adventures – with a handbook of 'facts'. They did, and through such professionally published books as 1981's two-volume *Programme Guide*, it was also made available to the production team itself. And second, *Doctor Who* itself had a new guiding hand. John Nathan-Turner took over as producer from Tom Baker's final season in 1980. He was eager to prove himself and equally eager to please, so *Doctor Who* fans were understandably delighted when he took time to visit their conventions and listen to their opinions, and those opinions almost certainly shaped the work he was to oversee in the coming years.

So when the fans went wild with excitement at the resurrection of the Master in 1981's *The Keeper of Traken*, Nathan-Turner felt happy and proud. He ensured his stories contained neat little continuity touches linking back with serials from long ago – it was now so easy to do.

An interesting measure of this can be found in Peter Davison's debut serial, *Castrovalva*. It is traditional that when the Doctor regenerates his body, his new incarnation spends a certain amount of time babbling confused memories in an incoherent fashion. In Tom Baker's first episode in 1974, this amounted to the new Doctor mumbling about 'Sontarans perverting the course of history' and bellowing, 'The brontosaurus is large, placid and stupid', both references to serials from less than a year before. In 1982, however, *Doctor Who*'s growing self-awareness allowed Peter Davison not only to stop to do impressions of Hartnell and Pertwee but also to play the recorder, talk about the Ice Warriors and make passing mention of Vicki, Jamie and the Brigadier.

Of course, if it had stopped there, this level of casual name-dropping would have been essentially harmless. But the archival plundering that brought back the Master soon did the same for the Cybermen, and to even greater fan acclaim. *Earthshock*, a hectic adventure story from Peter Davison's first year, revived the cyborgs for the first time in seven years. The serial was very popular, and thus the production team seemingly resolved to give these loyal and appreciative fans more of what they wanted. And they seemed to want old monsters.

This trend saw its greatest excesses with *Attack of Cybermen*, the serial which opened *Doctor Who*'s 1985 season. Although a reasonably diverting and fast-moving adventure in itself, the central conceit of its convoluted plot drew on aspects of both 1966's *The Tenth Planet* and 1967's *The Tomb of the Cybermen*. In a nutshell, the Cybermen in *Attack* attempt to change the course of history and prevent the destruction of their original home planet, which took place in the 1966 story. It was possible to follow the spirit of the story without knowing all the references, but less well-informed viewers were left with the nagging feeling that they were missing out on something; that *Doctor Who* was a show you had to be a full-time fan of to appreciate fully, a show you had to commit to in order to 'get' all the references.

Some have identified this trend towards self-referencing as a cause of the gradual decline in *Doctor Who*'s popularity through the 1980s, but the reasons for that gradual slip in ratings are far more complicated. What is certain, however, is that as the *Doctor Who* scripts filled with in-jokes and nod-and-wink comments about old friends and enemies, there came a significant shift in how the series was perceived by the audience at large. In 1980 *Doctor Who* was still simply a 'family show'; by the end of the decade it was a 'cult show', and no longer easygoing, easy-access entertainment.

To see how much things changed, one has only to look back to 1977, when the BBC2 popular art programme *The Lively Arts* broadcast its documentary *Whose Doctor Who*. Presenter Melvyn Bragg made an in-depth and considered investigation of the first thirteen years of *Doctor Who* with help from a psychologist, an educationalist, a physicist, families, schoolchildren and students. When *The Late Show* team produced their 1992 review of *Doctor Who*, *Resistance is Useless*, for the same channel, they instead offered an empty snorkel anorak on a stand reciting 'interesting' facts about the series via a droning voice-over. Two years after the series' cancellation, this was to be the image that summed up public perception of *Doctor Who* and the kind of personality you had to possess to enjoy it.

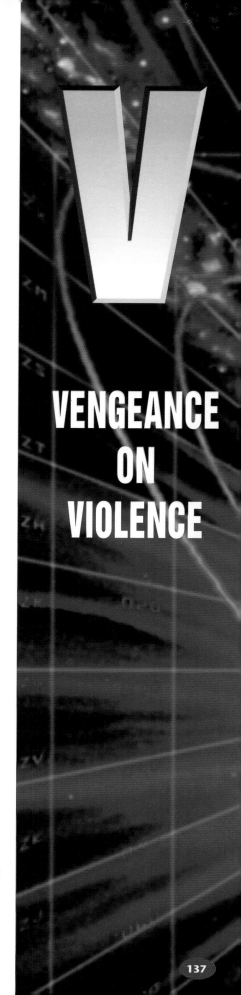

I**n 1985, _Doctor Who_ writer Eric Saward strove to bring what he described as 'a sense of realism' to _Doctor Who_'s previously bloodless round of woundings and deaths. But was this new approach part of a genuine quest for reality or just so much sensationalism?**

'The people who make Doctor Who _have got rather complacent. The show has got rather violent and lost a lot of its imagination and a lot of its wit… relying rather too much on straightforward on-the-nose violence.'_

This is not a complaint from a concerned viewer or parent, the commentary of a sensitive newspaper critic or the grumbling of a conservative TV watchdog. No, these are the words of Michael Grade, Controller of BBC1, when interviewed on Jimmy Young's BBC Radio 2 show in September 1985. The broader context of this criticism is explored in Chapter W; suffice to say here that it needed exceptional circumstances to draw a member of the BBC Board of Management into publicly criticising the attitudes of his own programme-making staff on a national radio station.

Nonetheless, it was an unprecedented remark. Although _Doctor Who_ had been called to account on many occasions during its first twenty-two years for its levels of violence, never before had it been attacked in public and 'on the record' by one of its own line managers within the BBC. They had previously been forced to defend the series' stance on such matters – even apologise sometimes – but never before had any senior figures felt the need to distance themselves from the content of the programme so forcefully.

Even if the comments were made by Grade as part of a broader political agenda (resulting perhaps in a more virulent tone), his was not the only voice to be raised in criticism of the six stories broadcast in Colin Baker's first full season as the Doctor in 1985. Even the devoted fans – who, one can imagine, would feel obliged to defend their beloved series against any assault – were aghast at what was seen as the employment of excessive graphic violence. A typical criticism came from Tony Howe, President of the Australian _Doctor Who_ fan club, in his society's newsletter in 1985: 'The 1985 season with Colin Baker is NOT the scary, stylised horror of the mid-1970s _Doctor Who_. The new style is sick, shock violence like Andy Warhol's: the Cyberleader crushes a prisoner's hand until it oozes blood; two men die in a vat of acid in _Vengeance on Varos_; there is an attack with a kitchen knife in _The Two Doctors_; and in the Dalek story someone is stabbed in the chest with a hypodermic needle. These incidents occur unexpectedly, they are not part of a total atmosphere for the whole story, they do not make the story interesting.'

Whether the overall number of acts of violence in these 1985 stories is any higher than those for previous years of _Doctor Who_ is doubtful – the series had always claimed a higher body count than even the most famously homicide-driven Hollywood films. What was actually being called into question by viewers as varied as loyal Australian fans and the Controller of BBC1 was the presentation of such deaths and the Doctor's attitude towards them.

In _Attack of the Cybermen_, broadcast in January 1985, the Cyber Controller discovers that the alien mercenary Lytton has betrayed him and orders that he be tortured until he is willing to reveal the extent of his treason. Two Cybermen approach Lytton, taking a fist each and slowly squeezing. The scene is presumably intended to demonstrate the awesome strength of these cybernetic soldiers, but the results on screen are gruesome and gratuitous. Blood is seen trickling down Lytton's wrists before he screams out in agony and collapses, vivid red smearing across the floor.

Challenged regarding the inclusion of such a scene in the script, Eric Saward, the series' script editor at the time, replied, 'I always felt that if you are going to show violence, you should also show the horrific effects of it. If you hit somebody, it hurts… If you hit them in the face, they're going to get a black eye or a bloody nose. Similarly, if you shoot somebody's hand, they're going to lose fingers, as Davros did in *Revelation of the Daleks*… To pretend there is no consequence to violent conflict is cheating the audience.'

But surely no one believed that the Cyberman torture scene could possibly teach viewers anything about the effects of real violence, unless of course they were addled enough to think that the Cybermen were real, so Saward's arguments fall down here. In comparison, 1975's *Revenge of the Cybermen* has one of the creatures grip the Doctor tightly by the shoulders and force him to the ground in pain. In this way viewers learn that a handshake with a Cybermen could leave you in agony, so they are not to be trifled with – surely all we need to know. Basically, Saward seemed to think that to make the Cybermen a credible menace, the times now demanded an ocean of blood.

He refers specifically to a scene in his own *Revelation of the Daleks* – the final story of the 1985 season – in which Davros has several of his fingers shot off during a bungled assassination attempt, but in this he also contradicts himself. Viewers are asked to believe that someone who has just had most of his hand severed can sit calmly, in no apparent pain, and carry on a conversation, having had the flow of blood from their grisly, mangled hand deftly staunched with a little gauze. It seems much more likely that the scene was included simply because Saward liked the idea of showing Davros losing his fingers; it certainly doesn't further the plot in any way.

What also marks these sequences is a feeling that the camera is *lingering* on the pain and the bloodshed in a ghoulish fashion. Davros's dismemberment is mercifully brief in execution, but his bloody stump then becomes the focus of a number of shots, and his detached fingers are seen littering the floor later in the scene. This would have required a member of the visual effects team to spend time producing the prop digits – surely not an exercise that adds anything to the story. There are even two sick jokes made about the injury. When Davros has to evacuate his base at the behest of some rebellious Daleks, the Doctor offers to shake his hand and the evil scientist seems to be about to reciprocate before realising – oh, how funny – that he doesn't have a hand any more. The Doctor's response to one of Davros's final threats comes in the quip, 'No 'arm in trying.' This kind of humour only serves to make the Doctor appear gloating and cruel, as if he is enjoying the whole, ugly spectacle, and as he is our hero, this suggests we are supposed to be enjoying it too.

In the action climax to the same year's *The Two Doctors*, the Doctor lies in wait for a homicidal pursuer, chef Shockeye (who had long wanted to serve sautéed Time Lord for lunch), with a cotton pad soaked in cyanide. The Doctor, at a physical disadvantage, is trapped in a traditional 'kill or be killed' situation and has had to improvise a last defence from the materials to hand – this generally being the only time when he can be judged justified in taking life. This he does, choking Shockeye on the poisonous fumes. As the chef's body twitches to stillness in his hands, the Doctor mutters, 'His just desserts…' The line doesn't feature in writer Robert Holmes's script for the episode – not even in the finalised camera script – so it must have been added by Saward, or pehaps even actor Colin Baker himself, at a very late stage. It's interesting to note that when the episode was screened by a more sensitive and censorial New Zealand broadcaster it was the Doctor's post-mortem quip, and not Shockeye's actual death, that was considered inappropriate and cut.

Similarly, in the previous serial, *Vengeance on Varos*, we see the Doctor wake just as two guards are preparing to tip his supposedly dead body into a vat of acid. In a resulting struggle, both guards accidentally fall in themselves, and while the Doctor cannot really be blamed for their deaths, it is more than a trifle disturbing to see him smile down at the bubbling liquid as he delivers the parting shot, 'Forgive me if I don't join you' – appearing to derive pleasure from the tragedy.

Producer John Nathan-Turner, writing for *Doctor Who Magazine* in 1996, said of *Vengeance on Varos*, 'I liked this story very much. How on earth some people can complain about its violence is beyond me. It really is a lesson against. I think the story has a message with extremely apt and good intentions.' Sadly, those 'good intentions' fail to come across, making the complaints he mentioned entirely justified.

Top: On the planet Varos, cruel and unusual punishments include being turned into a parrot, as almost happens to Peri (Nicola Bryant)…
Above: …or a lizard. Rebel Areta (Geraldine Alexander) gets half-way there. *Vengeance on Varos* (1985)

Main: Lytton (Maurice Colbourne), broken by his torture at the hands of the Cybermen. *Attack of the Cybermen* (1985)
Inset: Chef Shockeye (John Stratton), who gets his just desserts from a homicidal Doctor. *The Two Doctors* (1985)

Far left: A revealing shot of the vividly realistic 'acid-burn' make-up applied to one of the Varosian guards seen off by the Doctor in *Vengeance on Varos*

The story introduces us to the citizens of the planet Varos, who, bar a few revolutionaries, live obediently within the diktats of a totalitarian regime, both controlled and entertained by nightly TV footage of the torture and execution of rebels. Writer Philip Martin commented in 1987, 'What the story was trying to do in its own way was say, "Look, if you watch video nasties all the time, if you pump violence and poison into a population… this is the kind of society you'll get." I was astounded that some people didn't see this, that they actually thought I was peddling violence, when in fact I was saying it all as a warning.'

Martin's cautionary message is conveyed chiefly through a number of scenes where we discover that the viewing citizens of Varos are bored and desensitised by the scenes of torture broadcast to their living rooms, swapping listless remarks about whether a given night's slice of prime-time punishment is a repeat or not. What is chiefly lacking, however, is any strong moral response from the Doctor and companion Peri. They, not the Varosians, are the characters the *Doctor Who* audience are supposed to identify with, and their lack of outrage makes the whole awful business of Varos seem somehow acceptable.
So much for Martin's parable!

Moreover, the serial's production team as a whole seems out of step with the writer's noble vision. The scenes of punishment watched by the people of Varos are all 'fantasy' tortures – a man dodging a laser, women mutated into birds or snakes – and we are expected to feel revulsion at the idea that this sort of thing might one day be considered entertainment, even though we have no reference point for the 'agonies' of the ordeals depicted. However, in the acid-bath incident referred to previously, we see the skin of one of the guards burn and blister as he dies – pain with which we can much more readily identify. And when the Doctor smiles at the incident, it is *then* that viewers feel revolted. In a story which, through a series of ironic, show-piece commentaries, seeks to point out the dangers of presenting violence as entertainment, it is a terrible thing to realise that it is just what *Doctor Who* had begun to do itself.

Perhaps the production team were bravely crusading to bring a note of cautionary realism to the series. Perhaps they *were* trying to teach viewers that 'good' and 'evil' are not always black-and-white concepts and that sometimes terrible random things can happen to the nicest of people. Perhaps they *did* genuinely believe that lingering on the consequences of violence was the best way to desensationalise it.

But what they didn't seem to understand was that *Doctor Who* has *always* shown the sobering consequences of violence: that is, the ultimate consequences of terror, pain, retribution, guilt and grief – a cautionary message more suited to its youthful audience and tea-time scheduling. In 1985, it seemed, the 'consequences of violence' were judged to be merely the blood and the viscera, not the anguish or the remorse, and by lingering on this stickiness and mess, much of the series' moral core slipped away, leaving the Doctor looking like little more than a bullying, wise-cracking killer.

Top: Fantasy violence and its effects in *The Two Doctors* (1985) as a fake Doctor is tortured by a coloured light...
Above: ...and a Sontaran suffers after an attack

Far left: The Doctor (Colin Baker) confronts Davros (Terry Molloy) in 1985's *Revelation of the Daleks*, seconds before the wheelchair-bound scientist loses his remaining hand

Main: Orcini (William Gaunt), responsible for the shooting, loses his artificial leg in the final showdown. Unfortunately, any viewer who missed the preceding episode would not *know* it was artificial – rendering the moment of dismemberment especially shocking

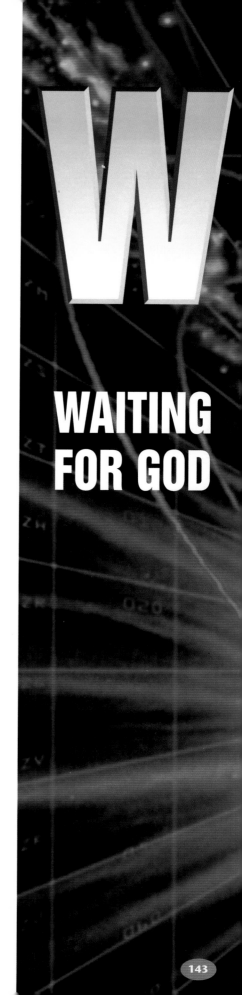

In the mid-1980s, a financial crisis at the BBC obliged a new, go-getting Controller to rest *Doctor Who* for a year. While the series could have easily survived this short break, the decision set in motion a chain of bizarre events that would have terrible consequences for the show's future . . .

1984 was a difficult year for the BBC. A confrontational Conservative government, freshly invigorated by a landslide general election victory, seemed set to take the organisation apart, viewing it as a lazy, left-wing and partisan institution ripe for privatisation. The BBC was, of course, used to fighting such political battles – having in its history faced and rebutted criticism from all of the major parties over perceived bias in current-affairs coverage. This time, however, the battleground was wider. The Corporation was finding itself under attack from the Government for not only perceived political differences but also all manner of programming and financing decisions – even in the fields of drama and light entertainment. When the frothy and expensive Australian mini-series *The Thorn Birds* was purchased that year for screening on BBC1, the Home Secretary himself, Douglas Hurd, took time to criticise the broadcaster for such 'foolhardy' expenditure: 'This is simply not the sort of thing the licence fee should be spent on.'

Scenting blood, the national press joined the chase. The London *Evening Standard* took its cue from Hurd, claiming that the purchase of *The Thorn Birds* demonstrated the BBC's 'remorseless mediocrity', before going on to describe the Corporation as like 'a juggernaut out of control... pitifully out of ideas and lost for a cause'. Never one to miss out on a chance to seize the moral high ground, the *Daily Mail* rained righteous indignation down on the BBC's 'sleazy' drama department. 'Alongside the sadistic sex,' alliterated columnist Paul Johnson, 'the BBC slips in the political message. It not only lies, it lies for the left. It not only rapes, it rapes for the revolution.'

In the midst of this, the BBC's audience share was sinking rapidly toward 35 per cent – seen as a critically low level even within the organisation. ITV was making successful forays into many of what were traditionally seen as the BBC's fields of expertise; most notably scoring high-profile hits with such lavish costume dramas as *Brideshead Revisited* and *The Jewel in the Crown*. Attacks from a fickle government and the right-wing press could be reasonably easily predicted and parried; long-term loss of the confidence and support of the viewing public was a far more serious matter.

There was still another battle to be fought. The licence fee had been held at £46 since 1981, although in the intervening years the BBC had dramatically increased its total number of hours per day of broadcast material through the launch of breakfast television and an expansion of its radio network. Now keen to fill both of its television channels right through morning and afternoon – replacing hours of testcard and pre-empting the commercial network's own expansion into daytime programming – the BBC was lobbying for the fee to be raised to £65, an increase of over 40 per cent. The Corporation knew it would have a difficult job selling this price hike to an unimpressed audience and a staunchly anti-inflation Conservative administration.

The falling ratings were a key problem. How could the BBC possibly justify the new licence fee if they weren't seen to be producing programmes that people actually wanted to watch? In the autumn of 1984 the final fee negotiations were still over a year away – giving the BBC time to set about restoring its pole position in the race for ratings. It was clear that a wise and inspirational general would be required to spearhead the fight back. The BBC needed someone who not only understood the opposition but could also sweep away the creative cobwebs.

Enter Michael Grade, an entertainment impresario of the old school. His uncle, Lord Lew Grade, had been a leading figure in British commercial television throughout the 1950s and 1960s. Michael's father, Leslie, had been one of the country's most successful theatrical agents, representing some of the major talents of the post-war variety circuit – including Billy 'Wakey! Way-key!' Cotton, whose *Band Show* had been one of the most popular light-entertainment TV series of the 1960s.

After a brief career as a sports journalist, Michael followed in his father's footsteps and became an agent himself. In 1974, at the age of thirty, he joined the commissioning staff of LWT, holders of the London weekend commercial-television franchise, and in less than three years rose to become the station's programme controller, a position he held for a further four years. Ironically, in 1980, Grade was a prime mover in the development of ITV's first fully networked Saturday night schedule; a line-up that, with the merciless deployment of the flashy American import *Buck Rogers in the 25th Century*, had cut *Doctor Who*'s ratings in half for Tom Baker's final year and forced the wounded series to become a midweek movable feast from its following season (see Chapter S).

In 1981, Grade left Britain for Hollywood. After a brief stint with Embassy Television, with a reported annual salary of nearly $1 million, he set up his own Los Angeles-based production company, whose chief output during this period was an expensive mini-series version of Jeffrey Archer's novel of feuding family empires, *Kane and Abel*.

In 1984, Grade found himself courted by the BBC for the post of Controller of BBC1 by none other than the Corporation's new Managing Director of Television, Bill Cotton – son of the chipper band leader managed by Michael's late father, and a long-time friend of the Grade family.

Grade was initially reticent. He wanted to move back to the UK, but the BBC job offered a salary of £50,000 – a pittance after the £250,000 his own production company had been bringing in, and pocket money compared with the six-figure pay packet from Embassy that Grade had once referred to as 'a living wage'.

To sweeten the pill, Cotton offered the young mogul a generous budget for new programming, and a remit to develop and schedule material on the principal channel as he saw fit – almost completely free of interference from the BBC's upper management or Governors. With these pledges, Grade accepted the post without further hesitation and was quickly installed on the sixth floor of BBC Television Centre.

Grade's bred-in-the-bone showbiz pizzazz swiftly invigorated the bruised Corporation. In his trademark red braces and matching socks, a massive cigar never far from his hand, Grade exuded confidence and charm; dominating planning meetings as he briskly engineered change after change to BBC1's moribund schedule.

Right: Colin Baker as the Doctor in 1985, just before the Time Lord was forced to take a year out...

Far right: In 1986, *Doctor Who*'s fourteen new episodes told of his second trial before a court of his own people. His prosecutor was the evil Valeyard (Michael Jayston)

Nothing was sacred in this long-term drive for ratings, audience appreciation and the £65 licence fee. In his first three months in the job, Grade fought for and won the right to move the flagship current-affairs series *Panorama* out of prime time and into a new slot after the *Nine O'Clock News*. He cleared the decks for the launch of *EastEnders* – the muscular new soap opera the BBC had had in development for three years. Flagging old warhorses such as *Crackerjack*, *Come Dancing* and *The Good Old Days* were put out to pasture. The whole BBC1 schedule was stripped down and rebuilt from scratch.

It was in this spirit that, in early February 1985, the planned winter 1985–6 series of *Doctor Who* was cancelled – seemingly without a second thought. 'We make a million of these decisions every day of the week,' Grade was to say later.

Typically, it was full-time fans of *Doctor Who* – with friends in high places at the Beeb – who were the first to hear about the cancellation. When Ian Levine, then friend and unofficial fan adviser to the production team, phoned John Nathan-Turner on Thursday 14 February to tell him the news, the producer refused to believe it, insisting that if it were true, he would have been informed first. It wasn't until after Nathan-Turner returned from a weekend trip to an American *Doctor Who* convention the following Monday that he was summoned to the office of Jonathan Powell, Head of Series and Serials, to be told the news. Powell assured Nathan-Turner that the series was not to be cancelled outright, merely shifted into the next financial year to allow BBC1 time to balance the books in preparation for the launch of daytime television.

The news reached the pages of the London *Evening Standard* the next day, presumably via Levine, who was quoted in the coverage, and then found its way to the front pages of the *Sun*, the *Daily Express*, the *Daily Telegraph* and the *Guardian* by Thursday; the *Sun*'s headline from reporter Charles Catchpole bellowing 'Dr Who is Axed in a BBC Plot'. Unluckily for the BBC, 28 February was rather a thin day for news, and the papers made use of the chance to take another swipe at the Corporation. Just a day later, the story would have been nowhere near the front pages, justifiably eclipsed by news of the death of nine men in an IRA mortar attack on Newry police station and the collapse of the eleven-month-long coal miners' strike.

Nathan-Turner was to confess later: 'I helped Levine to contact sympathetic Fleet Street luminaries and I explained how he might retain anonymity throughout the whole affair, should he wish. I certainly wanted to. For once in my career I wouldn't even talk to my mates on the London papers, lest I say something on the record that I might regret.'

Levine led a group of fans who were convinced that the announcement of the cancellation of one season indicated that Grade and fellow BBC mandarins were actually plotting to do away with *Doctor Who* for good. Although quite what they believed Grade's logic to be in taking such a step-by-step approach remains unclear, it is suggestive of the high level of reactionary paranoia washing around the *Doctor Who* fan network at this time. This fear made Levine a willing accomplice in Nathan-Turner's arm's-length inveigling of Fleet Street. The details as later recounted by Levine verge on the surreal: '[Nathan-Turner] told me there were codenames within the BBC that Charles Catchpole at the *Sun* would know, so I phoned him and said that I worked under Michael Grade and that my name was Snowball. I said that there was a plot to get rid of *Doctor Who*. While I was talking John and Gary [Downie, a close friend and colleague of Nathan-Turner's] were busy scribbling away telling me what to say... Then we did the same thing with Geoff Baker at the *Daily Star*.'

All primary evidence clearly indicates that the long-term future of *Doctor Who* was under no real threat at that time, and even though Nathan-Turner didn't subscribe to Levine's conspiracy theories, he certainly hoped that the BBC would be forced by a large-scale public outcry to return the series to production sooner rather than later. Tragically, however, although they did indeed provoke an immediate reaction at the highest levels of the BBC, with hindsight it seems that 'Snowball' and friends ultimately did more harm than good.

Facing the music...
Top: Recording with Who Cares: (back) actress Faith Brown and Colin Baker; (front) John Rocca from Freeez, *Man About The House* actress Sally Thomsett and singer Miguel Brown
Bottom: The sleeve for their remarkable record

Main picture: Doctor in the dock; the Time Lord justifies his return to TV in 1986 to The Inquisitor (Lynda Bellingham) and The Valeyard

In his 1988 autobiography, Alasdair Milne – the BBC's Director-General at the time of this fuss – recalled that there was a series of incidents at the time that 'gravely disturbed' the working relationship between the Board of Governors and the BBC management: 'Some were trivial, others less so. Together they began to look like a case law of management failure.' From the details given, it is clear that Milne considers the *Doctor Who* business to be one of those 'trivial' matters, but he went on to say, 'Grade decided *Doctor Who* needed a rest to allow for a rethink and refurbishment… and provoked a furious response from the series' fans, of whom there are a great many the world over. The Governors found themselves under attack for something of which they had no advance warning.'

This was the turning point. It is important to note that the BBC Board of Governors is a politically appointed body broadly charged with the protection of the public interest that only very, very rarely interferes in detailed matters of programming and scheduling – this being entirely the remit of the full-time management. But these were sensitive times, and the Governors, in the middle of a serious political and public-relations war, were unprepared for this latest damaging tabloid uproar. As Milne makes clear, the Governors expressed no concern with Grade's actual decision to freeze *Doctor Who*, merely with the fact that they hadn't been properly briefed.

To calm the Board, Bill Cotton pledged to contact the co-ordinator of the Doctor Who Appreciation Society and set his mind at rest regarding the series' long-term future, hoping that this would soothe the troubled fans and dissuade them from causing any further unnecessary fuss. And so, on the afternoon of 1 March, the Managing Director of one of the world's largest and most powerful broadcasting companies telephoned a north London librarian by the name of David Saunders to assure him *personally* that his favourite TV programme would be back soon – a bizarrely extreme over-reaction.

Alas, it seemed the Doctor Who Appreciation Society was not appeased by the personal touch. Saunders continued his attack on the BBC on Radio 4's *Start the Week* programme a few days later,

before hand-delivering a letter to Cotton's office demanding further assurances and clarification. As Cotton had already personally pledged that *Doctor Who* would still be on TV in 1986 – as it had been in 1985 and for twenty-two years previously – it's difficult to imagine what else the DWAS hoped to hear.

Over the following weeks Michael Grade and colleagues received a stream of hate mail, ranging in tone from the vitriolic to the downright deranged – including at least one letter apparently written in human blood. Ian Levine co-composed a protest song, 'Doctor in Distress', with a lyric that repeatedly complained that 'Eighteen months is too long to wait' like some bored and petulant child. The single used the same mass-chorus format of the Band Aid hit 'Do They Know It's Christmas?' – as if the two causes had equal merit – but rather than employing a host of A-list pop stars, Levine and friends drafted performers such as Bobby G from Bucks Fizz, one of the cast from the musical *Starlight Express* and the group Time UK, who had scored a blistering number 63 in the charts in the previous October. With around twenty others, this unlikely team recorded under the laughably double-edged name of Who Cares?, and the single they spawned sank without a trace.

In September 1986, the twenty-third series of *Doctor Who* premiered on BBC1 – as had always been promised – but by this point serious damage had been done. Although most were well meaning, an aggressive subset of *Doctor Who* fans had managed to label their entire ilk as an at best ungrateful, at worst borderline psychotic group who did not deserve any kind of favourable treatment. In the years to come, they would be sought out by the press only to criticise the series, something which many did all too willingly. Michael Grade, forced repeatedly to defend and justify his decision to rest the programme, began publicly to criticise its standards and content – suggesting that the cancellation was as much for artistic as financial reasons.

All in all, it added up to a terrible battering – one from which *Doctor Who* would never quite recover…

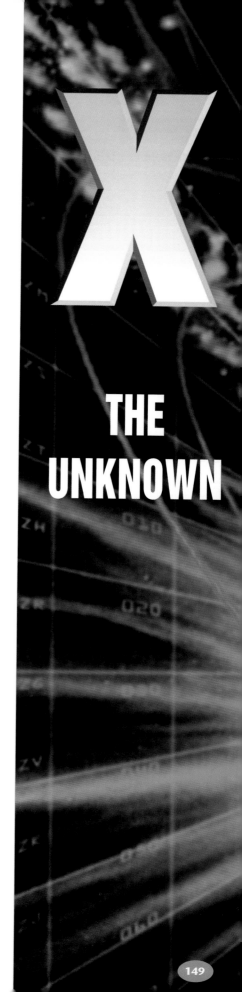

The Doctor was once an enigmatic man of mystery, his origins and history the stuff of speculation. Then, it turned out, he was a rebellious alien cut loose from his Time Lord race. In the late 1980s, a new guiding creative force on the series began to wonder if we'd been told the full story...

In late 1987, *Doctor Who* script editor Andrew Cartmel had finished work on that year's run of fourteen episodes and his thoughts began to turn to the next. He had a still-fresh Doctor – largely untested – a brand-new companion, Ace, and *carte blanche* from his producer to select his own team of enthusiastic, open-minded young writers. Cartmel decided that the time was right to begin to sketch out a whole new format for *Doctor Who*, and to introduce a range of changes in style and approach that would, perhaps, stand the series in good stead for its next twenty-five years.

While looking forward, Cartmel also looked back. A letter from a *Doctor Who* fan told him that, whatever else he did, he must take time to watch the Tom Baker serials *The Seeds of Doom* and *The Talons of Weng-Chiang* and Peter Davison's *The Caves of Androzani*. Discussing this later, Cartmel would comment, '*The Talons of Weng-Chiang* blew me away. It soon became obvious to me that Robert Holmes was a special writer. The story shows how good Holmes was and really gives you a good grasp of what the Doctor is capable of. I probably would have seen the story eventually, but it was better to see it sooner rather than later... I began to formulate the Doctor in a better way, or at least in a more interesting way.'

Cartmel looked back even further into *Doctor Who* history, trying to see past the clutter of continuity the series had built up around itself – the sticky shell of trivia that had made the programme such an unwieldy and unwelcoming beast during the mid-1980s – and into its heart, looking to identify its fundamental purpose and drive, its very *raison d'être*.

This intellectual 'strip-down' of the series showed that there were few sacred cows for Cartmel. None of the trappings mattered. The TARDIS could be seen as no more than an insignificant device to deliver the Doctor to the scene of his next adventure, remaining happily out of frame thereafter. New monsters and menaces created by his own team of writers were bound to be more interesting to viewers than dragging some long-forgotten foe back from the dead. (Not long-forgotten by the fans, of course – they loyally tended the graves of B-list baddies, often pestering for a resurrection.) Even the character of the Doctor could change – *must* change, thought Cartmel – if the series was to seem fresh and relevant for a new generation of viewers.

Taking this reductionist philosophy to the limits, Cartmel found himself left with little more than the series' title as a given. 'Doctor Who,' he would later say, 'Doctor *who*? That's the key question. He should be an enigma – mysterious, powerful and scary.' Cartmel believed that the sense of mystery that had surrounded and shrouded the Doctor when the series launched back in 1963 was central to what had captivated and excited viewers of the programme. It was a trick that had worked before, and there seemed to be no good reason why it shouldn't work again.

But the world in which Cartmel had to work was very different from that of the series' first story editor, David Whitaker. To create *his* enigma, Whitaker merely had to leave a space in his central character, to sketch him lightly, to avoid offering details of background or personal history. It was a passive process where the mystery of the Doctor would simply expand to fill the space available to it, like a gas. Whitaker, literally, had to do nothing.

Silliness in 1987...
Top: The Doctor (Sylvester McCoy), seconds away from another prat-fall, fends off a foe in *Time and the Rani*
Above: A comic confrontation with Richard Briers's Chief Caretaker in *Paradise Towers*

Main: 'A literal cliffhanger', we think, 'how hilarious!' *Dragonfire*

For Cartmel, on the other hand, creating a sense of mystery had to be an active process. A large volume of information regarding the Doctor had been made available since the veil over the character first began to lift in 1969. By 1987, an attentive viewer might recall a vast amount of trivia about the once impenetrable world of the Doctor. He was now known to be a Time Lord of Gallifrey – a member of the Prydonian Chapter no less. He had teachers called Borusa and Azmael and was friends with a hermit who lived up a mountain behind his house who told ghost stories about vampires. He studied at assorted academies with such nefarious classmates as the Master and the Rani, and was given the hilarious nickname Theta Sigma. He scraped through his courses on the second attempt with 51 per cent, less than Romana, and with a lower grade in Cosmic Science than the Master.

In short, most of the Doctor's CV had already been revealed, and if Cartmel really wanted to re-pose the question 'Doctor who?' there was an awful lot of background information he was going to have to ignore, contradict or sidestep.

This left the script editor in a tricky situation. Given the ferocity with which many fans of *Doctor Who* protected and fought for their continuity, Cartmel knew it would be a brave man who took it upon himself to 'reboot' the series from scratch, wiping away every revelation that had gone before. However, he was also certain that a more mysterious and enigmatic Doctor would give an interesting twist to what had become a rather predictable formula. It was clear, therefore, that he had to find a middle way – he had to add in an unknown and unpredictable element to the mix that would engage the floating viewer but not alienate the loyal devotee.

Cartmel's answer was to accept all of the established mythology. The Doctor *was* a Time Lord and he *did* come from the planet Gallifrey. The secret of time travel *had* been discovered by ancient Time Lords Rassilon and Omega. These 'facts' – bolted to the core of *Doctor Who*'s holy writ – remained inalienable. Cartmel's approach was to suggest that behind these truths there was another, bigger truth – to hint that, thus far, only a small part of the picture had been glimpsed.

However, whereas all David Whitaker had had to do to keep the Doctor seeming enigmatic and alien was maintain a dignified silence and steer his central character away from any questions regarding his background, Cartmel had to be more heavy-handed and interventionist. With everything short of the Doctor's inside leg measurement now a matter of public record, any new

'mystery' had to be clearly signposted in the dialogue. But it would be impossibly arrogant for the Doctor himself to suddenly start suggesting that he was anything other than a Time Lord with a poor degree and a charming smile. Anyone who says, 'Oooh, I've got a secret but I'm not telling you what it is,' looks like they are actually begging to be asked about it. It's not 'mysterious', just plain irritating. What Cartmel needed to do was either to have the Doctor let slip hints accidentally or to introduce characters who knew some of his secrets and could threaten to expose them.

But there were broader changes required before all this could begin. The Seventh Doctor as played by Sylvester McCoy during his first year in the role did not seem to be the sort of man likely to be troubled by a mysterious past or guided by a hidden agenda; he was too busy dancing at 1950s discos or searching for somewhere for Mel to go swimming. Inspired by the work of Robert Holmes, Cartmel realised that the Doctor could be a much bigger, less human and less predictable character, a man on a noble voyage of discovery into unknown lands and shadowy places rather than simply an excitable tourist on a cheap package tour around the universe.

The first year of the Seventh Doctor had served up a likeable if insubstantial Time Lord, but Cartmel knew that viewers gauged the scale of any threat within a *Doctor Who* story by the nature of the Doctor's reaction to it. If a danger or dilemma was addressed by the Doctor in a trivial way, it would be seen as a trivial threat, whereas if the Doctor was more serious, he must be caught up in a serious business. Better still, if the Doctor's feelings and attitude were left ambiguous, viewers would be kept truly on their toes. What the Doctor needed, therefore, was a dark half – a new mode of behaviour that would call his moral position and personal agenda into question until the final reel of each story. Cartmel was later to observe, 'If you have the Doctor wandering around, manipulating everything, being responsible in a shadowy kind of fashion, it's a great plot device... he's playing this chess game, which makes him an interesting character, quite potent, dark and powerful.'

This new approach was put into action from the beginning of McCoy's second year as the Doctor, and is key to the tone of the first of these new serials, 1988's *Remembrance of the Daleks*. The actor's volume of dialogue was effectively cut in half as his character, rather than gabbling trivia and racing to explain what was afoot, was left to brood in silence as the supporting characters discussed the plot. There was rarely any doubt that the Doctor didn't know precisely what was happening, or about to happen, almost all of the time. His replies to direct questions would be enigmatic and unhelpful, and he would quietly slip away on his own private missions. A beneficial side effect of this was that his companion became a much more empowered character. Ace was a girl frequently forced to take matters into her own hands, taking the initiative in situations when the Doctor steadfastly refused to outline his own agenda. If he wasn't prepared to respond to her questions, she had to go out and find the answers for herself. This would make Ace one of the most interesting and important companions the series had offered since Ian and Barbara first tumbled into the TARDIS twenty-five years earlier.

DOCTOR WHO – INTERGALACTIC MAN OF MYSTERY?

For a once mysterious and aloof alien, we now know an awful lot about the Doctor. Here are some useful facts gleaned from TV episodes...

○ He comes from the planet Gallifrey in the constellation of Kasterborous. Gallifrey is in the same galaxy as Earth, and is either twenty-nine thousand or 250 million light years away (the latter about 10 minutes by TARDIS).

○ He was born under the sign of 'Crossed Computers', and his mother was human. We do not know for sure if the Doctor's father was Gallifreyan, but we can assume this from his physiognomy (body temperature of sixty degrees, a pulse rate of ten-a-minute, two hearts, respiratory bypass system, some telepathic powers, the ability to regenerate his body – but he has a human retina).

○ In his education, the Doctor learnt the dead language Old High Gallifreyan, but his speciality was in thermodynamics. He scraped through one of his academies with 51% on the second attempt, and the Master got a higher grade in Cosmic Science than him. But then, the Doctor was always a late developer.

○ He became a pioneer among his people, campaigned for the banning of Miniscopes and went on diplomatic missions for the Time Lords. At some point he found time to have a family, and eventually a granddaughter, Susan.

○ The Doctor eventually fled Gallifrey because he was bored, or possibly exiled, and stole a Type 40, Mark One TARDIS, taking Susan with him.

Left: A more sombre and troubled Seventh Doctor dictated much of the 1988 and 1989 series, here seen pondering the fate of his companion in *The Happiness Patrol* (1988)

Top: Mrs Pritchard (Sylvia Syms) and her maids in 1989's atmospheric *Ghost Light*. The serial gives clues as to how Andrew Cartmel's and writer Marc Platt's version of Gallifrey would have been presented
Above: By contrast, Cartmel's first year had seen such light-hearted serials as *Delta and the Bannermen*, with guest star Ken Dodd

Main: In 1989's *Survival*, the Master (Anthony Ainley) was to challenge the Doctor's identity as a genuine Time Lord. Unfortunately, key scenes were dropped at a late stage

With a Doctor more likely to lurk in the background nursing secret plots and schemes than run around discussing his schooldays on Gallifery with anyone who could stand to listen, Cartmel had an ideal base from which to build what would later be referred to by fans, rather grandly, as his 'master plan' – his scheme to suggest that all we had come to know about the character might be only a simplified version of a more mysterious truth. This sometimes disingenuous new Doctor was someone we could really believe had a secret past; all Cartmel needed to do was drop a few clues. The first can be found as early as the third episode of that opening Dalek serial.

The Doctor has been browbeaten by Ace into filling in a little of the background to the conflict raging around them. The Daleks, says the Doctor, are on Earth searching for the Hand of Omega, a powerful Time Lord device that had been key to Rassilon and Omega's mastery of time, way back in Gallifreyan history. 'And didn't we have trouble with the prototype...' he adds. 'We?' queries Ace. 'I mean "they",' corrects the Doctor with a worried sideways look.

Very much a hint to the fan cognoscenti – who knew that the Doctor was supposed to come from a time long after that of the fabled Rassilon – Ben Aaronovitch's script also needed to label this new theme more clearly for the less well informed. In his final confrontation with Davros, the Doctor would respond to the mad scientist's description of the Time Lords as 'impotent' with the revelation, 'Oh, Davros, I'm far more than just another Time Lord' – which is about as bold a challenge to the established order of things as one could get. Unfortunately, this section of dialogue was cut from the finished episode, seemingly for timing reasons, so the slow, early build of this plot strand was lost, leaving another story later that year to, effectively out of the blue, bang the audience over the head with it.

Silver Nemesis was planned from the outset to celebrate the series' twenty-fifth anniversary and to end the year's batch of four stories on an enigmatic final note (which it failed to do after later being shifted up to run in third position). The storyline was a messy affair, with Cybermen, an Elizabethan sorceress, a group of latter-day Nazis and the Doctor all scrabbling for control of yet another powerful Gallifreyan artefact from Rassilon's time – in this case, a sentient metal called Validium.

The rather deranged sorceress, Lady Peinforte, seems to know a great deal about the Doctor's history and frequently rattles on about his 'secrets', happily without actually ever getting round to saying what they might be. It all comes to a head in her brutally unsubtle and inadvertently

hilarious final scene in which she spends a great deal of time threatening to reveal everything. 'I know your secrets,' she reiterates. 'I shall tell them of Gallifrey. Tell them of the Old Time. The Time of Chaos…' Luckily, *Doctor Who*'s new ongoing mystery is protected when Peinforte finally goes completely bonkers and charges off to her inevitable, if largely incomprehensible, doom. At the end of the serial, Ace challenges the Doctor on this matter, asking simply, 'Who are you?' The Doctor puts a finger to his lips, leaving the question unanswered.

And that, largely, was it for the voyage round this new riddle-ridden past of Cartmel's dark Doctor. A later story called *Lungbarrow* from new writer Marc Platt planned to take the Doctor back to his Gormenghast-like family home on Gallifrey but was abandoned at an early stage. *Survival*, the final serial to be broadcast before *Doctor Who* ceased regular production in 1989, was to have seen the Master challenging the Doctor's identity as a Time Lord – the Doctor replying that he had simply 'evolved' – but the scene was again lost before it could reach the screen.

Whether Cartmel ever really had a concrete 'master plan' is doubtful. Kevin Clarke, the writer of *Silver Nemesis*, was convinced that the Doctor was really God – a rather sweeping and even blasphemous interpretation of the character that Cartmel for one didn't support. The script editor had certainly brainstormed ideas with writers Ben Aaronovitch, Ian Briggs and Marc Platt, but whether any of their conclusions were ever laid out as 'gospel' is questionable. Certainly, given that Cartmel was preparing to move on from the series had it continued after *Survival*, it is likely that his successor would have had his or her own agenda.

The most beneficial side effect of this 'stirring up' of accepted wisdom by Cartmel took a few years to show itself. In 1991, Virgin Books launched a series of 'New Adventure' novels, designed to recount the Doctor's exploits from where BBC Television left off. This range became the true inheritor of Cartmel's legacy, his complex Doctor and gutsy Ace standing as perfect characters to drive Virgin's more adult storylines. It is difficult to imagine what approach such a range would have been able to take if *Doctor Who* had been cancelled at the end of McCoy's frivolous first year, rather than his thoughtful third. It was also for Virgin that a master plan of sorts was finally committed to paper by Aaronovitch, Platt and Cartmel – forming a writers' guide to the books' slowly unfolding investigation of the Doctor's (and his people's) secret history. In 1996, a book version of Platt's *Lungbarrow* finally saw the light of day, and suggested that the Doctor was possibly some complex form of reincarnation of an unnamed contemporary of Rassilon. It was a neat, fan-pleasing idea, but there is little to suggest that the TV series itself would ever have reached such a revelation.

It's a tragedy that Cartmel wasn't offered the chance to work on *Doctor Who* for just one more year. His drive and commitment refuelled the series in way that only the best of his predecessors had done. He was willing to challenge preconceptions about the programme and to look for new ideas, new methods of storytelling, a new idiom, for the more sophisticated young audience of the 1990s. And as the series' ratings began to rally in that final year, there is evidence that he had begun to achieve his ambition.

However, it wasn't enough to stop the axe from finally falling, and only dreams of what might have been would survive.

During its long run on BBC television, millions of children watched and enjoyed *Doctor Who*. Most would find themselves called away by other interests as they reached their teens, but others would remain devoted to the series for the rest of their lives. How did *Doctor Who* maintain such a strong hold over this loyal minority? And why were so few of them girls?

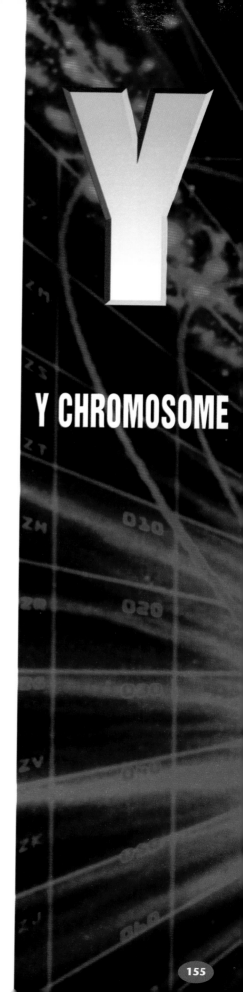

Y CHROMOSOME

'Although I never got to see it in the early days, I know it's not as good as it used to be – but I'm still terribly interested!'

The character of Whizzkid in 1988's *The Greatest Show in the Galaxy* was obviously intended by the story's writer to be a send-up of the most hardcore type of full-time *Doctor Who* fan. It is an interesting insight into how such individuals were viewed by the series' production team at the time. Commenting on the character later, script editor Andrew Cartmel would say, 'We did the rather cruel thing of destroying a young fan. There was a lot of laughter on the set when we finally executed that one, I can tell you! Well justified!'

By 1988, the relationship between the fans of *Doctor Who* and its makers had turned sour. Having accepted years of highly outspoken and often personal abuse from 'enthusiasts' in the pages of fanzines and, later, the national press, the production team apparently decided – not to put too fine a point on it – to stick up two fingers back at their critics, and the tedious, tank-topped, whining Whizzkid was the result: an unfashionable, bespectacled boy who had been a fan of a certain 'Psychic Circus' his whole life. He could reel off trivia regarding the show's long history, happily criticise the current management to their faces without a shred of embarrassment and, most tellingly of all, casually dismiss their work as not being nearly as exciting as earlier performances he had only read about.

But how much of this parody is rooted in truth? Is it a stereotype that *Doctor Who* fans would recognise, or would they dismiss it out of hand – claiming perhaps that Whizzkid was just *too* pathetic, more like a trainspotter or *Star Trek* fan than the laid-back, lager-swilling crowd they hung out with at *Doctor Who* conventions.

We all have our own obsessions – those very personal blind spots that help to define who we are – but we remain remarkably intolerant of other people's. A sombre *Star Trek* fan may see little of interest in the light-hearted antics of the Doctor, while a 'Whovian' may point and giggle at a 'Trekker' dressed up as a Klingon. Every obsessive instinctively knocks other people's other seemingly more trivial pursuits as a way of validating their own – even though, of course, they have much more in common than each would ever want to admit.

But what turns an ordinary consumer into a fan? What distinguishes the man who goes to see Tottenham Hotspur play at home every other Saturday from the one who can tell you the name of every member of their FA Cup/League double-winning team from 1961? What turns a youngster who enjoys travelling by train into a man who seeks to tick off every bogie number currently in use in the UK? How did the boy who ran home from the park every Saturday to watch *Doctor Who* grow up into the man who can recite more than 150 story titles in order of broadcast?

You'll notice that the word 'man' is employed throughout the previous paragraph. This is not to suggest that there are no female football enthusiasts, trainspotters or *Doctor Who* fans, but merely an admission of the fact that such areas are primarily the domain of the male. Exactly *why* such obsessive trivia-collecting behaviour is generally a masculine trait is difficult to say. As Nick Hornby has charted so well, males certainly have a greater inclination towards the anal-retentive, mildly autistic traits that underpin the collating and analysing of the endlessly spurious. Whether this hunger for fixture lists and episode guides is coded on to the male Y chromosome at conception is doubtful, as many men seem to live their lives quite happily without feeling the need to compare different pressings of Beatles LPs or discuss whether Daleks should have three discs on their eyestalks instead of five. No, it is more likely that such behaviour is a side effect of nurture rather than nature – men feeling safer with their cheery lists, fanzines and neatly labelled video collections (all in broadcast order, of course) than with anything that might require an expression of real personal feeling or a degree of empathy. Of course, there is such a thing as the anal-retentive woman, but she is vastly outnumbered by her masculine counterpart. And women can naturally also be obsessive, but – and here's another generalisation – they are more likely to be obsessive about people and relationships than about 'things'.

It is a fact that women comprise only a tiny minority of the *Doctor Who* fan base. A detailed market study commissioned by Marvel Comics' *Doctor Who Magazine* in 1996 revealed that less than 4 per cent of the title's readership was female. It is reasonable, then, to assume that sales of *Doctor Who* videos and books follow the same pattern. Although as children girls may have watched and enjoyed the programme, it is rare for their enthusiasm to survive beyond adolescence.

It is easy to see why *Doctor Who* may have limited appeal to women. Broadly speaking, its stories offer little in the way of realistic emotional interaction and are more clearly driven by plot and way-out ideas than by character or expressed feelings – and as the composition of soap-opera audiences demonstrates, it is emotional issues that interest women. Further, there are precious few strong, self-possessed female characters in *Doctor Who*, the vast majority of the Doctor's companions being – despite the often expressed good intentions of the series' many production teams – little more than insubstantial ciphers overshadowed by the Doctor's outsized personality. Conversely, America's *Star Trek: The Next Generation* – a series that might be placed in the same category of TV programme as *Doctor Who* by the viewing public – offers not only more emotional, 'soap-opera' types of storyline but also more confident female characters and so has, unsurprisingly, a much larger female following. So although it would not be right to say that science fiction *per se* fails to appeal to women, it is true that *Doctor Who*'s special brand of whimsical fantasy doesn't.

This lack of resonance for the female viewer probably has something to do with the fact that only a handful of women ever worked on the series in key creative positions. There has been only one female producer (Verity Lambert), only three female directors (Paddy Russell, Julia Smith and Fiona Cumming) and no female script editors at all. Only two serials in twenty-six years were solely written by women, 1983's *Enlightenment* (by Barbara Clegg) and 1989's *Survival* (by Rona Munro), both of which – surely no coincidence – offer more sophisticated and emotionally complex material than normal for the

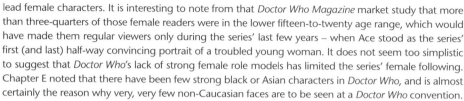

lead female characters. It is interesting to note from that *Doctor Who Magazine* market study that more than three-quarters of those female readers were in the lower fifteen-to-twenty age range, which would have made them regular viewers only during the series' last few years – when Ace stood as the series' first (and last) half-way convincing portrait of a troubled young woman. It does not seem too simplistic to suggest that *Doctor Who*'s lack of strong female role models has limited the series' female following. Chapter E noted that there have been few strong black or Asian characters in *Doctor Who*, and is almost certainly the reason why very, very few non-Caucasian faces are to be seen at a *Doctor Who* convention.

It is fair to say, then, that *Doctor Who* was a TV series written by men for the entertainment of boys. But we are still no closer to understanding what turns that boy into a 'fan': what it is that drives him to make lists, buy books, write stories or haggle over otherwise long-forgotten points of continuity; that makes him, maybe thirty years or more after watching his first *Doctor Who* serial at a parent's knee, re-watch those same episodes on video any number of times.

For each year that *Doctor Who* was on air, the series captivated a new, loyal young audience with its homely and 'safe' adventures. At the same time, it would lose another, older, batch of viewers to the more complex and unpredictable thrills of adolescence. While *Doctor Who* was always followed by an audience that included toddlers, teens, adults and OAPs, its most responsive viewers were between the ages of eight and eleven – effectively, those old enough to follow a twisting plot but young enough to ensure that often low-budget effects and sometime shaky performances did not fall victim to withering teenage criticism. This is the age at which fans are formed.

Of course, not every ten-year-old who ever watched *Doctor Who* went on to become a dedicated fan. The vast majority left it behind in much the same way they abandoned the reading of fairy tales or playing hide-and-seek, finding it hard to see that it could offer them anything in their adult lives. But those who became card-carrying adult *Doctor Who* fans will swear that their lives have been enriched by their enduring enthusiasm for the series. So how did it all start?

Initially, the programme's action and eye-catching monsters will have been the series' most important draw – that clichéd but no less genuine 'behind the sofa' factor. This was then coupled with a willingness on the part of these youngest of viewers, if not to actually *believe* that what they were watching was real, to at least trust that the storyline unfolding before them was a matter of great seriousness and very much worthy of their attention.

With age, this ability to entirely immerse oneself in fiction falls away. This occurs at perhaps the same time a child stops thinking that slavering monsters are lurking under the bed, but instead begins to fear that a mad axe-murderer is hiding in the wardrobe. Fantasies and fears at maybe eleven or twelve – or younger if you are particularly unlucky – become grounded, however loosely, in reality. Playground games that may turn the school dustbins into a TARDIS and the teachers into Voord, Zygons or Haemovores can no longer hold any appeal as children come to understand their place in the world. This self-consciousness, coupled with a need to appear mature in front of peers, will force children, maybe initially against their will, to put away childish things or, at the very least, hide them from view.

Y

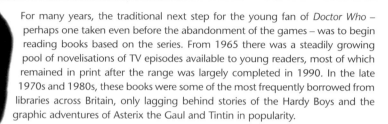

For many years, the traditional next step for the young fan of *Doctor Who* – perhaps one taken even before the abandonment of the games – was to begin reading books based on the series. From 1965 there was a steadily growing pool of novelisations of TV episodes available to young readers, most of which remained in print after the range was largely completed in 1990. In the late 1970s and 1980s, these books were some of the most frequently borrowed from libraries across Britain, only lagging behind stories of the Hardy Boys and the graphic adventures of Asterix the Gaul and Tintin in popularity.

Those boys who were eight during the height of 'Dalekmania' in late 1964, and loyally followed the series afterwards, celebrated their twenty-first birthdays in 1976 and 1977. It is no coincidence that 1976 saw the formation of the Doctor Who Appreciation Society (DWAS), and, the following year, the organisation of the world's first ever *Doctor Who* convention.

At this point *Doctor Who* fans created, literally, a society and culture of their own. Coming-of-age followers of the series who had already exhausted all the professionally published material on the subject now had access to a wealth of fan writing and opinion, and were in turn encouraged to put their own thoughts on paper. *Doctor Who* appreciation could make the leap from being a largely solo activity – reading books out of the sight of more 'mature' friends – to one defined by its new community of conventions, magazines and local clubs. This is a network of friends, acquaintances and social activity that exists to this day, but now with a core membership who were not even born at the time of DWAS's inception. Once it is possible to observe *Doctor Who* fans in groups, to take an overview of the thoughts and opinions published in the countless fanzines of the last twenty or so years, one key behavioural characteristic emerges.

At the core of the collective *Doctor Who* fan experience is something of a minor human tragedy. Although the nature of their response to *Doctor Who* changes as fans grow older, with innocent wonder giving way to detailed inspection and analysis, it is generally true that their taste in *Doctor Who* – their judgement regarding what makes a 'good' episode – is coloured by an often unrecognised drive to recapture the feeling the series gave them when they were that awestruck, accepting eight-year-old. The tragedy comes from the fact that this, of course, is something that they can never again achieve. This problem manifested itself primarily in the form of a bitter culture

of criticism that soured much of late 1970s and 1980s fan writing. Those who had grown up alongside the series would fill pages with attacks on any perceived 'childishness' in the series, bemoaning, for example, that the blobby monster Erato from 1979's *The Creature from the Pit* or the stomping Myrka from 1984's *Warriors of the Deep* was less convincing or worthy than the fantasy creatures the series had conjured ten years before. Of course, from a more objective viewpoint, there is little difference in 'quality' between a *Doctor Who* monster from the 1960s and one from the 1980s. No one can *really* argue that the fun-fur Cheetah People from *Survival* in 1989 are any more or less realistic than the vulcanised Voord from 1964's *The Keys of Marinus*.

As fans grow into adulthood, they find it difficult to be objective about the TV programme that has been part of their lives for so long. If it can be said that *Doctor Who* had two great phases of mass popular appeal – one around 1965 and the other around 1976 – the disproportionate number of die-hard fans created out of the ten-year-olds of those times would be the ones who, as young adults, battered the series through its most poorly received phases within fandom in the late 1970s and mid-1980s respectively. They could not see that *they* were the ones who had changed, not the series.

Fans have always sought to categorise and classify, to neatly label eras of *Doctor Who* as 'golden ages' or 'all-time lows'. But it can never be as simple as that. One generation's disaster was always the next's fan epiphany. In 1987, for example, while reviewing the first Sylvester McCoy serial for the *Daily Mail*, the co-ordinator of the Appreciation Society, Andrew Beech, used the occasion to lambast the show's production team for over half a decade of what he considered to be flawed decisions – even calling for them to be replaced. In the midst of this blistering attack, the '28-year-old solicitor' paused to observe that he had to represent 'a society divided', commenting, 'There are those (usually the under-20s) who enjoy the bright colours, the starry cast and the glitzy "production values"… But others believe that there is something radically wrong with a show that 24 years ago had something indefinable.'

It is revealing as a measure of a fan's lack of objectivity that the main change Beech noted in *Doctor Who* was an absence of 'something indefinable'. Perhaps this 'something' was nothing the show had in or of itself, but was instead an attitude brought to it only by open-minded, enthusiastic viewers. It was obviously still there for those 'under-20s', several of whom would later grow up to become co-ordinators of the DWAS themselves.

Happily, in more recent times, *Doctor Who*'s fan base has become more reasonable and accommodating. The series' extended leave from our TV screens has led to the evolution of a new, more laid-back kind of fan who can be a little more objective and see the strengths and weaknesses of the series as a whole. *Doctor Who* has even found fans purely through its availability on video, bringing in new followers who have taken a more individual, non-linear trip through the show's history – and see few of the 'trends' identified by their older brethren.

But back in 1988, perhaps Whizzkid *was* a fair and accurate depiction of a carping *Doctor Who* fan. Although he didn't know *why*, he was *so* certain that his favourite show wasn't as good as it used to be, he told everyone. If he hadn't been so cruelly murdered, maybe he would even have found the time to let the readers of the *Daily Mail* know how he felt.

The Peter Davison years divided opinions across *Doctor Who* 'fandom'…
Top: While the return of Nicholas Courtney in *Mawdryn Undead* (1983) was popular, the story is now best remembered by fans for its rewriting of 1970s continuity
Middle: Anthony Ainley's take on the Master was well-liked at first, but later suffered unfavourable comparison with Roger Delgado's version. *Planet of Fire* (1984)
Bottom: Many fans took time to warm to Davison, ironically judging him to have only hit his stride in time for his final serial, *The Caves of Androzani* (1984)

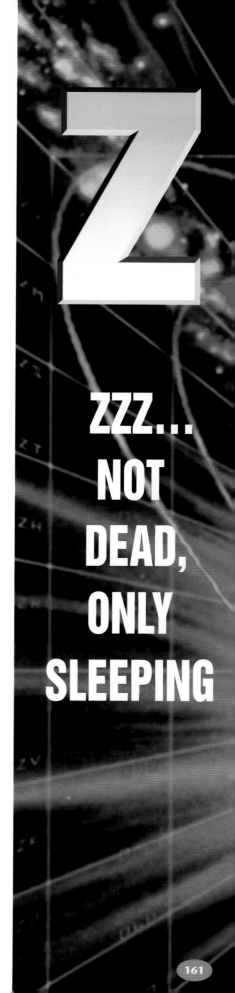

In 1989, *Doctor Who* vanished from television while the BBC looked for someone else to make it – or perhaps just somewhere to bury it. Then, a would-be saviour made an appearance, a driven man determined to bring life to a programme that seemed dead and forgotten. The Doctor, it seemed, needed only to emigrate...

'Where to now Ace?'
The girl looks up at the Doctor. 'Home,' she says wistfully.
'Home?'
'The TARDIS,' she affirms.
The Doctor smiles. 'Yes,' he says approvingly. 'The TARDIS.'
Ace stands and takes the Doctor's arm, they turn and walk off over the hillside towards 'home'.
'There are worlds out there,' proclaims the Doctor, 'where the sky is burning, and the sea's asleep and the rivers dream. People made of smoke and cities made of song. Somewhere there's danger, somewhere there's injustice, somewhere else the tea's getting cold. Come on, Ace – we've got work to do.'

In many ways, the end came unexpectedly. Although the axe had been hanging over *Doctor Who* since the 1985 crisis-of-confidence (see Chapter W) and the series hadn't achieved double-figure ratings in millions since 1982, Sylvester McCoy's Doctor seemed to have found a reasonably happy home at 7.35 p.m. on Monday or Wednesday evenings opposite *Coronation Street*. The two series were scarcely in competition with one another, the BBC providing what could be described as 'complementary programming' to the soap – the unquestioned king of the ratings. The production team had begun to find a faster, action-oriented storytelling style more suited to a new generation of viewers. McCoy was earning respect from fans and public alike as he settled into his role and Sophie Aldred's Ace was the most popular companion in years. *Doctor Who* had escaped from a mid-1980s rut and seemed fresher, cleverer and healthier than it had in some time. It was more than ready to approach a fourth decade on TV.

And then, at the end of 1989, *Doctor Who* was cancelled.

The members of the production team were only partly surprised. While plans for the next year's stories had begun to take shape, there was at least an element of doubt in the crew's minds that they may not be coming back. Script editor Andrew Cartmel wrote the dreamy if somewhat trite speech that opened this chapter, which Sylvester McCoy recorded some months after completing work on the season proper so it could be dubbed over the closing seconds of the final story of the year, *Survival* – the producer, aware that it might stand as the final serial ever, decided to strike an optimistic note at the end. Appropriately for *Doctor Who*, the speech offers undeliverable promises – people of smoke, cities of song – so, even at the end, the series was dreaming of the very strangest and bravest of new worlds.

It is not known when precisely the decision to kill the series was taken, nor the identity of the decision-maker. At a mid-season press launch during that final year, BBC Head of Serials Peter Cregeen seemed optimistic enough. '*Doctor Who* has lasted twenty-six years,' he said. 'I can't see any reason why it shouldn't continue. The BBC is committed to more *Doctor Who* in the future.' Otherwise, the BBC remained staunchly 'off the record' on the series at all times. Even if they had no desire to see *Doctor Who* back in production, they had even less desire to be called upon to justify that decision – the lessons of 1985 had been learned well. The first real inkling in the national press that the end had finally come – bar some exclamation-mark-ridden prophecies of doom based on reports of the Doctor's poor viewing figures compared to those of *Coronation Street* – came in tiny articles in the *Daily Mirror* and *Today* newspapers of 5 February 1990, reporting that BBC contract options on McCoy and Aldred had been withdrawn, their services no longer required.

'Cancellation' didn't seem the right word. From November 1989, Cregeen had suggested that the time had come for *Doctor Who* – like much of the BBC's output – to be turned over to an independent production company. 'There may be a little longer between this series and the next than usual,' he told *Radio Times*. This was to prove the greatest understatement in the show's history, but at the time the move towards external production seemed to be quite proper, positive and rather liberating.

In early 1990, Cregeen told a freelance journalist, 'We are looking for a format to keep *Doctor Who* on our screen for the next ten years. This could mean using an independent production company but as yet no formal tendering process has been instigated, although several interested parties have come forward with their own proposals.' Chief among these 'interested parties' was a consortium led by two former *Doctor Who* writers, Dalek creator Terry Nation and Cyberman co-creator Gerry Davis, and Cinema Verity, the successful film and TV production company headed by *Doctor Who*'s first producer, Verity Lambert. The Nation/Davis bid apparently came with the support of, variously, Disney, Columbia, the Turner Network and Fox TV (the last of these would come, by an entirely different route, to play a significant role in this saga some years down the line). With such high-profile interest, Cregeen must have had particular reasons for not initiating a formal tendering process, but the only one that appears to make sense is that he did not wish *Doctor Who* to be part of his department's portfolio no matter *who* made it – perhaps the series was 'tainted' by the perceived failures of its last few years. Gerry Davis was later quoted as saying he met with 'a wall of silence' from the BBC while attempting to find someone willing to discuss the future of the programme.

A number of ill-judged fan campaigns served only to make matters worse. A 'Day of Action' was supposed to jam the BBC switchboard on 20 November 1990 with '25,000 fans each making twenty phone calls each', and although the BBC actually took steps to prepare for this, the duty office log noted only 996 calls on the subject over two days. The following year, a small group of particularly outspoken fans formed a self-styled 'Doctor Who Action Committee' and announced their plan to sue the BBC for £30 million – the charge being 'blatant apathy and insensitivity in the face of strong demand from customers'. Naturally, this ludicrous scheme came to nothing and did little to persuade BBC management that any future production of *Doctor Who* would really be worth the trouble.

In the months that followed, statements from the Corporation certainly became increasingly uncompromising. James Arnold-Baker, then Head of BBC Enterprises, commented on the Channel Four discussion programme *Right to Reply*: '*Doctor Who* is an old property, it has had its day and is no longer commercially viable.' Mark Shivas, Head of Drama, whose department had overseen the production of *Doctor Who* for twenty-six years, was to respond to a fan enquiry, '*Doctor Who* has nothing to do with us.' By 1991, the BBC Press Office's official line, which for nearly two years had been the encouraging if patronising, 'We're not closing the door on the TARDIS yet', had become, 'In a competitive market environment… one cannot continue to support a programme of this sort that is not able to achieve a substantial audience.' *Doctor Who* – like those who meet the Boojum in Lewis Carroll's *The Hunting of the Snark* – had softly and suddenly vanished away.

But far across the Atlantic, there was one man who had other ideas, one man for whom the chance to make *Doctor Who* would be nothing less than a childhood dream fulfiled, one man who – however much the BBC vacillated – wouldn't take 'No' for an answer.

Philip Segal grew up in the melancholic seaside town of Southend and had watched *Doctor Who* from the knee of his much-loved grandfather. A complex career path had taken Segal to the United States, where for some years he was just one of thousands of jobbing freelance producers desperate to make a break into the big time. His moment came when he visited Steven Spielberg's Amblin Television, a relatively young company keen to develop new, often fantasy-based series for the US networks. Segal offered Amblin his 'big idea', *SeaQuest DSV* – basically *Star Trek* in a giant submarine – and found they were willing to gamble on the project. Such is the rate that American television develops and burns up new ideas, Segal was to find himself in a senior commissioning role at Amblin in double-quick time.

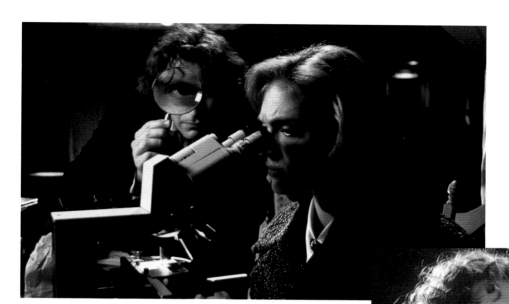

Amblin had already approached the BBC and asked them for a list of available programme properties they might consider letting go. When the paperwork passed over Segal's desk, one particular title leapt out at him, one about which his colleagues knew very little. Segal saw an opportunity to do something his grandfather would have been proud of, a chance to make a TV series he could watch with his own children. With Spielberg's blessing, Segal decided he would take on *Doctor Who*.

Even though the series was on the list of properties for independent exploitation, Segal initially had great difficulty finding anyone within the BBC willing to discuss *Doctor Who*. Eventually he began to speak to Tony Greenwood, then in charge of Children's International Projects at BBC Worldwide. As a former Head of Home Entertainment, Greenwood was aware of the success of *Doctor Who* in overseas markets – through the sale of episodes for broadcast on foreign TV stations – home videos, and licensed merchandise. BBC Worldwide had developed from the old BBC Enterprises and was a much more proactive organisation than its predecessor, as the BBC directorate were keen it should achieve ever more healthy profit margins and so supplement the Corporation's licence fee income, which, under a Conservative administration, had been decreasing in real terms for some time. Various BBC series, ranging from *Match of the Day* to *Antiques Roadshow*, were now seen as 'brands' in their own right, properties which could be exploited across different media – magazines, books, videos and so on.

Furthermore, despite resistance elsewhere in the BBC, Worldwide was keen to move into programme-making themselves, almost turning the whole merchandising process on its head, as programmes could be produced to support their associated product. With a healthy market in home video, *Doctor Who* must have represented the ideal project with which to test the politics and possibilities of this new system. To BBC Drama, *Doctor Who* seemed to have had its day; to Worldwide, it was a tried and trusted success – a known and manageable quantity. More importantly, a charming, experienced producer from one of the world's most important production companies was just begging for a chance to make it for them. Segal and Worldwide were perfect for each other: he had enthusiasm and determination, Worldwide was keen to flex its muscles as an independent programme maker. Without this synergy, *Doctor Who* may have slipped away for ever. As it was, work began on a script for a possible pilot film almost immediately.

In 1993, Alan Yentob was appointed Controller of BBC1. Yentob was a younger man than many of his predecessors in the role and *Doctor Who* had been part of his own childhood television landscape. Segal said later of him, 'Yentob believes that there is life in the old Doctor yet. In some ways Yentob is nostalgic, but he is also concerned that *Doctor Who* is not written down to and is not a parody of itself, because that's why it failed in the first place. Alan has been terrific – he is really concerned and has been the one who cared enough to say "yes".' It was Yentob who made a commitment to purchase Segal and Worldwide's film for screening on BBC1.

Moments from the 1996 TV movie…
Far left: Eric Roberts – brother of *Pretty Woman* star Julia – played the latest incarnation of the evil Master

Above left: Daphne Ashbrook took the role of troubled cardiologist Grace Holloway, who turned down the chance to join the Doctor (Paul McGann) as his travelling companion
Above: It was the childlike sense of wonder brought to the role by McGann that so endeared him to fans of the programme

While the series proper was off-air between 1989 and 1996, the BBC kept fans occupied with a number of spin-off projects...
Top: Jon Pertwee recorded material for a number of specialised video releases...
Above: ...and reprised his role as the Doctor in two radio serials. Elisabeth Sladen and Nicholas Courtney also returned as Sarah and the Brigadier

Two particularly expensive aspects of the TV movie were:
Main: A lengthy chase sequence, filmed entirely at night...
Far right: ...and the impressive TARDIS interior

In 1994, Segal left Amblin and, again with Spielberg's blessing, took his option on *Doctor Who* with him to Universal Television in Hollywood. A co-production deal for a pilot and possible series of new episodes was set up between Worldwide and Universal, each to cover 50 per cent of the costs. The only factor still missing from the final equation was a screening commitment from a US TV network – Universal couldn't bankroll the project without a guaranteed sale for the finished product. In late spring of that year, the series was considered by CBS, the pitch coming exclusively from Segal, described at the time by Worldwide as, 'the man who has made this happen. He has convinced everyone of the likely success of a new series of *Doctor Who*. Now he only has to convince a network.' That proved to be a big 'only'. So far, two different pilot scripts had been considered and assorted network executives had wrestled with Segal's revisionist 'bible' for the series – a series of character studies for the Doctor, his father Ulysses and his half-brother the Master, and background notes for likely plots, including the Doctor's quest to find his missing dad, his first encounter with the Daleks and his battles with the Cybs of Mondas. Perhaps understandably, floor plans of the TARDIS and drawings of unfolding 'spider' Daleks did little to impress CBS, who replied to Segal with a polite 'Thanks, but no thanks.'

But at Fox TV, Segal hit lucky again. There he met Trevor Walton, another Englishman abroad, who knew *Doctor Who* well. Walton was a vice-president in charge of stand-alone movie production and, although he was unable to commission a whole new series from Segal, he gave the green light to a one-off TV movie which, if successful, could serve as a launch pad for more episodes. One requirement was that Segal throw out his tortured, quasi-mythical early scripts and start afresh with 'a simple story to allow a new audience to get to know the Doctor'.

The rest was comparatively easy. The new script – from British writer Matthew Jacobs – was accepted by Fox and the BBC and the principal details of their contract and budgets were ironed out by autumn 1995. Liverpudlian Paul McGann was chosen to play the Doctor, while, in a concession to the film's schizophrenic transatlantic needs, the rest of the cast would be American. On 10 January 1996, the BBC formally announced McGann's selection to the British press, a story which made the pages of every single major newspaper. Only five days later, he was filming his first scenes in Vanier Park, Vancouver, Canada – the city inexpensively doubling as San Francisco for the project.

The TV movie, when it finally reached the screens of Britain on 27 May 1996, two weeks after its première in the US, was a strange mix of the old and new. Much of its first third is clearly inspired by Jon Pertwee's debut serial from 1970, *Spearhead from Space* – as the Doctor is taken to a hospital and has his alien biology explored before he steals some clothes and makes for the hills – while the final third has much in common with 1976's *The Deadly Assassin* – where the Doctor struggles to prevent the Master from winning a new lease of life, at enormous cost to innocent lives, from the powerful Eye of Harmony before the villain is cast into the pit. These two main sequences are linked by a late-night motorcycle and ambulance chase, the theft of a plot device from a huge, glitzy West Coast party and much showing off of the extravagant and

Gothic new TARDIS interior set – three elements which undoubtedly ate up the lion's share of the gargantuan (by *Doctor Who* standards) £3 million budget and are, not coincidentally, the only three elements that make the film seem in any way different from the series of old. Otherwise, it was typical 1980s *Doctor Who* with an expensive gloss – slightly too little exposition, slightly too much violence, a few too many unnecessary references to a largely forgotten continuity. Although very entertaining, stylishly directed and perfectly played, the TV movie perhaps tried a little too hard to be what *Doctor Who* once was, rather than crusading to demonstrate what it could be in the future.

That aside, the film was a major hit for BBC1, watched 'live' by 8.19 million viewers and video-recorded to be watched later by a further 0.89 million. This represented a healthy 36 per cent audience share for the time-slot and placed the film fifteenth in the week's rating chart. It did, however, receive a rather sniffy response from the national press, with only McGann's performance singled out for unguarded praise: 'The best since Tom Baker' was the general feeling.

If the film had been made to a suitable budget by the BBC alone, there is little doubt – on the above figures – that a series would have been instantly commissioned for a 1997 launch. But the complex production deal that had been instrumental in getting the project off the ground in the first place was also to spell its downfall. In America, the movie vanished without trace, attracting only 9 per cent of the available audience on transmission; Fox and Universal were understandably less than entirely bowled over. BBC Worldwide, meanwhile, funding the British end of the deal, hoped to recoup much of their expenditure through sales of a video of the film. This had been planned to reach the shops some weeks before the film's TV transmission, but a stream of certification problems delayed the release, so the video eventually hit the shelves only some 140 hours before viewers could happily tape it at home. Worldwide had hoped to sell hundreds of thousands of cassettes in those first weeks, as potential viewers' curiosity got the better of them. The shrinking of their window of opportunity meant that, to date, only 45,000 units have been sold.

And so, in the final analysis, the film could be described as something of a disappointment for its production companies. Despite the fact the movie was very poorly advertised and marketed in the States, the lukewarm response was enough to demonstrate that the series wasn't likely – or perhaps just wasn't ready – to become a true global phenomenon in the manner of *Star Trek* or *Star Wars*.

Nevertheless, it did prove one thing. Back in its ancestral home on BBC1, *Doctor Who* could, even after thirty-three years, still cut it. Its chart placing was the highest since *The Robots of Death* in 1977, bringing back memories of a time when everyone seemed to watch the programme and had something to say about it.

On that evening in May, the British public demonstrated that they were more than ready to rejoin the adventures of the Doctor, that they had been sad to lose him and that he was welcome in their homes once again. Sadly, they had no knowledge of the complex politics that would allow them only this brief taste of what they had been missing.

For even before they had a chance to see and enjoy the frenzied yet stylish ninety minutes for themselves, the US screening ratings had been logged by Fox and the series' future decided. The news was not good.

A little before 10 p.m. on 27 May 1996, viewers saw the Doctor slip away from Earth again in his TARDIS. The witty, brave, mysterious traveller in space and time had been sorely missed and his return visit had been so painfully brief. They didn't know where he was heading next – that was rather the point – but they would surely have been more than happy to travel with him for just a little longer. ◖

POLICE PUBLIC CALL BOX

POLICE TELEPHONE
FREE
FOR USE OF
PUBLIC

ADVICE AND ASSISTANCE
OBTAINABLE IMMEDIATELY

OFFICERS AND CARS
RESPOND TO
URGENT CALLS

PULL TO OPEN

FROM A TO Z

AFTERWORD

In the years that have followed Paul McGann's all-too-brief appearance as the Doctor, it has been up to the fans of *Doctor Who* to fill the void left by their favourite programme's enforced absence from TV, much as they were obliged to do between 1989 and 1996. The marketplace for *Doctor Who* merchandise is as healthy as ever, Marvel's *Doctor Who Magazine* still sells in excess of twenty thousand copies every month and BBC Worldwide has extended its commitment to the series by taking on the publishing of *Doctor Who* fiction, issuing twenty-two original novels per year, the majority written by long-term followers of the series who have managed to couple their creative talents with their knowledge of the series – embarking on what will, in many cases, be long and successful writing careers.

Neither has interest in *Doctor Who* among the press and the general public diminished. The most bizarre and unsubstantiated of rumours regarding the series' possible revival can make the pages of the major newspapers. Even while 'resting', the series still managed to win that BBC 'people's choice' award – the presentation ceremony for which formed the focus of the introduction to this book.

That introduction also posed a number of questions regarding the possible reasons behind *Doctor Who*'s longevity and popularity. It also suggested that we might find some answers. Perhaps we have.

The story told across our twenty-six chapters has been, by necessity, a complex and often bewildering one. While each chapter has investigated its chosen theme and attempted to draw some neat conclusions in the process, they have often had to trade on generalisation and sweeping statements. *Doctor Who* was the product of too many hands – a sum of ideas from too many minds – for us to expect much consistency from its content, or look for any measured development in its execution.

And that, when all is said and done, is the point. Twenty-six topics have been chosen for this book, and it would have been easy to choose twenty-six more. While *Doctor Who* doesn't have the infinitely variable format its admirers claim for it – its own rules of logic, decency and rationalism dictate that there is much it cannot do – it has certainly been able to present itself in many guises. Sometimes comedy, sometimes historical drama, sometimes sombre science-fiction, *Doctor Who* has indeed, to paraphrase C.E. Webber, taken the best of any style and category as it suited. It is that ability to change and to adapt that kept *Doctor Who* alive for so long on television and, even while away from our screens, will still allow it to entertain its fans. Only on the occasions when *Doctor Who* lost sight of that need, and wasted its energies elsewhere, did it ever struggle to find an audience.

And the future?

Well, it's worth remembering that *Doctor Who* was created simply to fill a gap in the BBC's schedule, a gap which required a dynamic adventure serial that would entertain both children and adults together. A serial that would excite as it amused, delight as it amazed.

Now that gap exists again. There is only one programme that can possibly be called upon to fill it.